At Grandma's House

At Grandma's House

THE WORLD WAR II HOMEFRONT IN HAVANA, ILLINOIS

H. BYRON EARHART
With illustrations by JOHN MICHAEL DOWNS

Saluki Publishing | Carbondale, Illinois

Saluki Publishing
1915 University Press Drive
Carbondale, IL 62901

Cover illustration: Grandma standing by her house. ILLUSTRATION BY
JOHN MICHAEL DOWNS; COLOR ADDED.

ISBN 978-0-8093-7007-8

Library of Congress Control Number: 2019918237

Printed on recycled paper ♻

This book is dedicated to my parents,

Kenneth and Mary Earhart

and to

my maternal grandparents,

Ruth and Charles Haack

for Their

Courage, Bravery, Humility, and Love

Contents

At Grandma's House

Prolog

Growing up in Illinois during World War II gave me a firsthand view of life on the homefront. In those days everyone focused on two scenes: the warfront where our military fought battles, and the homefront where civilians supported "our boys." (In this book I use "homefront" as one word, because in the 1940s that's the way we pronounced it and thought of it, as the opposite of warfront.)

Our family, like all Americans, feared the loss of life for loved ones and fellow countrymen. Because my father served in the Navy, we felt the pangs of anxiety all the more sharply. We lived through a terrible time.

Although we paid attention to every bit of news about the war, we had to go about our daily life—school, work, gardening, shared meals, leisure. In spite of the raging battles around the world, we managed to keep our daily routine, and we even had a lot of fun. We enjoyed good times.

Shortly after our father enlisted in the Navy, my two older sisters and Mom and I moved in with our mother's parents. They were Grandma and Grandpa, but we always said we lived at Grandma's house, because her warm heart defined the center of our home.

I look back at 1943–1945 as the time of my youth spent at Grandma's house. The events of those years mark off a period and place set apart, a storehouse of reminiscences. Episodes from those days lie waiting in a special chamber of my memory. When I look back through a mental window to that part of my recollection, the incidents of more than a half century ago reappear. From these scenes come many of the stories about World War II and Grandma's house.

These tales cover a wide range of emotions, from happiness at getting Daddy's letters, to fear that he would be killed. We felt proud that he had enlisted and was serving our country, yet at the same time we worried about losing him.

This book tells how my family, as well as fellow Americans, lived through the war years on the homefront. It does not describe the military conflict between allies and enemies. From Pearl Harbor in late 1941 to the surrender of Japan in late 1945, much that happened to me, my family, friends, and fellow citizens, followed the pattern of everyday life—the minor happenings as well as the festive occasions. Not all that happens during spans of military conflicts takes place in battles on the warfront.

People in all situations, military and civilian, in wartime and peacetime, find time for joking, recreation, and pleasure. My experiences from 1941 through 1945 include a mixture of what Charles Dickens would call the best times of my life, as well as the worst times. This story records the highs of enjoyment and the depths of anxiety while I was growing up in Havana, Illinois. My hometown, a county seat in the heart of the Midwest, located near the geographic center of the country, can be seen as a miniature United States: its life and values are typical of much of mid-twentieth century small town America. Fellow countrymen shared the rapidly shifting emotions that my family and other people in Havana experienced.

Most of the veterans of World War II, like my father, have passed away, and many of my generation who lived through the war have joined them. These pages preserve memories of events, experiences, and attitudes of wartime America.

We are who we remember ourselves to be. Recalling the wartime era enables Americans to see who we were, who we have come to be, and who we may become—no matter what challenges face us.

Writing down anecdotes from my boyhood made me realize the limited viewpoint of my own eyes and ears, making me wonder what others had seen and heard and written. I found a number of accounts of people who spent the war in central Illinois. These first-person records proved helpful in gaining a wider appreciation of wartime Illinois.

I also wanted to go beyond my own experiences and recollections to a contemporary record of the Havana area. The 1941–1945 issues of *The Mason County Democrat,* a weekly newspaper serving Mason County and some of neighboring Fulton County, provide an overview of the life, attitudes, and events of the region during wartime, as described by its reporters and editor. The articles and editorials in this paper enabled me to place my personal anecdotes in perspective.

World War II, both on the battleground and on the homefront, has been thoroughly researched and interpreted in numerous articles and books. I read through many of these works, and have used them as background for seeing the local situation in a wider context. Some of these writings are listed in the Suggestions for Further Reading for those who wish to pursue specific aspects of the war. I have not attempted to sum up quickly what others have covered in greater detail. This book focuses not on the war as such, but on what it was like for ordinary citizens to live through war.

Recalling the activities and scenes of childhood prodded my mind to bring up forgotten details of what I have seen, read, and lived through in the postwar era. The story begins with my memories of wartime experiences. The narrative also goes back and forth from episodes of the 1940s to what I learned in later readings, and to my reflections on how the conflict influenced my outlook on life. My remembrance of World War II is not a linear account of sequential events, like a freight train of linked railroad cars, but more like a panoramic web of incidents, sights, sounds, smells, and tastes, all interconnected, both past and present. For those of us who spent our formative years during the early 1940s, we never completely forgot the war, we just stored it in our gray matter. Occasionally we consciously call up past scenes. Also, quite unexpectedly, past wartime experiences surface of their own accord, triggered by something that reminds us of that era.

For example, even nowadays, when I eat very good corn bread, it calls to mind the kitchen in Grandma's house and the taste of the corn bread she baked in a skillet on her coal-fired cast iron stove. When I write about the kamikaze plane that hit the USS Missouri on which Dad was stationed, it reminds me of the books I have read about these suicide pilots.

Several times as I watched my grandsons as actors in the play *A Christmas Story,* the tale of a boy who has his heart set on a BB gun for Christmas, I think back to the drama at Grandma's house when I wanted a BB gun. When I hear the distinctive rattle of a diesel engine in a pickup truck, I am transported back to 1940 and the first time I heard the pucka-pucka-pucka made by the diesel in the basement of our locker plant.

Watching a television ad for a lottery conjures up images of the one-armed bandits in my hometown, then known as "Little Reno." During the wars since the 1940s—in Korea, Vietnam, Kuwait, Iraq, Afghanistan—reading or viewing the news of injuries and deaths makes my stomach churn and my heart ache with the same fear and dread I felt for Dad when he served in the Navy.

For me, the past of World War II runs together with my later experiences and activities. My mind commutes back and forth between distant events and more recent occurrences. Personal memory for me is like a patchwork quilt of earlier scenes, sounds, smells, episodes, and phrases, cobbled together with later reading and experiences. Maybe a better label for the pages that follow is a crazy quilt, a sewing together of contrasting elements, textures, and moods. The individual patches or segments of this story may seem quite unrelated, but as an interconnected pattern they offer a picture of our confusing wartime experience. On the homefront, we did not experience the war as a neat blueprint of geometrical precision and logical progression from start to completion. The war had its ups and downs, advances and retreats, which created an emotional roller coaster, filling those years with contradictory attitudes and actions, like the different colors and shapes of a cloth collage, yet we managed to make sense of our situation and live through it.

Eyewitness accounts like mine, shaped by personal experience and perspective, are selective and limited, so it is good to be candid about the source and viewpoint for my observations. Grandma's home—the house itself and the household—provides the setting in which these memories appear. The members of our extended family take the roles of key players. Post-Depression America forms the backdrop. The narrative follows the drama of our daily life, acted out on the wider stage of American life during wartime.

The story begins with a page from a typical day in 1943.

CHAPTER 1

Last One Home's a Rotten Egg

When I saw Mom nearing the house, I asked, "Did we get a letter from Daddy today?"

During World War II, when my mother came home from work at the family business she managed, right away my older sisters, Rosemary and Sylvia, and I wanted to know if we got a letter or package from our father in the Navy.

If Mom said, "No, no letter today," we wailed our disappointment.

Too young to understand about war and international politics, we only knew that evil people across the ocean had attacked our country, and our dad joined the Navy and went away to protect us.

He mailed his letters to our business, Earhart Food Locker, which Mom ran during his time in the Navy. On days when Mom returned home empty handed, we felt down. But when she smiled and said, "Yes, we got a letter today," we hooped and hollered, and could hardly wait to go in to the kitchen table to hear her read the letter out loud, and then pass it around and read it. We looked forward to every bit of news the Navy allowed him to share with us. My sisters and I kept going over what Daddy had written, trying to imagine his life as a sailor in the Navy.

Our father didn't graduate from high school, so his spelling tended to be creative. He signed his letters, "Love, Dady." We kids liked to say it the way he wrote it, "Love, day-dee." He always joked with us, and his unintended humor cheered us up. His letter, a brief picker-upper for our spirits, also reminded us just how much we missed him.

* * *

As young children in the 1940s, my sisters and I didn't know about the earlier decades of American life that had molded our family members into strong, self-reliant people. The Depression shaped the character of our parents and Mother's parents, Ruth and Charles Haack. Grandma had come from a rather well-to-do family. She married late at age 28 to Grandpa, whose family owned a paint store. Grandpa wanted to farm. He sold the paint store to buy a farm, and did well for a few years. With the drop in grain prices and economic hard times, they lost the farm in the early 1920s.

Grandma and Grandpa did not talk openly about this dark background of the early days of their marriage. The loss of the farm injured their pride so much that they never completely overcame it. Grandma had not been in favor of the move from the city to the country, and never forgave Grandpa for this misfortune of trading a paint store for a farm. They returned to the city, but never owned a house or a car. Neither of them had a driver's license.

After that, Grandpa fell back on what he knew, painting and wallpapering, enabling them to pay rent and buy groceries, but with no money for luxuries. He had to depend on his daughter and son-in-law to drive him to all his home decorating jobs. Like so many Americans who lived through the hard times of the 1920s and 1930s, they worked hard to survive, making do with little money, yet generous with care for their family. Parents and grandparents alike reminded us frequently that life in the 1940s could not match the tough times of the previous decades.

If we kids dared to complain about some food shortage or minor sacrifice, Grandma would come down hard on us. "Hah! You don't know hard times. Why, during the Depression . . . ," and she would tell another tale of people standing in long soup lines or suffering some other indignity of hunger and poverty.

My wife and I remember an unwritten rule of Depression times in the Midwest: Never turn away a hungry person. In those days, we didn't know the word "homeless." Havana, with a railroad running through it, had more than its share of "hobos" or "tramps" who rode the freight trains from town to town. When one of these transients knocked on the door and asked for food, our family always gave them something, such as a sandwich and an apple. Usually we had some minor chore such as raking the yard, or other make-work task we asked the guy to do before he got the food. Our family followed the other side of the rule of not turning away the hungry: there was no free lunch. If you ate, you worked for your food.

In 1930 at the beginning of the Depression, shortly after my mother graduated from high school, she married my father, who did not have a high school diploma. Both had been raised on farms, and had personal experience with hard work. It took a lot of love, courage, and optimism to start a marriage with the country in such severe economic turmoil. Dad tried various jobs, finding his vocation in meat markets and retail business. Mother always found time to help him. They soon had two daughters, by the time I was born in 1935. While raising three children, Mother continued to help him in the store, preparing displays and serving customers. When he managed the meat market in an A & P (Atlantic and Pacific) store in Mason City, Illinois, the two of them increased sales so much that they won a company trip to the World's Fair in New York City in 1939, and a tour of the Queen Mary.

Dad continued to work all through the very difficult decade of massive unemployment from 1930 to 1940. Relying on his good business sense, in 1940 Mom and Dad decided to move from Mason City, Illinois, to the larger town of Havana, population 4,500, and open a frozen food locker plant. Havana sits on the east bluff of the Illinois River in the center of the state.

They pioneered a new business at the end of the Depression in a small town, a daring venture, relying on faith in their hard work ethic to make

This 1937 photo shows Kenneth Earhart (on right) at work in his meat market at the back of an A & P Store in Mason City, Illinois. FAMILY COLLECTION.

ILLUSTRATION BY JOHN MICHAEL DOWNS.

a go of it. Although most Americans had begun to use refrigerators, they had little familiarity with frozen foods. In small towns like Havana, the only common frozen foods were ice cream and popsicles. In 1942 when Daddy joined the Navy, our three-generation family centered around two locations, Grandma's house, and Earhart Food Locker.

Moving from the south side home of my parents at 533 South Orange Street to Grandma's house at 223 West Market Street, one block from Main Street on the north edge of the downtown business district, only a matter of eight blocks or so, to a seven-year old counted as a major event. The transition to a three-generation household also meant a dramatic change for my mother and grandparents. Mother gave up some of her independence, resuming the role of daughter, and my grandparents once more became parents and partly responsible for raising youngsters.

For me, the biggest adjustment in this move meant leaving Oak Grove School, on the corner of First Street and Plum Street, a short block away from my parent's home, for Rockwell School, about eight blocks farther north of Grandma's house, on North Broadway. Although only several miles separated the two homes, our grandparents' residence seemed to be located in a different world, right next to the bustling business district and just a few minutes from Riverfront Park.

Havana during the 1940s and 1950s, like many small Midwestern cities, had a bustling Main Street with a number of grocery, drug, hardware, clothing, and other stores, along with movie theaters, restaurants, and taverns. This early 1940s picture was taken from the intersection of Main Street and Orange Street, looking east. As the county seat of Mason County, it was a financial and shopping magnet for all of Mason County and also some of neighboring Fulton County to the west just across the Illinois River. PHOTO COURTESY OF NANCY GLICK AND THE HAVANA PUBLIC LIBRARY.

This 1940s picture was taken from the intersection of Main Street and Plum Street, looking north. The lawn and trees at the right are at the west side of the square block for the county court house. Among the trees at the right of the picture is the base of the commemorative stone for soldiers of the Civil War. Barely visible at the very end of the street on the right is the belfry of the First Baptist Church. PHOTO COURTESY OF NANCY GLICK AND THE HAVANA PUBLIC LIBRARY.

Our grandparents' house stood at the center of a very large corner lot on West Market Street and Schrader Street with a smaller house on each side. Doc lived across our grassy play area to the east. An old bachelor with a bad leg, he made his living pushing a hand cart around town picking up rags and papers to sell, and doing odd jobs. With so many able-bodied men gone to the war, he never wanted for work. Doc, a friendly old guy, always had time to talk to us children. Grandma often had us take him leftovers from our meals.

The Watkins lived back of us a dozen yards to the southwest, a feisty old couple who had been married for sixty years. Always bickering, they often complained about us pre-teen children. The Watkins provided a good source of gossip and jokes at the dinner table. "Did you hear what they were fighting about today?" one of us would say, and we added a new story to the collection of Watkins folklore.

We had a large yard, perfect for having plenty of friends over to play. To the west of the property and running down the center of Schrader Street, which everyone called "Railroad Street," lay the tracks for the Illinois Central Railroad. To the south was a miniature version of rural and small town America in the first half of the twentieth century. A sprawling vacant lot extended from our back yard to the alley behind the businesses on Main Street.

In the days before supermarkets and suburban development, almost all stores and businesses were concentrated downtown on and around Main Street. A half dozen grocery stores competed for housewives' shopping budgets. Havana National Bank was the only financial institution. Several hardware, drug, and clothing and shoe stores lined up next to each other like the sections on a Monopoly board. Every block had its restaurants and taverns. Grandma's house stood just a few minutes away from all these places of business.

Grandma loved flowers, so in summer, flowers bloomed all around the house, especially varieties such as four-o'clocks and geraniums. The back yard held a large vegetable garden and two storage sheds.

Grandpa's painting equipment occupied one of the large sheds, the other large shed we used for storage and chickens. No matter that south a couple hundred yards and across an alley were the backs of buildings that fronted on Main Street. Here we gathered eggs for breakfast, and killed chickens for dinner.

A large vacant lot behind the sheds held Allis Chalmers trade-in equipment for a farm implement dealer. Overgrown with weeds, and

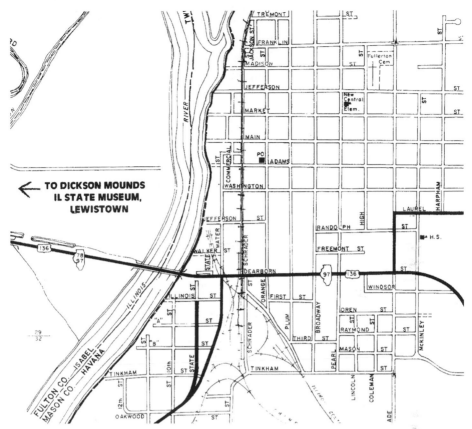

This map of Havana, Illinois includes street names, highway routes, railroad tracks, and the adjoining Illinois River, the boundary between Mason County and Fulton County. Locations cited in the text can be found by referring to this map. MAP COURTESY OF CHRIS TROXELL, VICE PRESIDENT, HAVANA CHAMBER OF COMMERCE.

cluttered with discarded implements, for a seven-year old, this seemed to be wild country. We could make it anything we wanted to. With large groups of children around we would play in the side yard between the house and the railroad tracks, but my buddies and I always wound up in the vacant lot. That's where we dug worms, told stories, and when the mood visited us, peed on the back of Grandpa's paint shed. This open area and our carefree fun and games gave us the time and space to be kids, and to completely forget about the war.

One day we had fun clambering around the rusty farm implements. Climbing up a broken-down combine, my buddy Art said "Hey, look at this!" Nestled in the machinery of the combine, faded orange, stained with brownish-red rust, a chicken had made a nest and laid an egg. The tan-speckled egg stood out against the darkish weeds of the nest. I figured, since we always kept our chickens penned up, a hen must have built its nest in the combine and laid an egg while it was still on some farm. Then, before it could hatch the egg, the farmer bought a new combine and the implement dealer pulled the old combine here.

We laughed until our sides hurt. "Can't you see that hen running around looking for its egg?"

"Yeah, and just think, the egg didn't break on the long trip into town."

The tan-speckled egg stood out against the darkish weeds of the nest.

More than the humor of the frantic hen or the miracle of the egg's trip, we wondered what to *do* with that fragile egg. The combine seemed to be saying to us: *Boys, I've been saving this egg for you for an awfully long time. Here it is. Do with it what you will.*

This presented a rare opportunity, something to be handled properly. We agreed it couldn't be good to eat, but that's all we agreed on. Finally, Art, the most venturous of us boys, reached down into the machinery and plucked the egg out of the nest.

We all craned our heads closer. I don't know what happened next. Maybe someone bumped Art. The egg slipped out of his hand, glanced off one of the uprights and hit flat metal with a "poof" sound. The egg didn't break. It *exploded* and splattered all over us.

What caught us off guard was the *smell!* The rotten egg engulfed us in a stench so powerful we couldn't believe it had come from something so small. We paused only a second before turning tail and running away. Surprise changed to revulsion and then just as quickly to laughter and jokes.

Using an outside faucet from the house to wash the egg off our hands and clothes, we kidded each other about what scaredy-cats we were for running away. Rough and tumble boys, with all the things in the world to be afraid of, we couldn't get over the ridiculous reaction of fleeing from the stink of a putrid egg.

We got rid of the odor, but for the rest of that day we laughed, kidding each other. "Art, I never saw you run that fast before."

This backyard adventure added color and odor to one of our favorite sayings: "Last one home's a rotten egg."

CHAPTER 2

Corn Cobs, Coal, and Ice

Grandma's house, rather large for its day, stood tall as a two-story white wooden clapboard structure with a front entrance that opened onto the central hallway, and a stairway leading upstairs. On the first floor on each side of the stairway, doors right and left led to a small and large parlor. Behind the left parlor was the bathroom, back of the right parlor the large dining room, which also had a door to the bath, and at the far end of the house, the large country style kitchen.

In the three years we lived there I only recall a few times when we had formal company and someone entered through the front door facing Market Street. Our family always used the back door as an entrance into the kitchen, our main gathering place.

Grandma standing by her house. ILLUSTRATION BY JOHN MICHAEL DOWNS.

A coal-burning cast iron range dominated the kitchen. Grandma cooked on this stove. She placed pans and skillets on the flat top or "range," and baked bread, cakes, and pastries in the oven. At the right end of the stove, the "reservoir" held hot water. A warming oven above the stove top kept prepared dishes warm.

We used corn cobs for kindling to light the coal. The stove top had four large holes in it through which we dumped cobs and coal from

Grandma cooking a holiday meal on the kitchen range. The buckets for coal and cobs are at the left. ILLUSTRATION BY JOHN MICHAEL DOWNS.

nearby buckets. Then we covered the holes with lids, to make a flat cooking surface. Each lid had a slot or groove into which a lifter could be inserted to raise and move them. Our lifters had attractive silvery metal coils around them, to keep hands from getting burned. Controlling the heat on the range called for skill and art, balancing a number of factors: how much coal was used, how long the fire had been burning, and the adjustment of the damper for air intake. Allowing more air made the coal burn faster and hotter. When the desired temperature had been reached, partially or completely shutting the damper would bank the fire.

Kitchen ranges had no "simmer" function like modern stoves, but a good cook could place pans or skillets in the center of the range for frying and boiling, then move them toward the edge of the flat surface for simmering. Grandma cooked with heavy cast iron metal skillets that retained heat, keeping a consistent temperature. For baking, an oven thermometer helped gauge the temperature.

In spite of all the difficulties of stoking and tending a kitchen range, Grandma prepared all kinds of delicious dishes. To take just two examples of Grandma's downhome cooking, her corn bread, cooked in a large covered skillet on the range top, ranks as the best I have ever eaten, her angel food cake baked in the oven—heavenly.

As one of my jobs, winter and summer, I kept a full bucket of cobs by the stove. We stored cobs and coal in the shed out back. Grandpa handled coal and ashes. A full bucket of coal was too heavy for me to carry. A third bucket held ashes, that had to be removed daily.

When we got low on cobs, we hired Doc to go to the grain elevator with his cart to bring us cobs. The cart had two iron wheels, and a long U-shaped wooden handle he used to balance and push it. The grain elevators gave the corn cobs away for free, because otherwise they had to burn them.

We had four unheated rooms upstairs. Three we used for bedrooms— one for my sisters, one for Grandma and Grandpa, the third one for Mother and me. A fourth room we used for storage. In the mornings, Mother and grandparents got up early and started the fire in the kitchen. We dressed quickly and hurried down to get warm by the kitchen range. In winter the range made this room toasty; in summer it became ungodly hot. From late spring to early fall, we did some cooking on the back porch with a kerosene (or "coal oil") stove. The range had a reservoir, an attached tank for heating water. We washed

Doc with his pushcart. ILLUSTRATION BY JOHN MICHAEL DOWNS.

dishes in the kitchen sink with hot water dipped from the reservoir. The sink had only cold water.

In the days before refrigerators, an "icebox" meant a box (usually a wooden cabinet with metal lining) in which ice was placed to keep food cool. This icebox has been refurbished for sale as an antique. Through the open door can be seen the metal-lined cabinet. AUTHOR'S PHOTO.

Grandmother had an old icebox before we moved in with her. She needed to buy a chunk of ice every other day or so, putting her sign in the window to tell the iceman how many pounds she wanted. The square sign had four numbers on it, 25, 50, 75, and 100, arranged in a circular fashion. She rotated the sign to display vertically the number of pounds she wanted. When the iceman pulled up to the curb by the house he could see at a glance from the sign in the window how much ice to bring in. Grandma's little icebox surely couldn't have held more than fifty pounds at a time.

The hundred-pound slabs of ice in the truck had four evenly spaced notches, so that a few quick stabs of an ice pick in a notch split off the exact size block of ice a customer wanted. The iceman needed no scales. Ice tongs with steel teeth biting into opposite sides of the block made it easy to handle. The iceman had a piece of leather over his right shoulder, to protect it from the cold and dripping ice when he hefted it and carried it to a customer's icebox. In my old neighborhood, even before we moved to Grandma's, on a summer's morn we would run to the iceman's truck and beg, "Can we have a piece of ice to suck on?"

About the time we moved in with Grandma, she got a second-hand refrigerator. Our family had an advantage during the war years, because our parents had just opened the locker plant. We could keep meats, vegetables, and fruit in the locker plant, and each evening Mother brought home something for dinner. The nearby location of the locker plant on North Orange Street, only a block and a half from Grandma's house, made it a five-minute walk.

An iceman carrying a block of ice from his truck to a home. ILLUSTRATION BY
JOHN MICHAEL DOWNS.

The kitchen had a cupboard, with spices, flour, sugar, and other
cooking and baking ingredients. The range, the centerpiece of the
kitchen, stood opposite. The large round kitchen table occupied the
other end of the room. We ate all our meals here, except for holidays
and Sunday dinner. In central Illinois, as in some other parts of the
country, dinner is at noon, supper in the evening. We used the kitchen
as our meeting and socializing place. We had a snack at the kitchen
table after school, and might do some homework there. Grandpa usually
started reading the newspaper seated on a kitchen chair while waiting
for supper to be served. When we had washed and dried the dishes
after the evening meal, in warmer weather we often played some cards,
especially rummy or pinochle.

In cold weather, we let the kitchen range fire go out after supper,
walking through the unheated formal dining room to one of the parlors.
The east parlor was smaller and easier to heat, the west parlor was larger
and harder to heat, but had enough room for a card table. Grandma and
Grandpa made the decision of which parlor they would use that year. Because the house had no central heating, each fall we had to install a large
round coal stove in the parlor we used. From spring to fall we stored the

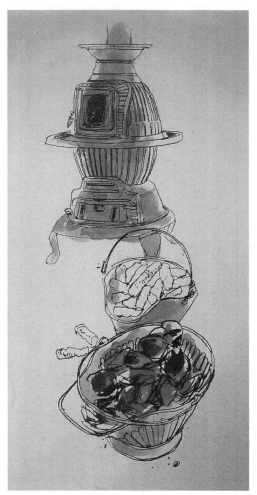

A parlor stove, with buckets of cobs and coal used as fuel in the stove. ILLUSTRATION BY JOHN MICHAEL DOWNS.

stove in a shed in the back yard. A silvery metal-clad asbestos pad was the fire-resistant base on which we set the stove, in front of the chimney, and Grandpa fitted a stovepipe from the stove into the round hole in the chimney, high on the wall close to the ceiling. In other seasons a decorative circular plate covered the chimney hole.

Before supper, Grandpa started a fire in the stove to get the parlor warm. After the evening meal, we gathered there for everything we did before bed: reading the newspaper, listening to the radio, doing school work, sewing. Mother loved to work jigsaw puzzles, and we liked to help her. We usually had a large puzzle "going" on a card table. We worked at it furiously for a few nights, then tired of it, and after several days came back to it again.

The stove had silver metal trimming, with small mica windows on the door so that you could see the flames. When bored, we kids liked to get close to the stove, watch the glow of the fire, and bask in the heat.

* * *

Most of the time we took sponge baths at the kitchen sink, or carried a basin of hot water to the bathroom. We had hot water in the bathroom only on weekends, when Grandpa fired up the water heater in the cellar. Grandma's house had no inside access to this crude basement. On the outside of the house, a wooden cellar door and steps led to the dirt-floored area and the coal-burning water heater. In Havana, as in many other towns in America, families set aside Saturday night as bath night, getting clean for church on Sunday morning.

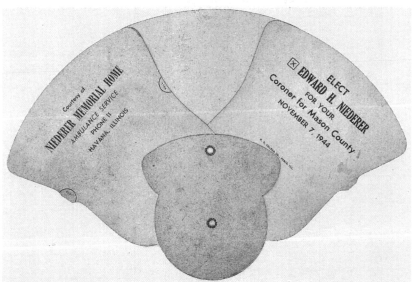

Most funeral home fans had wooden handles. This fan is unusual because of its design as three cardboard sections that collapsed to fit in a purse, and could be expanded for use by spreading the sections to form a triangular shape. This wartime example carries the familiar slogans of unity and freedom, along with the iconic Statue of Liberty and the protecting fighter planes and other planes in the distance. Church members could cool their pious brows while fanning the patriotic flames of war. The back of the fan advertises the services of the Niederer funeral home and promotes the candidacy of its owner for county coroner. PHOTOS COURTESY OF NANCY GLICK.

In winter, only the kitchen in daytime and the parlor in evenings had heat; the rest of the house remained cold. In summer, the whole house turned into an oven, the kitchen uncomfortably hot with its cast iron range. We had no electric fans, no air conditioning. Funeral homes vied with one another by giving away paper or cardboard fans with flimsy wooden handles. Summer in churches would have been unbearable without those fans. Most homes kept a supply of such fans. Friends and family members carried on conversations while stirring up a breeze to cool their faces.

When we lived at Grandma's house, blocks of ice and iceboxes had already become memories of a past way of life. But buckets of corn cobs and coal remained very much a part of our daily routine of heating, cooking, and eating.

CHAPTER 3

Pucka-pucka-pucka

During the war we split our time and lives between two locations: Grandma's home as the place for all family activities, and Earhart Food Locker where Mom ran the family business. After school, on weekends, or in the summer, my sisters and I would tell Grandma, "I'm going to the store," and she knew we would be spending time at the locker plant while Mother worked.

By opening this frozen food processing and storage facility in 1940, our parents undertook a risky venture. The early 1940s marked the early days of the commercial process of freezing and storing food. Many Americans, like Grandma, had just discarded their iceboxes and become accustomed to having refrigerators with reliable cooling for keeping milk, vegetables, and other perishables such as meat for at least a few days. However, the tiny freezer compartment of a refrigerator only had space for a few ice cube trays and a quart or two of ice cream. Home refrigerators had no room for frozen foods, and most grocery stores sold few or no frozen items. While some people had just emerged from the icebox age, our parents advanced into the new era of frozen food technology.

Building and running a food locker, an untested experiment, required successful mastery of financial, mechanical, and retail skills. It even called for educational patience, to teach people how to prepare food for freezing. At the end of the Depression, money was tight, and loans hard to come by. Somehow my parents convinced the local bank to provide them the startup funds to purchase and install the expensive equipment. My father's decade of steady employment during the Depression and his winning of the A & P sales trip to the World's Fair served as good credentials of his business abilities.

A complex link of mechanical devices made up the key components of the entire enterprise. I watched in wonder when our family gathered in the basement of the locker plant with a local mechanic to see the machinery started up for the first time. The mechanic cranked the flywheel of the diesel engine, it puck-puck-pucked into life, and finally settled down to a loud PUCKA-PUCKA-PUCKA, and turned huge belts that spun the generator, which produced electricity for the compressor motors. This scene remains one of the magical moments of my childhood.

A breakdown or faulty adjustment of just one of these links could result in disaster. If the diesel could not be repaired quickly, the frozen food would begin to thaw and start to spoil. We could switch the compressor motor to public utility electricity, but at much greater cost than diesel fuel. John Scarcliffe, the diesel mechanic, almost became a member of the family, always on call to make sure the diesel was pucka-puckaing in good form. The system ran 365 days a year, making it subject to wear and repair. Frequent breakdowns and maintenance strained the operating budget.

Even after our parents managed to obtain financing and the refrigeration equipment, they still had to convince people that you could freeze and store, then thaw, cook, and eat meat, vegetables, and fruit. Farmers from the region followed the downhome practice of canning

Preparing the diesel engine for its initial startup in the basement of the locker plant. ILLUSTRATION BY JOHN MICHAEL DOWNS.

fruits and vegetables as well as meats, and preserving meat by smoking and curing. The idea that you could freeze and then later eat perishables proved to be a hard sell to people who had survived the Depression without such facilities.

I witnessed conversations between some skeptical farmers and my enthusiastic parents about the merits of freezing foods.

"Ya mean ya can actually freeze a pork roast or hamburger and then cook it later?"

"Yes, you just let it thaw out and cook like you always do. And you can have frozen strawberries in January."

Some farmers decided to try out this newfangled process. Others just shook their heads in disbelief and walked out of the locker plant unconvinced.

For my parents, part of the challenge of opening a food locker meant persuading enough customers to rent individual lockers for a year, and bring their produce and meat to the plant for proper packaging. In the 1940s, convincing farmers that frozen foods tasted almost as good as fresh was not easy. Farmers, proud of sticking to their old-fashioned ways, had trouble believing city people like my parents telling them to change to new practices.

Mom and Dad also faced the problems involved in any business, such as hiring good help. As the government drafted more and more able young men, good workers became scarce.

Shortly after they opened the locker plant, unforeseen circumstances worked in the favor of their innovative enterprise. The ongoing military campaigns in Europe, and then the Japanese attack on Pearl Harbor on December 7, 1941, ushered America into a state of war that changed everything. Not only material goods and fuel, but also and especially, food became scarce.

By early 1942 the government promoted Victory gardens, asking everyone to grow extra food in order to save food for the armed forces. Even city folk cultivated their own back yards, rented ground, or raised gardens on public land. (Chapter 8 deals with Victory gardens.) During the war, not only farmers, but also small-town residents and large city dwellers grew much of their own food. Gradually, these people became accustomed to preserving such produce by storing it in a locker plant.

The government's implementation of rationing certain products, in order to provide more for "the boys over there," offered patriotic encouragement to grow your own food. Food rationing made life complicated for everyone. Housewives, in addition to budgeting their money, had to make sure they had enough ration coupons to present to a retailer for their purchases. Store clerks had to keep track of ration stamps and submit regular reports to the government. Families could save money and avoid the trouble of submitting ration stamps by raising their own food, and at the same time helping the boys in uniform. The government encouraged cooperation and enforced compliance, all in the name of patriotic duty.

Practicality, frugality, and patriotism helped make the frozen food locker a viable enterprise. Farmers might have been reluctant to try out frozen foods, but necessity nudged them to become customers of the locker plant. For city dwellers, meat became the most difficult food item to buy. Farmers who raised their own chickens, pigs, and cattle, could be self-sufficient with their own meat, not having to bother with waiting in lines, paying high prices, and handling ration stamps. And once they actually ate their previously frozen pork chops, hamburgers, and steaks, they enjoyed having "fresh" meat year-round. In the days before locker plants, butchering took place in late fall or winter during cold weather, the only time when farmers could eat their own fresh pork and beef. The rest of the year they could eat canned or cured meat, not nearly as tasty as fresh or frozen meat. City folk had to rely on the local meat markets; farmers liked to be self-sufficient.

As a boy I knew none of the economics of setting up a locker plant. I liked to go to the basement when the diesel was off, and there was absolute silence. I watched the mechanic connect the heavy crank to the huge flywheel of the diesel, then slowly set it spinning until it went past the first few pathetic puck-pucks, and finally came to life with a deafening PUCKA-PUCKA-PUCKA.

CHAPTER 4

Mrs. America, "The Weaker Sex?"

om and Dad saved every letter they wrote to each other while he was in the Navy. After they passed away, reading through some of these letters gave me a better picture of their new business. In 1942, Earhart Food Locker struggled as a young venture. Although the outbreak of war had helped boost the number of customers, repairs to the equipment and the need for loans put a strain on the owners. Our parents had to decide whether to try to make a go of the locker plant, or to cut their losses and give it up. At this time our father's mother, Grandma Earhart, offered to pay off the loans and let them close the business without going into bankruptcy, but my parents decided to go ahead and try to turn the locker plant into a profitable business. I only learned about this many years later. Our parents never troubled us children with money problems.

During this difficult time for my parents, in late 1942, the government called my father for induction into the military. We understood that, according to the draft rules, he could probably have asked for a deferment because he was providing an "essential" service, helping people preserve large quantities of food, and making more available for the armed forces. Instead, he chose to serve his country by enlisting in the navy. We felt quite proud of him.

In retrospect, I think practical factors may have influenced his patriotic decision to enlist, including financial incentives. As a married man with three children, he would receive pay for four dependents. And we rented out our house on South Orange Street when we moved to Grandma's house, an additional economic advantage. At the time, all my sisters and I knew was that Japan had attacked us, and Daddy had enlisted in the navy to help protect the country.

For Mother, this meant that she became immediately promoted from co-owner at the food locker to the businesswoman running the store.

In 1953, when I graduated from high school, I attended Knox College in Galesburg, Illinois. We used to joke that people like my dad had a "Knocks" degree, from the School of Hard Knocks. My father and mother passed the course in entrepreneurship by successfully setting up an innovative venture in Havana.

My mother's experience helping my father in a meat market and then the locker plant made her familiar with retail trade. When Dad joined the navy, every aspect of managing a fledgling business fell to her. She had to promote and sell the idea of storing frozen food to potential customers who had no knowledge of or experience with such a strange idea. And she had to hire and supervise workers to process the food entering the locker.

During the years we lived at Grandma's house, we never thought of Mother as doing something extraordinary. We assumed that just as Dad did his duty serving the country, Mom did her duty running the locker plant. In the decades after World War II, scholars have focused on the role of women in the war as a turning point in the status of American females. Many women in wartime America faced challenges like those Mother had to deal with. It was not so much a question of what they wanted to do, or thought they could do, but what they had to do. In almost every aspect of American work—in war plants, on farms, and in businesses—women took the place of men and did a very good job.

During World War II, the important role of women doing the work of men became

How To Prepare Foods For....
Frozen Food Lockers

Earhart's Food Locker

WHOLESALE — RETAIL

Locker Service — Meat Processing — Custom Butchering
Custom Curing

PHONE 148T

HAVANA, ILL.

Inquire about our home locker service and installations in your home.

This is a photo of the cover of a brochure that Earhart Food Locker provided to customers to help them prepare foods for processing and cold storage. THANKS TO DAVID C. EARHART FOR PROVIDING AN IMAGE OF THE COVER OF THIS BROCHURE. FAMILY COLLECTION.

memorialized in one of the most important poster icons of the times, Rosie the Riveter. In this carefully posed portrait, Rosie looks rather stern-faced, her jaw firmly set and eyes staring off into the distance, as if committed to helping the boys over there. The bandana wrapped around her head is a sign she doesn't have time for a fancy hair-do, because she's getting ready to work. She has rolled up the sleeves of her blue work shirt and flexes her biceps with a clenched fist. Rosie remains one of the most famous images of World War II. In a 1942 popular song, "Rosie the Riveter," singers alternate lyrics praising her patriotic war work with "brrrrrr, brrrrrr," mimicking the sounds of her riveting machine. (This song is available on Youtube.)

The official poster of Rosie has a simple message, "WE CAN DO IT." The picture of a determined woman implies that "we women" can do it— take over from the men and do a man's job. The "we" also refers to all of us in America, female and male, young and old, civilians and military personnel, who can pull together to win the war.

Everyone who lived on the homefront at that time became familiar with Rosie as a symbol of the mobilization of women. Before the war, females had rather limited employment options in service work, teaching, nursing, and clerical positions, but with America's young men gone to war, the "weaker sex"

IMAGE COURTESY OF NATIONAL ARCHIVES/WIKI-MEDIA.

was promoted to blue collar status in factories and managerial positions in businesses. When men went off to the warfront, women on the homefront took over where the men left off. Although some doubted that members of the fair sex could fill the shoes of men, women proved themselves more than worthy of the task. The military gave some women the rank of officers.

The image of Rosie the Riveter highlights the work of women in munitions factories and other war production plants. The War Production Co-ordinating Committee, the government agency that produced posters, carefully and deliberately crafted the official icon of Rosie. However, the day-in, day-out hard work of Mother and Grandmother shaped my small town memories of women during wartime.

On the other side of the Pacific Ocean, in postwar Japan, people said, "after the war, stockings and women got stronger." If we adapted this Japanese phrase to the American scene, it might also be true that in America stockings got stronger after the war. But my recollection is that American women gained their greater strength *during* the war. They didn't have to wait until postwar times. Four pieces from *The Mason County Democrat* for 1942, 1943, and 1944 document the fact that while men in the military fought the war overseas, some stateside people recognized the important role of women in the war effort.

A November 20, 1942 news item announced the designation of November 22–28 as "Minute Women War Week," urging the cooperation of all women's organizations in Mason County, especially to promote the sale of war savings stamps and bonds. "This is one week when every woman in America—the farmer's wife, the village school teacher, the soldier's sweetheart, the woman at home and the woman at work—must enlist her active support behind the gigantic plans to promote the sale of bonds and stamps."

The government borrowed the Revolutionary War notion of the "Minute Man," a member of the militia who in a minute could change from civilian to soldier, to create the "Minute Woman" of World War II. Although our family did not use the phrase "Minute Woman," our mother and grandmother acted as living examples of women who supported the war effort with their replacement of working men.

The April 16, 1943 issue of the *Democrat* took up this theme with its own editorial acknowledging the role of women, both in military service, and also as civilians, war workers, and housewives.

TO MRS. AMERICA

Seldom does a day go by that we who read the news and listen to the radio do not hear lauded the WAAC's, the WAVE's, and other Women's Auxiliaries of the various branches of service. We see their pictures in attractive poses, we see pictures of them at work and at play. We hear their daily schedules explained and we picture them as making an excellent contribution to the war effort. Doing a job that possesses glamour, and a job that appeals to the adventurous instinct of the American people.

To these women go the applause of the nation. However, there is another woman that is making a contribution to the war effort of which we hear very little. Her job possesses no glamour, no adventure. Her schedule is pretty much the same, year in and year out. Yet she goes about her work with all the seriousness of the man on the fighting front. We refer to Mrs. Housewife, whose job it is to keep her family well fed, well clothed and happy, that they may better perform their jobs.

No glamour job has Mrs. Housewife, but a vital one. She is a working girl and her uniform is the familiar apron. She works all three shifts, putting in up to 16 hours a day, seven days a week, and her only time-and-a-half is the satisfaction she gets out of a job well done for her family, her home and her country.

My own experiences can add to this praise of Mrs. Housewife, because our mother served both as Mrs. Businesswoman and Mrs. Housewife. After Dad left for the service, and before we moved to Grandma's house, for a while we still lived in our own home on South Orange. Because Mother needed to be at the locker plant to open the business, she had to rely on my two older sisters and me to wash, dress, fix our breakfast, and get to school on time. I could easily make it to school on time, because Oak Grove School was just a block away, and I liked to go to school early to play.

School came easy for me, and I got good grades. But on my first report card after Dad left, I received a low mark in conduct. Mother asked me what I had done to deserve that low grade. It puzzled me, because I didn't talk in class, throw paper wads, or get into fights.

Mother had to go to school to discover the problem. The teacher explained that a number of times she had noticed dirt behind my ears. In today's world that might seem unimportant, but to a 1940s mother, the scandal of sending a child to school unkempt amounted to utter humiliation. I promised Mother that in the future I would be more clean, and, "Yes, I will be sure to wash behind my ears." What I didn't tell mother was that I thought the teacher should keep her eyes on the blackboard, not on my ears.

Women involved themselves in a number of war-related activities. A brief article in the March 31, 1944 *Democrat* reports on the availability of "kits for soldiers" entering the Army. Members of the Business & Professional Women's club volunteered their time and effort to prepare kits for military inductees:

KITS FOR SOLDIERS STILL AVAILABLE

Announcement has been made that there are still a limited number of Kits for Soldiers available for men from Havana Township who are entering the Army. These kits, made and filled by the Havana Business & Professional Women's club, contain articles that the soldier will find very useful during his training.

Anyone entering the Army may have one of these kits by calling at the Harsman Electric Shop.

On June 2, 1944, the *Democrat* once more editorialized on the significance of women in the war effort:

THE WEAKER SEX?

Although most of the memories that we will have of the present conflict, when it finally comes to an end, will be the recollections of the suffering, dying and destruction that came to so many of the people and nations of the world, there will also be many thoughts that will fill us with pride. Among the greater of these memories will be the part that the American women played in the battle to save the world, but they never before had the opportunity to prove that they could be as resourceful, as courageous and as full of the spirit of competition as the members of the opposite sex. It is true that as far back as the American Revolution we have had war heroines, but not until this war did they arise in such great masses to assist in conquering an enemy.

Besides the women and girls that have joined the various branches of the armed forces in order to replace a man that he might go to the front, thousands have gone to work in war plants, exchanging their evening dresses for a pair of coveralls and their dressing tables for drill presses and many other machines that heretofore only a man was ever taught to use.

The housewives are also contributing in various ways, such as conserving food, abiding by all rationing laws and saving fats and other material used in the war effort. The mothers who have waited for their boys to return, so many in vain, are displaying the courage and spirit that is expected of the mother of any fighting Yank.

It goes without saying that American women have always had these qualities and now, as in the past, needed only to hear their country's need for them. We are proud of you, Women of America, and when the history of this war is over, we know that your courage and perseverance will remain among the other great accomplishments which, added together, brought defeat to our enemies.

Whether she was businesswoman or housewife, American women were certainly essential to the homefront as well as the war effort. One of the lessons of World War II, as demonstrated by my mother and grandmother, is that Mrs. America could not be called the "weaker sex."

CHAPTER 5

Rosie the Riveter

My small-town setting had no major factories for the likes of any would-be Rosies. But for the women of Havana the war also meant taking over what had always been considered men's work. For Mother, that meant running the locker plant. Moving back to her parents' home required another major adjustment, sharing a home and responsibilities in a three-generation family.

As a boy, I knew little of the larger picture of women's role in the war. But what I saw and heard of Mom in action at the locker plant, I will never forget. Workers were very hard to come by during the war. The main employee in our small business, Fred, a retired farmer, had butchering experience from the farm, and could cut meat. Fred took the place of our dad in the locker plant, and as is the case of any small business, he became part of our extended family. He had one shortcoming—a weakness for the bottle, something Mom and Grandma talked about at the dinner table.

Mom gave him some credit, "Well, he's a good worker, if he just wouldn't drink."

Grandma agreed, "Sure, he can drink at home, at night, but not during the day, when he's on the job."

Occasionally Fred would arrive with the smell of whiskey on his breath. From time to time he got drunk and didn't show up at all.

One day, too liquored up to work, he entered the Locker and insisted he could run the electric saw and cut meat with sharp knives. He created a real scene, and Mother had to send him home. The next day I happened to be at the Locker when he came in. Unfortified by alcohol, he had turned meek and humble.

Mother gave him a merciless tongue-lashing. "What in the world were you thinking of, coming to work drunk? Don't you know you give our business a bad reputation?"

Mary Earhart scolding Fred. My mother was about 5′1″, Fred was over 6 feet tall. At that time my mother weighed probably 120, Fred must have weighed over 200. ILLUSTRATION BY JOHN MICHAEL DOWNS.

I had never seen Mother so mad. She made Rosie the Riveter look like a cream puff. That day Mom could have whipped both Germany and Japan all by herself.

Fred had lost a son in the war, and people today might say he had good reason to drown his sorrows in booze. We did not accept that excuse during World War II. Everyone sacrificed and worked hard for the war effort. Dad was risking his life in the Navy. Mom gave Fred no slack for coming to work drunk.

She took a risk being harsh with Fred, because he could easily get a job in another store, and Mother would have a hard time replacing him. He did good work and could be trusted when sober.

She chewed him out like he deserved. She scolded him just like she would punish her child who had misbehaved.

Fred didn't make excuses or talk back. He apologized.

She didn't fire him and he didn't quit.

This was the first time I ever had seen a woman in such a position of power and authority laying down the law to a man. Just over five-feet tall and a little over a hundred pounds, Mom—only about half the size of six-footer Fred—showed no hesitation or lack of self-confidence in tearing into him.

During the time we lived at Grandma's house, I never heard my Mother complain once about the burdens of singlehandedly running the business. She surely must have worried as much or more than the rest of us about the safety of Dad. If he lost his life in the war, how could she continue? But I don't recall any time when she voiced concern for her husband. I never saw her cry. Instead, she kept her fears to herself, and focused on reassuring us kids that Dad would be fine.

Only much later, after my parents passed away, did I realize the difficulties of those years. Mom and Dad, compulsive savers, kept every receipt for anything they bought, and during the war, they stored away every letter they wrote to each other.

Sorting through a shoebox of their letters, I picked up one of Mom's letters to Dad. Its message shocked me. The background of the letter's content framed the dilemma of the locker plant, which had been much worse than I could ever have imagined: constant maintenance, the diesel fuel supply, expensive repairs, difficulties getting the loans to keep the plant open, and also labor problems with Fred and negotiations with customers. Frugal farmers and townspeople were all the more troublesome to deal with, because of the many OPA regulations, ration books, and general food scarcity. My folks discussed the possibility of simply closing the locker plant.

In today's world of cell phones and instant text-messaging, we cannot imagine the wartime situation of lengthy intervals in correspondence, mailing a letter to a serviceman and waiting weeks for a reply.

An August 22, 1945 letter from Father to Mother illustrates this time lag. It had been sent by V-mail, a photographic copy of his message recorded on microfilm, sent to the United States, and then printed and delivered. This wartime technique minimized and lightened postal matter. Note the date on the handwritten letter, August 22, 1945; the date on the US Postal Center envelope is September 8, 1945. Mom and Dad were separated not only by distance, but also by a communication gap of weeks while each had to stew over what to write, and wonder what the response would be.

Text of Kenneth Earhart's August 22, 1945 letter to his wife Mary.

> Dear Mary Aug 22–45
>
> To start with, this is going to be the shortest letter I have ever written. A fellow give me this paper and another gave me the stamp. I can't explain yet. This will probably be the last letter for a while. Thing aren't really that bad. I will be pretty busy for a while so don't worry if you don't hear from me for a while.

The envelope for a V-mail from Kenneth Earhart to his wife Mary. FAMILY COLLECTION.

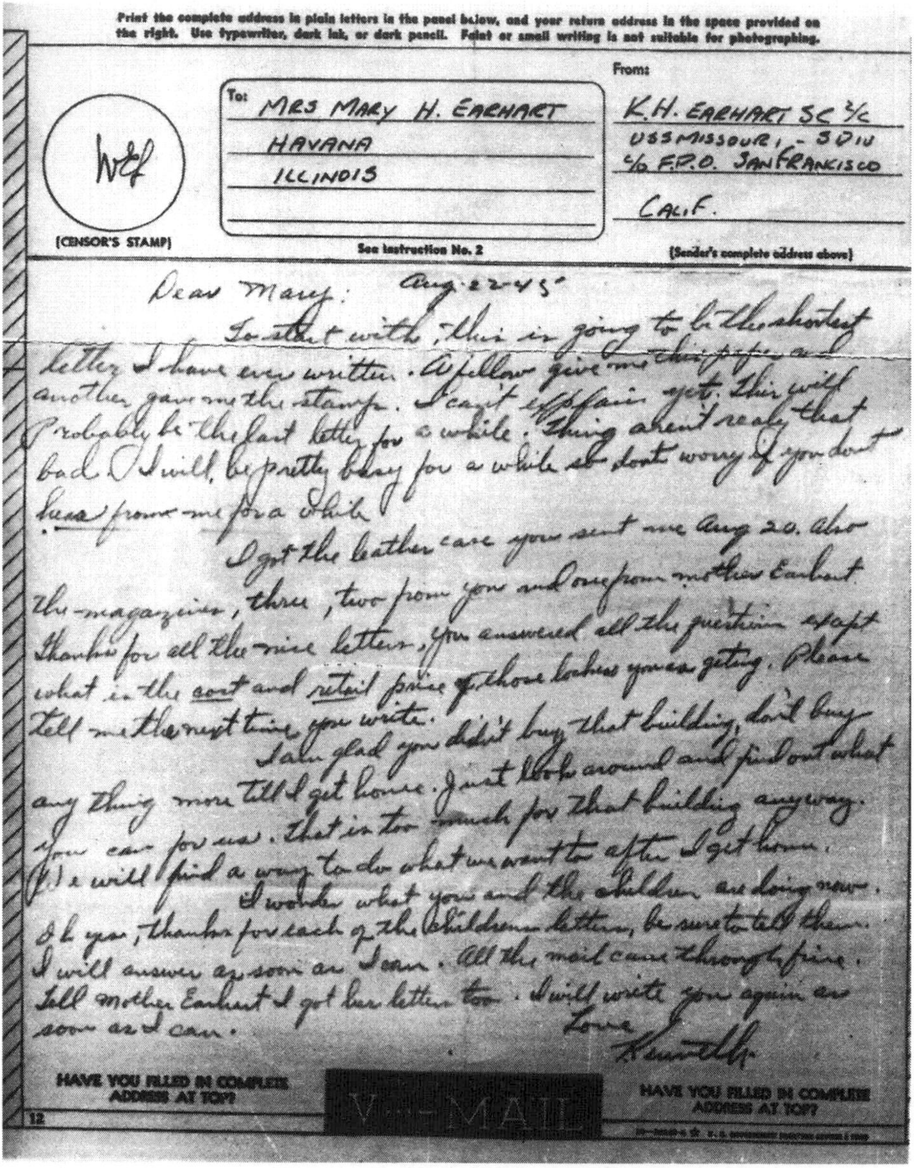

Print the complete address in plain letters in the panel below, and your return address in the space provided on the right. Use typewriter, dark ink, or dark pencil. Faint or small writing is not suitable for photographing.

To: MRS MARY H. EARHART
HAVANA
ILLINOIS

From: K.H. EARHART SC 3/c
USS MISSOURI, - 30 IV
c/o F.P.O. SAN FRANCISCO
CALIF.

(CENSOR'S STAMP) W.E.

See Instruction No. 2

(Sender's complete address above)

Dear Mary: Aug. 22-45

To start with, this is going to be the shortest letter I have ever written. A fellow give me this paper and another gave me the stamp. I can't explain yet. This will probably be the last letter for a while. Things aren't really that bad & I will be pretty busy for a while so don't worry if you don't hear from me for a while.

I got the leather case you sent me Aug 20. Also the magazines, three, two from you and one from mother Earhart. Thanks for all the nice letters, you answered all the questions except what is the cost and retail price of those lockers you are getting. Please tell me the next time you write.

I am glad you didn't buy that building, don't buy any thing more till I get home. Just look around and find out what you can for us. that is too much for that building anyway. We will find a way to do what we want to after I get home.

I wonder what you and the children are doing now. I [illegible] you, thanks for each of the children's letters, be sure to tell them I will answer as soon as I can. All the mail came through fine. Tell mother Earhart I got her letter too. I will write you again as soon as I can.

Love
Kenneth

HAVE YOU FILLED IN COMPLETE ADDRESS AT TOP?

V-MAIL

HAVE YOU FILLED IN COMPLETE ADDRESS AT TOP?

12

The handwritten text of Kenneth Earhart's letter, which the government photographed and sent by microfilm to the U.S., then printed out and mailed. Note the censor's stamp in the circle at the upper left. FAMILY COLLECTION.

I got the leather case you sent me Aug 20. Also the magazines, three, two from you and one from mother Earhart. Thanks for all the nice letters, you answered all the questions except what is the <u>cost</u> and <u>retail</u> of the lockers you're geting. Please tell me the next time you write.

I am glad you didn't buy that building, don't buy anything more till I get home. Just look around and find out what you can for us. That is too much for that building anyway. We will find a way to do what we want to after I get home.

I wonder what you and the children are doing now. Oh yes, thank you for each of the childrens letters, be sure to tell them. I will answer them as soon as I can. All the mail came through fine. Tell mother Earhart I got her letter too. I will write you again as soon as I can.

Love,
Kenneth

Early in the war, Mom and Dad discussed a shocking option: Dad getting a "hardship" discharge from the Navy. This kind of discharge was difficult to obtain, but could be arranged if a vital industry or essential service needed a man on the homefront. My parents could make the claim that keeping the locker plant open helped civilians feed themselves, providing more food for the war effort. Mom had written Dad, asking him to apply for a hardship discharge. Dad wrote back to her that he didn't want to leave the Navy, but if she really needed the help, he would go along with this petition.

In the letter I randomly picked from the shoe box, Mom wrote a poignant reply to her husband. She thanked him for being willing to accept her suggestion and do what he didn't want to do, give up his duty to country and leave the military, in order to come home and help her run the business. Mom had been getting ready to start her part of the application for a hardship discharge.

Before she completed the application, something she heard me say made her change her mind. According to Mom's letter, I had learned about another hometown man who received a hardship discharge. At the dinner table, I told the family that this was a disgrace. *My* Dad would never pull such a dirty trick. He was patriotic. He had *enlisted,* even when he was past thirty, and had four dependents, and would never have been drafted.

My Dad was in the service. He would never ask to leave the service. To this day, what is remarkable about this whole discussion of a hardship discharge for Dad is that I never heard about it during the war, or in the many years up to my parents' deaths when they were both past 95. Only in an accidental glance through my folks' exchange of letters did I fully realize just how much Mom had to put up with during the war, relying on her steel nerves and iron constitution. Even after the war, my parents never discussed this hardship application. I can only imagine the turmoil each of them experienced writing letters to each other, agonizing over how to put down on paper their best judgment of what to do, and then waiting weeks for a reply.

Looking back today, I find it hard to comprehend how she could do all of this. Part of the answer is that during the war people—especially women—simply did what they had to. No one told them what they were able or unable to do. They just went ahead and did it!

People like my parents and grandparents, who grew up or lived through the Depression, had faced hard times and knew that making a living presents a constant challenge. Another part of the answer to how Mother managed to run the locker plant is the help and support of Grandma and Grandpa, mostly Grandma. Grandpa assisted in building the individual "lockers," made of plywood. He varnished them. But Grandpa had no gift for business. He continued to paint houses during the war years, and never worked at the Locker.

Grandma was a dynamo, helping Mom in everything. Grandma took care of the house, which put her in charge of meals. This freed up my mother to go to the locker plant early and work late, depending on Grandma to be home when my older sisters and I returned from school. Grandma also worked at the Locker when needed, wrapping meat and waiting on customers.

People renting lockers would come into the store and ask for their key, before going into the cold storage, unlocking their rented locker and getting food from it. Then they locked up their locker and gave the key back as they left. Grandma often worked what we called "the front," the small area by the street where we kept keys next to the cold storage entrance. The processing part of the business took place in "the back," behind the cold storage and next to the alley.

Anyone familiar with a small family business knows they operate by no regular hours and no job limitations. You do what needs to be done when it has to be done for as long as it takes. And often you work beyond your limitations. Once, toward the end of the war, Grandma had a fainting spell while working at the locker plant. Everyone in the family worried about her. She laughed it off and returned to work in a few days.

Others may visualize wartime women workers as the national "poster icon" Rosie the Riveter, but my images arise from personal experiences. I think of my mother managing the locker plant and giving Fred a good tongue-lashing. I recall my grandmother shrugging off a fainting spell and going right back to work.

Rosie the Riveter, move over and make room for Mary Earhart the Ironwoman and Ruth Haack the Powerhouse.

I still hear these three chanting in unison: *WE CAN DO IT!*

CHAPTER 6

For the Duration

When our family moved to Grandma's house, we considered it neither temporary nor permanent. Our stay had no time limit of days or weeks or months. But we didn't expect to live there forever. We put our lives on hold until the war ended, and Dad came home.

For a young boy, who changed schools and had to make new friends, and watched the seasons come and go, it seemed like for all time, even though we knew it wasn't. Our family never really talked about it. We didn't need to, because we were living it. Everyone called this vague waiting period "for the duration."

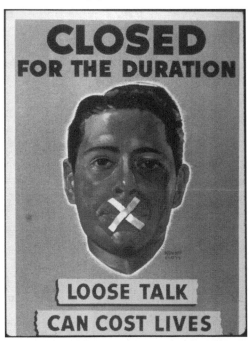

IMAGE COURTESY OF NATIONAL ARCHIVES/
WIKIMEDIA.

These three words became so familiar that people used them for any activity that spanned the indeterminate time between Pearl Harbor and the end of the war. The poster "Closed for the Duration" refers to a ban on "loose talk" for as long as the war lasted. "For the duration" defined the expanse in between temporary and permanent, a suspended animation with no conclusion in sight. December 7, 1941, with the Japanese bombing of Pearl Harbor, set the tone for our wartime life, a period that alternated between tense anxiety and dedicated patriotism.

A store could close "for the duration," because they had no goods to sell, or no employees (especially men), to run it. These three words justified the absence of goods, and served to explain strict wartime policies. During the war we had no new cars or bicycles. Although America had been the land of plenty, during the war many goods became scarce or simply not available.

Most of us just put up with what we had. Mom and Grandma helped set the tone for our household. Grandma would say, "Well, we don't have anything to complain about, giving up a few luxuries. Think of what our boys are doing fighting the war. And we're not starving, like some of the people in China."

Mom would chime in with her two cents. "Yes, we're very lucky. We have plenty to eat, and we want to help Daddy and others in the armed forces win the war."

The shortage of new goods made us much more appreciative of all material possessions. We noticed most some of the smallest things. Grandma loved to fish, and as soon as I went fishing with her, I was hooked, too. We fished with plain bamboo poles, tying a line to the tip and adding a bobber, sinker, and hook, and using fishworms for bait. Before and after the war, one of the familiar signs of spring was bundles of bamboo poles stacked in front of hardware stores, standing tall and proud like flagpoles. After the war started, with the interruption of shipping from Asia, the stores had no bamboo poles.

During the war years, even bats for playing ball became scarce. Everyone was on the lookout for the hard to get. As a boy, I had my eye out for fishing poles and a good bat. It pains me to remember how persistent I was in this quest. Mother had hired Fred, a retired farmer, to help her cut meat and run the store. His son joined the Air Force, and his plane got shot down over Germany, presumed dead.

Fred told me one day that his son liked to fish and play ball, too. I posed the inevitable question. "Do you still have his fishing poles and bats?"

Fred paused, as if thinking, then said, "Yes, I do."

I asked, "Would you sell them to me?"

Fred turned away from me, with a sad look on his face, mumbling, "Uh, well . . . we'll see."

At the time I could not imagine the pain I caused Fred by my innocent question. Hanging on to his dead son's belongings must have been one way of keeping alive memories of this only child. But Fred didn't mention what he was thinking or feeling. Throughout the war, people tended to hold back their raw emotions.

Looking back on the situation, I only did what other Americans were doing, trying to get through the war as best they could. Maybe my crude questioning of Fred can be attributed to a combination of boyish naivete and the scarcity of goods "for the duration."

We remember World War II as the good war, and that's the way I recall it. All the time we lived with Grandma, the war completely set the rhythm of life. We looked for mail from Daddy every day, and were happy when a package came from him. At school, teachers encouraged us to use our dimes for savings stamps rather than candy. Even when we went to the movies on weekends, we would hear a special plea from leading citizens of the community, such as the local bank president, to buy war bonds.

At the movie theater, from time to time, after the newsreels and before the main feature in the evening, they held a special auction for the services of leading citizens to do some cleaning or other menial task, all the proceeds going to support the war. Here are the first few paragraphs of a June 9, 1944 article in *The Mason County Democrat:*

"Slave Auction"
Added Attraction
At Bond Premier

The people of Havana and surrounding territory will have a chance to help in winning the war, and at the same time enjoy themselves, according to the announcement made by Ray Chadwick, manager of the local Kerasotes Theatres.

The Havana Rotary Club is sponsoring a "Slave Auction" where prominent men of the community will sell their services to the highest bidder for war bonds. This is in addition to the War Bond Premier "A Lady In The Dark," to be shown at the Lawford Theatre on Wednesday evening, June 21. This auction will be the same as that recently sponsored by the Rotary Club in Springfield where Governor Green was sold in bondage to cut twenty acres of timothy hay (with a lawn mower).

Admission to the Premier is by the purchase of War Bonds only. One ticket will be issued with each $25.00 bond, or a limit of four tickets to any purchaser.

"Any Bonds Today," a 1942 tune by Irving Berlin, was the official song of the National Defense Savings Program. Made into an animated cartoon featuring Bugs Bunny, Porky Pig, and Elmer Fudd, it was played at movie theaters before the main film, with ushers collecting money for savings bonds and stamps. A number of singers, including the Andrews Sisters and Gene Autry, recorded the song. Versions of "Any Bonds Today" can be viewed and listened to on the internet.

Local drives headed by prominent citizens matched a number of War Bond drives on the national level. The head of the First National Bank in Havana had been one of the "slaves" in the auction held at the War Bond Premier. Because Havana had always been an all-white community, and during the 1940s there was no awareness of later notions of political correctness, the term "slaves" could be used without a second thought of offending anyone.

The head of the bank also served as the leader of the local bond drive. This bank placed an ad promoting Savings Bonds in the December 12, 1942 *Democrat*, which ran continuously in every wartime issue.

From 1941 through 1945, I never once heard anyone criticize or oppose the war effort. We saved harsh words for those who didn't do enough. Some of this criticism might have been unwarranted, some was probably true. Once when an old peddler made his way through town, his strange appearance made us kids think he must be a gypsy,

Peddler with his goats and wagon. ILLUSTRATION BY JOHN MICHAEL DOWNS.

with his colorful dress and bandana around his neck, and his wagon pulled by goats. For days after he left town he remained a lively topic of conversation among us kids.

"He must be a spy."

"I bet he keeps war secrets hidden in the horns of the goats."

The ugliest talk—and action—we reserved for draft dodgers. The *Democrat* occasionally reported the names of men who the military police apprehended for avoiding the draft, and those who went AWOL after entering the armed forces. All men had to register for the draft at age eighteen. After medical examination for physical fitness, each man received a classification from 1-A to 4-F, depending upon his physical condition, number of dependents, and occupation. The young who were fit, with no dependents, and working at an "unessential" occupation, got a 1-A rank. These were the first to be drafted. To be 1-A was a matter of pride and patriotism, and also a romantic advantage, as a late 1941 popular song phrased it: "He's 1-A in the Army, and He's A-1 in My Heart." (This song is available on Youtube.)

Those with limited eyesight or hearing or mobility, or other infirmity, received a rank from 1-B to 4-E, and were lower priority for the draft, while men with 4-F rank due to some major physical, mental, or health condition were exempt from the draft. As the April 7, 1944 *Democrat* image of Uncle Sam indicates, those with 4-F status may have been relieved of military duty, but the government insisted that they answer the "Call To Duty!" to support the war effort with their labor, such as in war plants.

Those with many dependents received special consideration, and some people in occupations considered "essential" for the war effort were exempt from military service. Local draft boards had flexibility in their responsibility of determining which draftees were engaged in essential occupations. If a person with a higher draft rank who previously had been exempted from induction because of his work in an essential job, later left that position, he was subject to being drafted immediately.

Young men who appeared to be able-bodied, yet did not serve in the military, were always suspect. In a neighboring town, a rumor circulated that a younger man who ran the bank was "yellow" because he somehow qualified for exemption from service. Someone painted a yellow stripe on the bank door, but the police never made an arrest for this act.

Some young men who were sons of farmers and worked on the family farm managed to get deferments because of their claim of doing "essential" work raising food. City folk whose sons, husbands, and brothers had been drafted or voluntarily enlisted, shared with one another their criticism of these young farm men. "Hah, he got out of the draft by hiding behind the corn stalks."

My sister Rosemary remembers not only this phrase of "hiding behind the corn stalks," but even the names of several area farm boys who obtained deferment to help out on the family farm.

Because the issue of who served in the military was a matter of life and death, inevitably it provoked controversy over who was drafted and who got deferred. The *Democrat* in a July 18, 1943 editorial took the side of the "farm lad" who had been exempted from service due to his "essential" service.

HOMEFRONT ESSENTIALS

One of the most pathetic situations we have learned of during the war concerns a farm lad of military age who, the induction board has decreed, should remain on the farm. He comes to town occasionally, only occasionally, because the sight of boys his own age in uniform causes him untold agony.

He considers his job menial and he is not satisfied in the security of his agricultural duties. It is difficult for this lad to realize that there are jobs of vital importance which are not directly connected with the armed forces. In order for the people to eat—both the soldiers and the civilians—this boy and thousands of others like him must produce the food.

There are other important jobs that are void of glamour. The ability to coordinate these jobs and maintain a fighting force is what makes this country great, and it is that ability that will tell in the end.

I remember one pleasant fishing trip made unpleasant by friction over questionable support for the war. My grandmother had a good friend Elsie, who also loved to fish, and owned a 1936 Ford. Gas was rationed during the war, but because she seldom drove her car, Elsie always had gas to take us fishing. On one such outing Grandma and Elsie started talking about the war, which came up in conversation every day. Elsie told Grandma, "I know your son-in-law is in the service, but if my son Delbert had to go, I don't know what I'd do."

Grandma turned away and didn't say anything.

At the time it struck me as strange, because if my father—Grandma's son-in-law—was in the service, what was the difference if Elsie's son had to go to the war?

I soon forgot about it and got back to fishing, but Grandma was cool the rest of the afternoon. After Elsie took us home, Grandma really exploded. "Elsie doesn't mind if the men in other families go off to war, but she just couldn't stand it if her son Delbert was in the military!"

Grandma repeated that episode several times at the dinner table, using her imitation whiny voice of Elsie and her self-centered comment. Our family chimed in our agreement with Grandma, because if Dad could serve—*enlist!*—then Elsie had no reason to complain if her son got drafted.

World War II may have been the "good war," but we still had plenty of room for disagreement about matters such as farm lads—some city folk saw them as hiding behind the corn stalks—while the local newspaper editor viewed them as providing an essential service. The issue of who served in the military and who didn't was a touchy subject. Grandma didn't complain to her friend Elsie about not wanting her son to serve. Grandma waited until she was home, and vented her frustration to the family.

Our family was proud that our Father had enlisted in the navy, but not everyone shared our pride in this decision. One relative ridiculed Dad for leaving his family and business to enlist. "He didn't *have* to go into the service." My older sister, some seventy years later, still resents that unkind remark by a man who went to work in a war plant, making big money. I mention these two unpatriotic examples not to open old wounds, but to show that even during the "good war," people had sharp differences of opinion and occasional arguments.

Was an exempt "farm lad" just hiding behind the corn stalks? Or was he performing a job of vital, "essential" importance to his country?

Was our father's enlistment in the Navy a patriotic deed to serve his country? Or was it a selfish act of following personal sense of duty and thereby neglecting his family and business? Most of the time we kept these concerns to ourselves so they did not lead to open conflict. Nevertheless, these nagging questions lasted for the duration, and linger in memories even today.

CHAPTER 7

Rationing and the OPA

T he troublesome policies of price controls and rationing lasted for the duration. Government officials ordered rationing for most food items such as meat, canned goods, and sugar. They also rationed some wearing apparel such as shoes, and gasoline and tires.

Excerpts from a November 20, 1942 *Democrat* article told citizens how they had to comply with rationing. The article includes some of the bureaucratic maze of registration, ration books and coupons, dates, age limitations (for coffee), and special applications and certificates that citizens had to know and follow in order to purchase goods.

BOARD PREPARES FOR RATIONING OF MILEAGE—COFFEE

3125 BASIC "A" BOOKS WERE ISSUED IN THE COUNTY

A total of 3125 Basic "A" Mileage Ration books were issued during the regular registration period November 12, 13, and 14. Wilbur F. Wepner, Chief clerk of the Mason County War Price and Rationing Board announced today. . . .

Applications for supplemental mileage, non-highway rations, and transport rations must be mailed to the local office. Transport rations must be accompanied by a certificate of war necessity. . . .

Application blanks for fuel oil, including kerosene, should be obtained at the dealers and mailed to the office after being carefully processed. . . .

COFFEE

Coffee rationing, starting at midnight November 28, will set the amount of the beverage available to the individual at one pound for five weeks, according to word received at the local rationing office.

Beginning Sunday, November 29, and through Sunday, January 3, any person holding War Ration Book One, whose age is shown as 15 years or older on his book, may purchase one pound of coffee upon surrender of Stamp No. 27 from Book One. Coffee stamps in a book of a consumer whose age is shown on his book as 14 years or younger are not valid.

Consumers who have never received War Ration Book One because of a supply of excess sugar may obtain a book with all the sugar stamps 1 through 16, removed. . . .

These excerpts highlight some of the key provisions of a lengthy article with numerous requirements for punctual registration and proper utilization of these books and their stamps. The OPA issued a ration book to every person, and when you went to the store, you not only paid for each item, but also had to have the proper ration coupon. To prevent selling or trading of stamps, regulations required a customer to bring his or her personal ration book to the store and tear the ration stamps out in view of the cashier. In actual practice, families swapped stamps among themselves, and retailers looked the other way when customers handed over stamps already removed from books. Although our family carefully followed ration book rules, many people who have written

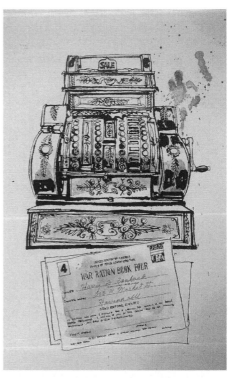

ILLUSTRATION BY JOHN MICHAEL DOWNS.

about wartime experiences confess that they and retailers often fudged on these regulations.

The complexity of food rationing is illustrated in an OPA guideline, "OFFICIAL TABLE OF POINT VALUES FOR PROCESSED FOODS," printed in newspapers across the country. It appeared in the February 26, 1943 issue of the *Democrat*. This directive's last line, in larger bold type, announces to all stores that "This Chart Must Be Displayed in a Prominent Place." Housewives and retailers had to present their ration books, tear out their stamps, and select the food items that matched the points on their stamps. The left side of this table of point values contains a list of fifty kinds of products: for example, fifteen kinds of "Fruits and Fruit Juices," from Apples to Pineapple; and fourteen kinds of Vegetables, from Asparagus to Tomato. The top of this table is divided into compartments by weight, in sixteen gradations from four ounces to four pounds. A housewife had to find her item, such as applesauce or peas in the list at the left, then read across the table to the weight of her purchase, in order to find the allowed points for that item. The fifty food items, bracketed by sixteen weights, make up a table of 800 cells. Both housewives and store clerks found this cumbersome table difficult to read and follow. (The Table appears as a large foldout between pp. 172 and 173 of the official government document, *Studies in Food Rationing*.)

A front-page cartoon in the February 26, 1943 *Democrat* bears the title "Cookin' with Numbers." A housewife sits at her kitchen table with cans of vegetables in front of her. She has a pad on the table, pencil in hand. Over her head are her mental calculations of which days of the week she will have how many ounces of what vegetables and their point equivalents. From the other room comes the voice of the husband, "How many points for dinner tonite, dear?" This illustrates a humorous portrayal of the daily dilemma for Americans, who never had to worry about starving, but did have to learn to plan their eating habits around rationing programs.

People tried to joke about rationing, and yet it became a serious matter with its complex regulations. A February 28, 1943 issue of the *Democrat* includes a half page set of instructions on rationing:

Use Your OLD Ration Book for SUGAR and COFFEE

HOW TO USE YOUR NEW RATION BOOK
TO BUY CANNED OR BOTTLED FRUITS,
VEGETABLES, SOUPS, AND JUICES; FROZEN
FRUITS AND VEGETABLES; DRIED FRUITS

1. The Government has set the day when this rationing will start. On or after that day, take your War Ration Book Two with you when you go to buy any kind of these processed foods.

This notice follows up with eight numbered instructions for using ration books when shopping.

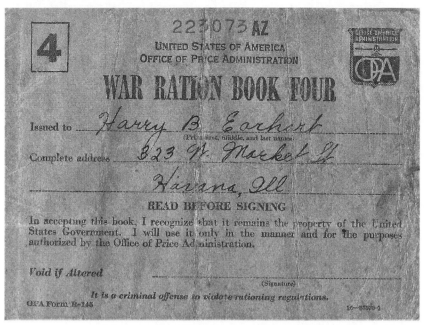

This is my ration book from World War II. Note the official "OPA" (Office of Price Administration) logo in the upper right corner of the front. On the front, the emphasis is on the fact that the ration book "remains the property of the United States Government." PERSONAL COLLECTION.

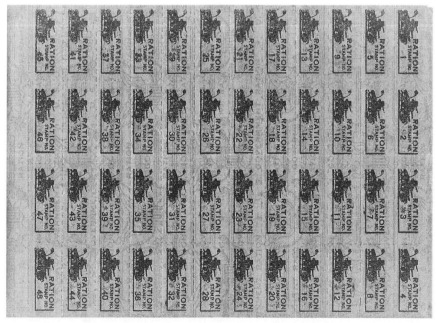

Even the ration coupons on the inside of the book have military symbols of tanks and ships. PERSONAL COLLECTION.

A May 21, 1942 *Democrat* article announces "New Book Designed As Aid To The Housewife Is Now Available At This Office." This book, "Home Budgets for Victory," is "designed as an aid to the housewife and to agriculture in general." By cooperating with the National Defense program, housewives will "speed our ultimate victory by lessening the use in the home of food and other commodities so necessary to the united nations' war effort." The book helps the homemaker stretch food and the home budget, including sections on "What Foods to Eat and Why," as well as chapters on Victory gardens and canning. Government regulations implemented the national policy on rationing, but in general, people supported this policy, for example, in the writing of the book on Home Budgets for Victory.

Our household fared better than many families, especially because we grew much of our own food, and could either can or freeze it. But we couldn't grow sugar, what we missed most. Everyone in our family kept their eyes on the sugar bowl. Grandma promised us, "If we have enough sugar at the end of the month, I'll bake a cake or pie."

INSTRUCTIONS

1 This book is valuable. Do not lose it.

2 Each stamp authorizes you to purchase rationed goods in the quantities and at the times designated by the Office of Price Administration. Without the stamps you will be unable to purchase those goods.

3 Detailed instructions concerning the use of the book and the stamps will be issued. Watch for those instructions so that you will know how to use your book and stamps. Your Local War Price and Rationing Board can give you full information.

4 Do not throw this book away when all of the stamps have been used, or when the time for their use has expired. You may be required to present this book when you apply for subsequent books.

Rationing is a vital part of your country's war effort. Any attempt to violate the rules is an effort to deny someone his share and will create hardship and help the enemy.

This book is your Government's assurance of your right to buy your fair share of certain goods made scarce by war. Price ceilings have also been established for your protection. Dealers must post these prices conspicuously. Don't pay more.

Give your whole support to rationing and thereby conserve our vital goods. Be guided by the rule:

"If you don't need it, DON'T BUY IT."

16—33299-1   ☆   U. S. GOVERNMENT PRINTING OFFICE 1943

On the back of the ration book is the combined encouragement of patriotism and threat of aiding the enemy: "Rationing is a vital part of your country's war effort. Any attempt to violate the rules is an effort to deny someone his share and will create hardship and help the enemy." PERSONAL COLLECTION.

All of us had to be sparing in our use of sugar, in morning oatmeal and corn flakes. One of the long-term benefits of this ration policy is that I learned to drink tea without sugar, and still drink it without sweetening today.

The reader may wonder, with foods rationed, and ration stamps so valuable, why my ration book seen in previous illustrations still has many stamps in it. That leads me to a shameful confession. As a boy I was absent-minded, always losing or misplacing things. Unfortunately, one of my ration books went missing, which meant that the entire family suffered for my forgetfulness. Until we received the next ration books, everyone had to skimp on essentials such as sugar. My sisters reminded me time and again, "Byron, if you didn't lose your stamp book, we'd all have more sugar." Somehow the book turned up, a bittersweet memory of wartime life.

Adults prized coffee as a luxury item. Some people turned to drinking imitation coffee, such as Postum, made from roasted grains. Grandpa remained a holdout. "I won't drink the damned stuff. If I can't have real coffee, I'll just do without."

We did not understand the complex regulations and changing decisions handed down by the OPA, which we feared like an all-powerful black box that we had to obey. Unknown to us, behind the scenes, government officials kept busy with paper work. Bureaucrats in the OPA seemed to enjoy creating tables, lists of regulations and statistics, and charts of distribution. The "Flow Chart of Coffee from Importers to Ultimate Consumers" is just one of many examples of such bureaucratic organization, which traces the path of coffee from the importer to the American coffee pot. (The chart appears on page 65 of the official government document, *Studies in Food Rationing*.) This chart has at the top one large box for "importers," from which channels trace the flow of coffee to compartments labeled "roasters," and flowing by various routes to compartments for "wholesalers," "chains," and "retail outlets," and finally to homes. The last compartment has a channel for the coffee to flow into "the American coffee pot."

The average American such as Grandpa had no knowledge of such bureaucratic efficiency. All he knew was that his own "American coffee pot" and cup were empty, and he refused to drink the alternative. Bureaucrats loved charts, graphs, and figures. Grandpa loved his coffee.

Coffee, like sugar, was a problem because we could not grow it. Other items we could not grow or obtain without coupons were gasoline and tires. Owners of cars had to apply for a gasoline sticker, which had printed on it a letter according to the amount of gasoline the person was allowed to buy. The lowest category was an "A" sticker, displayed on the lower right corner of the windshield. When a car with an "A" sticker pulled into the gas station, the station attendant required the driver to produce coupons of the "A" variety in order to buy gas. The gas station attendant supposedly had to watch the customer tear out

This October 13, 1943 *Democrat* advertisement for D-X gasoline illustrates stickers and coupons. This ad, like most wartime ads, was multipurpose, promoting a product, but also claiming that their gasoline "stretches your gasoline coupons." It also encourages motorists to save their old tires ("the carcass") and recap them. Below the car in the graphic is a text urging people to buy war bonds.

the coupon from a ration book. Legally, loose coupons could not be accepted, but attendants did not always follow this regulation. People who had to travel farther to work, or drive a car as part of their work, received higher letter stickers, which entitled them to purchase more gasoline. We heard many rumors about black market gasoline sales.

The Office of Price Administration oversaw the cost of most goods. At the time, Americans referred to this government bureau by its feared, sometimes hated, acronym, the OPA. The program was probably a good idea overall, because it served a dual purpose for the armed forces and for civilians. It gave first priority to the military for access to food and products. On the homefront, the OPA minimized hoarding and prevented gouging on prices of scarce goods. But it turned into a nightmare for people like my mother, who had to run a small business while following all the regulations of a complex bureaucracy. For children, the OPA represented the phrase for a government and its regulations that we could not understand but knew we had to obey. We experienced rationing through the use of ration books that determined what canned goods and sugar we could buy. I regretted losing my ration book, because the whole family let me know that everyone suffered due to my absentmindedness.

Hindsight always allows people to criticize bureaucratic organizations and policies. It should be noted that in spite of false starts and changing regulations, the rationing and price controls proved effective in assuring rather equitable distribution and pricing of goods. Nevertheless, any bureaucracy can be so bureaucratic that it leads to its own ridiculous extremes. One such case is found in the *OPA MANUAL for Typists, Stenographers & Secretaries*, published by the Office of Price Administration in 1943.

The booklet begins with the serious tone of a military manual for soldiers disassembling and reassembling a weapon: "At a time when every minute must be made to count, Standardization is especially needed to facilitate flexibility in personnel assignments, to save operating time and to serve as an instrument of efficient supervision." The absurd extreme to which this manual subjects typists is highlighted in the many details of "OFFICE HOUSEKEEPING." Quoting just one of many "housekeeping" requirements is sufficient to demonstrate bureaucracy run amok: "PENCILS, PENS, ETC. Keep a supply of well-sharpened pencils. Keep your fountain pen clean by irrigating it with warm water once or twice a month, and see that it is always filled. See that any other equipment which you may need is ready for immediate use." (Page I-4 of *OPA Manual for Typists, Stenographers & Secretaries.*)

Bureaucrats in Washington obsessed over details like typists irrigating their fountain pens regularly. On the homefront, we had no knowledge of such efficient directives. We paid more attention to the sugar bowl and the coffee pot.

The regulations for wholesale beef regulation ran to 40,000 words of rather obscure details of how meat should be processed, priced, and sold. One example:

> The excess loin (lumbar) and pelvic (sacral) fat shall be trimmed from the inside of the full loin by placing the full loin upon a flat surface, with no other support to change its position, meat side down, and removing all fat which extends above a flat plane parallel with the flat surface supporting the full loin and on a level with the full length of the protruding edge of the lumbar section of the chin bone.

Meat packers had difficulty following such complicated details. Retailers like my mother had trouble buying and pricing cuts. And the housewife didn't know how to spend her valuable points for cuts of meat whose technical names she did not know (such as "yoke, rattle, or triangle bone in"). Many cattlemen, independent slaughterhouses (with no inspection), and farmers who slaughtered their own cattle, managed to avoid such restrictions. Some sold directly to the black market. Farm-slaughtered meat alone counted for about 12 per cent of the civilian supply, which found its way into frozen food lockers like ours, with no exchange of points. Meat was the most scarce of all rationed food items. Some butchers saved their limited supplies for regular customers, telling others they did not have the requested cuts. (Some of this information on meat rationing comes from Lingeman, *Don't You Know There's a War On?*, pp. 257–267.)

The precious nature of meat is borne out in the memory of one of my schoolmates. In 2014 this woman went to the Easley Pioneer Museum for a Camp Ellis Day celebration (Camp Ellis will be discussed later). The director of the museum, Marion Cornelius, told a party of visitors from Havana about a rough draft of the present book, which he had read. The woman remarked that she remembered me, because I was the rich kid from the locker plant who gave his teacher a pound of bacon for Christmas. This jogged my memory. I remembered the

1942 Christmas present of bacon, but not being rich. I had given my teacher some bacon for Christmas, maybe a pound. Bacon was hard to come by, and at that time anyone who could give a gift of a pound of bacon would have been thought of as rich.

As with gas rationing, there was a black market in meat, and some violators were prosecuted. It is estimated that one in fifteen businesses were charged with illicit transactions, and one in five of all establishments received some kind of warning. (Detailed accounts of the black market and prosecutions are given in Lingeman, *Don't You Know There's a War On?*, pp. 257–267.)

The government charged Mother with overpricing, and she paid a hefty fine. Mother complained bitterly about the injustice of this penalty. "I'm just trying to do my job, run a business, but it's impossible to follow all the rules. I wish Kenneth [our father] was here." This is one of the few instances Mother ever spoke openly to us children about difficulties with the locker plant.

I never heard the details of this infraction, but it must have been because she just could not follow all of the ever-changing rules and price restrictions. Knowing how conscientious our mother was, I am sure she would have bent over backwards not to break any OPA rules, but just got caught in the complexity of the regulations while trying to run a business.

Of course, very few of us on the homefront knew the details of official regulations. We only heard and obeyed the mighty voice of the OPA. Nevertheless, one wartime incident changed my mind about the sacred cows of bureaucracy and officialdom.

I went with my mother and sisters on the forty-five mile drive to Peoria, where Mother needed to discuss some of the OPA regulations at their regional headquarters. Retailers like my mother had to keep detailed records of prices and amounts of sales, and submit them for inspection and approval. Keeping up with the changing restrictions and price guidelines was time-consuming and difficult.

This trip to the OPA office presented a good opportunity for combining a business appointment with a rare shopping trip to Peoria's large department stores. We arrived in Peoria during a heavy fog. Mother parked the car and we walked to the office for the OPA, took an elevator to an upper floor, and looked out the open window while waiting our turn. The fog was so thick we couldn't see buildings across the street. We soon learned that the foggy weather obscuring our vision outside the building was matched by conditions inside the office. We could not see through the red tape or get around the highhanded abuse of an OPA administrator.

We had to wait for one of the lower level clerks of the OPA to handle Mother's questions. He was a middle-aged balding guy with a paunch, sitting behind a large desk. At this time, most men not in

A wartime OPA official mistreating a young woman. ILLUSTRATION BY JOHN MICHAEL DOWNS.

the military were either disabled or too old for the draft. This clerk, obviously past the prime of his manhood, seemed to be unaware of his less than handsome appearance. An attractive younger woman sat opposite him, meekly asking about some OPA rules, trying to submit the proper materials. She had presented official papers to him, related to the business she worked for, but he rejected them. He announced loudly, "You don't have all the right forms, and what you have aren't filled out right."

He toyed with her, giving her a hard time. Although too young to understand the way men in power often mistreat women, I realized he was being mean, giving her a hard time for no reason, making us wait. What made me mad was that I knew in a few minutes he might be just as mean to my mother.

He stood, scooped up from the desk the woman's papers, and after waving them in front of her, placed them on his chair, slowly sitting down on them and scolding her, "I'm going to sit on these papers, and won't get up until you give me the right answers."

I hated that man. My mother and sisters and I didn't dare say anything, but I wished someone would drop him out the open window, letting him disappear in the fog.

He finally shifted his weight to get the papers he had been sitting on, used his rubber stamp to mark his approval on them, and let the young woman leave.

Fortunately for us, this man was not so cocky when faced with a woman and three children. Mother submitted her papers, received a stamp of approval, and we were all glad to leave that office.

For the most part, the idealized label for World War II as the "good war" and the perception of unified cooperation holds true. The officials of the OPA were on our side, friends helping us win the war. However, in ambiguous situations like this nasty bureaucrat in Peoria, we might move him from the category of friend to foe.

We couldn't wait for the end of the war and the end of rationing and the OPA.

CHAPTER 8

Victory Garden

The experiences of our family during the war, and postwar writings about it, include a variety of attitudes toward government programs.

Not only our mother, but the entire population, hated the OPA, because everyone had to obey this all-powerful agency. The restrictions of rationing and concern for the equitable distribution of food and goods led to much grumbling and criticism. Some of the discontent seems to have been due to the fact that at first they made the regulations too strict, then either relaxed or rescinded them, and then invoked new rules. They played the same rationing game, but the rules seemed to always be changing. Americans did not like having the government and its bureaucracies telling them how to shop, clothe, and feed themselves.

In sharp contrast to discontent with the OPA, the Victory garden program became the most widely and enthusiastically accepted wartime project. I think a major reason for its popularity stemmed from the fact that in this activity, ordinary people like our family members could take initiative, control the process, and reap the benefits—right on the kitchen table. Every time we planted a seed, hoed a weed, or picked a tomato, we performed our patriotic duty helping the servicemen overseas win the war. My sisters and I, Mom, and Grandma and Grandpa supported Victory gardens one hundred percent.

Without our Victory garden, life—that is, eating—would have been much more difficult at Grandma's house. The garden we had in the back yard was just the usual large garden that our grandparents would have had anyway, war or not. But after the war started, every able-bodied citizen on the homefront should be as frugal and productive as possible. And to be patriotic, you had to have a Victory garden.

Although it may seem strange to think of agriculture as a weapon of war, central Illinois formed part of the heartland of American farming, and local residents knew the great importance of crops. At the very beginning of the war, a December 26, 1941 article in the *Democrat* proclaimed that "Illinois farmers believe that 'food will win the war and write the peace.'" On the governmental level, the Department of Agriculture announced that "food production goals will be reconsidered as a result of America's entry into the war. . . ." Rural and city folk worked together in the fight to supply both civilians and military personnel with sufficient food.

The government recruited everyone on the homefront in the campaign of Victory gardens. The poster "Victory Garden Plots" highlights the way officials provided urban people the land, tools, and advice to do

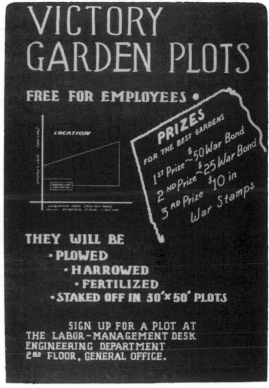

An urban poster encouraging employees to plant Victory gardens, even to the point of offering them ground and assistance in planting. IMAGE COURTESY OF NATIONAL ARCHIVES/WIKIMEDIA.

their part in increasing food production. The government promoted Victory gardens, not just in big cities, but also in small towns like Havana. A March 5, 1942 *Democrat* article's title asks, "Have You Planned Your Victory Garden?" The article declares a Victory garden a "must," especially as a measure guarding "against the probability of no canned vegetables available for civilian consumption and also as a means of conserving the supply for our armed forces and to assist in feeding our allies. . . . People with extra garden space, or those needing space can pass along this information to the Victory Garden Committee by communicating with the *Democrat*. The Mason County Farm Bureau has gardening literature available."

Government officials even encouraged young people to participate in the war effort through gardening. One of the means of mobilizing young people was the Junior Victory Army, promoted through newspapers, radio, special insignia, and registration cards. An article in a 1942 Los Angeles newspaper announces the "Orders of the Day" from the Chief Adjutant of the Junior Victory Army; on the same page, a separate article on "Junior Army Gardens" gives planting and watering tips to the novice agricultural soldier.

Large city residents and small town people alike paid some of their war dues by tending Victory gardens. Residents of smaller cities either

Where seedlings of broad, heavy-foliaged species are being handled, some of the top of each plant should be trimmed off, to compensate for the partial loss of roots which is inevitable when plants are transplanted.

The soil should be soaked, not merely sprinkled, after the transplanting operation is completed. A little dry soil then sprinkled on the surface immediately around each plant will aid in checking evaporation.

If the sun is hot, seedlings should be provided with partial shade for a day or so, until the roots begin to absorb enough moisture to balance the evaporation which occurs through the plants foliage. Paper tents, berry boxes or split shingles are handy or this purpose.

Observe distances carefully in transplanting the various flower and vegetable varieties to the open garden. The little plants may appear lonely when set a foot, or two or three, apart, but bear in mind the normal size they will attain at maturity, and thus make sure they will have enough room to develop properly.

Vigorous growth in seedlings of all species will be additionally certain if a complete, balanced plant food is applied while they are still small and young. It will enable them to develop a strong root system, which is essential to their proper feeding.

Here again, however, the general gardening rule holds true that small applications made frequently are better than large feedings at long intervals.

A handy garden gadget for use in transplanting small seedlings is the dibber. Fashioned of steel or hard wood, with a round, blunt edge, it is stabbed into the ground, twisted and withdrawn—and the hole is ready.

The Junior Victory Army (or Junior Army) was recruited and instructed in the Victory garden campaign. THIS ARTICLE APPEARED IN THE MARCH 21, 1942 ISSUE OF THE *LOS ANGELES EVENING HERALD AND EXPRESS*.

had or could find land for a garden. Government agencies offered growing space and tools to people in larger metropolitan areas. National policy and local groups encouraged everyone to carry out their civic and patriotic duty to produce food. Seniors and youngsters, like the Junior Victory Army and their Junior Army Gardens, pitched in to raise crops. The rationale of Victory gardens was to make civilians more self-sufficient, in order to provide more food for the boys over there.

An example of the "boys right here" growing their own food took place at nearby Camp Ellis. In 1944 the soldiers at this camp had their own Victory garden, with an "amazing yield of 525,825 pounds of more than 30 varieties of vegetables," having an estimated value of $58,000 at 1944 price levels. An article from the October 27, 1944 *Camp Ellis News*, "Garden Nets Half Million Pounds of Food," gives details of this Victory garden. This information is reprinted in *The Story of Camp Ellis*, p. 124.

ORDERS OF THE DAY

From: Chief Adjutant
To   : Junior Army

1. Salvage is of the utmost importance. Remember that old rubber, salvaged, makes new rubber for planes, tanks and battleships. Bear that in mind constantly.

2. Junior Army members are to be thoughtful of those who work at night and sleep during the day. Such workers, most of them in airplane factories, must be at their best. Do your part by playing noisy games at your nearest playground rather than in the residential district.

3. You are ordered to complete your Home Safety Survey, sign your name, address and registration number and send the report to W. G. Kennedy, Safety Engineer, State Compensation Insurance Fund, 501 State Building, Los Angeles, Cal.

SECRET ORDERS

Carry your Registration Card with you and keep your Code Card secret.

CODE

55-14-23-23*24-45-31-22-41*41-32-14*24-31-12-41-44-45-14*21-33*
41-32-14*33-31-45-42-41*31-44-22-31-21-45*13-45-25-51*
25-14-25-15-14-45*33-31-22-31-42-32-31-22-35*13*25-21-11-14-23*
24-23-13-22-14*33-21-45*41-32-14*22-13-53-51**

RADIO

Hear the story of a Lockheed test pilot on the Junior Army Radio Program over Station KHJ at 8:30 tomorrow morning.

MODEL PLANE EXHIBIT

A model plane exhibit, with motion pictures, was held this morning at the State Exposition Building. These planes will be kept on exhibit all next week.

Those desiring to have Junior Army insignia pins mailed can send 10 cents to the main office of The Herald and Express, 1243 Trenton street, or they can call in person at branch offices and get pins for 5 cents on the presentation of their Registration Card. Branch offices follow: Downtown office, Arcade Building; Hollywood office, 1103 North Serrano; Southwest office, 5314 South Figueroa; South Side office, 10061 South Main street; Whittier boulevard office, 907 South Leonard; Alhambra office, 305 North Garfield; Glendale office, 312 South Brand; Inglewood office, 309 South La Brea; Long Beach office, 819 Pine street; Pasadena office, 42 South Fair Oaks; Santa Monica office, 406 South Broadway.

On the same page as the previous article appears this set of "Orders of the Day," complete with "Secret Orders" to be decoded by the Junior Army member using a Code Card.

In the countryside, the loss of able-bodied men to the war effort threatened farm production. The government singled out women to play a major role in the domestic agricultural blitz. Every member of the traditional family farm had work or chores to take care of. Before the war, farm women took care of chickens, milked cows, separated cream, churned butter, and took eggs to market. Men usually handled field work, such as driving tractors and trucks. During the war, many young farm men enlisted or were drafted—those who did not "hide behind the corn stalks." With the draft or enlistment of husbands and sons, government programs encouraged women to move from the chicken coop and milk barn to the fields and the tractor seat. On the farm, as in factories, what had been considered a man's work now became a woman's work.

Although most of us in the cities knew little about the new role of women in agriculture, they became crucial to the planting, harvesting, and delivery of farm products. About three million women worked on farms in 1943, almost a third of the agricultural work force. Washington had its disagreements about whether to urge women to do farm work (as it disagreed about almost every aspect of the war and mobilization). Nevertheless, the government eventually, with the help of President Roosevelt and the support of first lady Eleanor Roosevelt, organized the Women's Land Army. Americans patterned this program after the successful model of the British Woman's Land Army of World War I, and the establishment of the Woman's Land Army of America in World War I. In the early 1940s, officials proposed a special "uniform" for the Women's Land Army, but this style of dress was not widely adopted.

During World War II, the Women's Land Army turned farm wives into what were then called "farmerettes," and recruited and trained non-farm women from the cities (and from colleges during the summer) to keep the crops growing and to maintain the supply lines to civilians and the armed forces. Younger people from the ages of fourteen to seventeen worked as Victory Farm Volunteers. Although at first some government officials and many oldtime farmers had been skeptical of the usefulness of women doing men's work, by the end of the war both administrators and farmers praised women for their hard work in keeping agriculture alive and productive during a difficult period. The full story of female farmers during World War II is told in Stephanie A. Carpenter's *On the Farm Front: The Women's Land Army in World War II.*

My reason for including the role of the Women's Land Army is not because it has a prominent role in my memory of the 1940s. Quite the contrary, most of us during the war knew little of the larger picture of the war effort. To be candid, I think we were as self-centered as we were patriotic. We were totally committed to supporting our loved ones in the conflict overseas by doing what we could on the homefront, and one small help was growing a Victory garden. By comparison, the contribution of the Women's Land Army and the Victory Farm Volunteers, as well as foreign workers and prisoners of war, were more directly responsible for agricultural output during the early 1940s than Victory gardens. However, Victory gardens did play their part, not only in supplying material goods but also in instilling pride and in cultivating civilian morale.

What exactly was a Victory garden? The usual garden didn't really count. A Victory garden meant the extra effort, what you did beyond what you ordinarily grew. If a family planted more potatoes than they usually did, the potatoes they didn't buy and eat could be sent to the boys overseas. This principle held for everything we could grow in central Illinois, from potatoes and tomatoes to green beans and corn.

Grandma rented her house from a wealthy family in town. Grandma asked this family for permission to use a large plot of land behind their fancy house as our Victory garden. Its location only two blocks north of Grandma's house, on the east side of the railroad tracks, made it very convenient. We carried our tools—hoes and the like—the two blocks to our Victory garden. There we planted, weeded, and eventually harvested our garden.

Grandma, belonging to the old school, watched the signs of the moon on the calendar and planted in harmony with the phases of the moon. During the dark of the moon, the time of month when the moon was not visible, she planted root crops such as potatoes, radishes, and carrots. On days during the phase of the moon when it was visible, she planted vegetables such as lettuce, peas, and beans.

Grandma also grew and ate vegetables that my sisters and I were not familiar with. We loved tomatoes and couldn't wait for them to change color from dark to pale green, then pink and finally red. It seemed that once they got to eating size it took them forever to ripen. Grandma said, "Well, if you want to eat tomatoes, we can pick green tomatoes and fry them."

We had never heard of such a thing, and thought she was "funning" us, which she liked to do. When she actually picked green tomatoes, we knew she was serious, because she would never waste any food. We tried her fried green tomatoes. As a boy, I never did take to them. I couldn't get used to the idea of eating *green* tomatoes.

Eggplant was a vegetable we had never eaten before we lived with grandma. Her fried eggplant made a hit with us. Grandma peeled the large eggplants, sliced off round slabs, dipped these vegetable discs in beaten eggs and covered them with flour or cracker crumbs, frying them to a golden brown in a hot skillet. Topped with syrup, eggplant tasted as good as pancakes or French toast. Grandma laughed at us when we polished off the fried eggplant. "You wouldn't eat my fried green tomatoes, but they're no different than my fried eggplant."

In my senior days, I have learned to cook and fry green tomatoes. After I experimented, and got the greased skillet hot enough, they turned out pretty good. But they can't compare to Grandma's down-home cuisine, the tomato slices crispy brown on the outside, juicy and delicious on the inside.

We raised lots of white potatoes and sweet potatoes, and all kinds of beans and peas. Peas and lima beans were a pain to pick and then shell, but we did freeze some. Lettuce and tomatoes we ate fresh, and tomatoes we canned or froze. By watching Grandma, we learned that the easiest way to get the skin off tomatoes was to scald them, which reminded me of scalding chickens.

Tomatoes also provided the main ingredient for ketchup. Grandma had always made her own ketchup, and we preferred it to store bought ketchup, especially when we ate it on her pot roast. The war forced everyone to become more creative with recipes. Ketchup calls for a lot of sugar, which we didn't have. And if we used much of our sugar ration on ketchup, there wouldn't be enough for baking. So Grandma experimented with saccharin in place of sugar. We used tomatoes from the Victory garden, but her saccharin ketchup was not a great victory. She used too much saccharin. It tasted good at first, as it went down, but after the food reached your stomach, the saccharin sweetness lingered in your mouth and turned strange on your tongue.

We dreaded the tiresome chores of planting and hoeing in the hot sun. As children we couldn't see beyond this hard work to the more abundant vegetables it would help grow. Making ketchup was fun. We enjoyed picking tomatoes, like all harvesting, more than the day-to-day care of the garden. Grandma cooked ketchup in the kitchen on her range. It was hot in the kitchen but we didn't mind so much, because we always liked the family togetherness in this homey setting. Grandma reigned supreme as the Queen of the kitchen, turning work into play. What I liked most about making ketchup was putting caps on the bottles, and pulling down the lever on the special tool to crimp the caps and seal the bottles.

Cucumbers tasted great fresh, and also were made into pickles. As with ketchup, the problem was sugar. Dill pickles don't call for sugar. For sweet pickles and spiced pickles, saccharin had to be used instead of sugar. A real treat was her pickled beets. She liked to put a few hard boiled eggs in with the beets. And her pickled water melon rind was delicious. Grandma was much more successful with pickles than with ketchup. Maybe the spices in the pickles overpowered the saccharin.

People who have grown and eaten their own sweet corn, boiling it soon after picking, are spoiled for life. The sweetness and fresh taste of this corn is not matched by any corn bought in a store, because within a few hours the corn changes. For the connoisseur, "fresh" sweet corn means within an hour or two of picking. Store-bought sweet corn is never really fresh, because it takes at least a day or two to harvest, ship, and stock in a store. The time lag turns the tender sweet corn tough and starchy.

Frozen corn is no match for fresh picked corn, but it's a lot better than canned corn. We experimented with all kinds of foods during the war, partly because we had plenty of produce from our Victory garden, and also because we could use the locker plant and advise other customers. Frozen corn was a real winner. We blanched the corn, cut it from the cob, and put it in airtight freezer containers. Our family became quite familiar with blanching, because we blanched a number of vegetables in preparation for freezing. Briefly dipping vegetables in boiling water without thoroughly cooking them preserves the freshness, so that after freezing they can be cooked and taste almost like fresh-picked items. You can even blanch corn on the cob and then wrap it in cellophane and waxed paper. This takes up more space in the freezer, but we liked to enjoy corn on the cob at least once or twice during the winter.

Frozen potatoes were not a winner, because they turned dark. Freezing them in water helped prevent them from discoloring, but they still didn't process satisfactorily, and we gave up on potatoes. Today's frozen potatoes in grocery stores are mainly cooked or processed potatoes, which keep much better.

Growing up in a family with a locker plant provided us with interesting experiences, because we were always "trying" things. Our experiments in eating were not limited to the harvest of the garden. Dad butchered both hogs and beef, and processed them. He was very good at curing and smoking meat, especially bacon from pigs. From cows he made what we called "dried beef," usually known today as chipped beef. Dad's bacon and dried beef tasted much better than commercially available products. Our employee Fred had a farm with some woods. We bought hickory wood from Fred, because it was the best wood for smoking.

Corn fed pigs had a large layer of fat under their skin. Dad trimmed this fat off the hog carcass, cut it into cubes, and placed it in a large metal vat heated by gas. The grease "rendered" from the chunks of pork fat became lard, which in the 1940s was a major form of shortening. Mom and Grandma insisted, even decades later, when vegetable shortening (oleo margarine) became available, that lard was a key ingredient in pie crusts. Our family agreed that their pie crusts were flaky and tender, never soggy and doughy.

A saying about the processing of hogs, adopted by some meat packing companies, is they used everything from the pig except the squeal. Dad didn't cite this phrase, but he did act it out, especially when it came to rendering lard from pork fat. After the lard drained out of the vat, pieces of skin remained. Dad placed these pieces of skin in a large circular press with a screw mechanism to put pressure on a round wooden form to compress the pieces of skin, forcing the remainder of lard out. In the bottom of the press, the leftover pieces of skin were reduced to fat-laden brownish scraps. These bits of cooked pork skin, known as "cracklins," were a delicacy for the locals. Dad didn't have to advertise the availability of cracklins, because the rendering process took several days, and the odor of hot pork fat filled the whole downtown area. Customers dropped by from time to time, wanting to know, "Are the cracklins ready?" Most people just munched on the cracklins, like some people today eat roasted pigs' ears. Grandma took cracklins home, ran them through a food grinder, and added them to biscuit dough to add flavor.

The nicest part of our experimenting with frozen foods was fruit. Properly packaged and processed, then quickly frozen in our "sharp freezer" which stayed about -30 Fahrenheit, frozen strawberries, raspberries, and peaches had good taste and texture. Ascorbic acid (vitamin C) helped some fruits such as peaches, enhancing the flavor and preventing the fruit from turning brown.

In the early 1940s, fruit in the winter consisted mainly of apples, and citrus fruit like oranges and grapefruit. Bananas were a luxury. Local grocery stores did not sell frozen products, and fresh fruit was not shipped and sold year-round the way it is today. The only alternative was home-canned fruit or fruit in tin cans from the store, or dried fruit. Frozen fruit, especially frozen strawberries, tasted much better than any canned fruit. Jellies and jams were favorites in our family, but they called for so much sugar that Grandma could make them only in small amounts.

When our family was busy combating crawling and flying pests in our victory garden, we had two allies. As seen in the previous Office of War Information poster, we were supported by government advice to protect our garden. On the local scene we had the help of the druggist Bernhard Walters, whose store was on Main Street just a block from Grandma's house. His advertisement in the May 22, 1942 *Democrat* offered for sale various insecticides as ammunition in the "war on insects." Individual families, national policy, and local businesses presented a united front in safeguarding our valuable produce.

For us kids, some of the greatest battles were with bugs in the garden. In this case, violence was a virtue. We knocked striped orange and yellow potato bugs off the potato plants and squashed them under a heel. The large green tomato worms with the prominent horn on the end made for a great kill. When we found one, our hoes turned the worm

While many of us on the homefront—seniors and youngsters, men and women—were waging our battles with bugs in the garden, the Office of War Information was distributing posters to encourage these civilians in their war against insects. IMAGE COURTESY OF NATIONAL ARCHIVES/WIKIMEDIA.

into green mincemeat. We couldn't go to war, but in our Victory gardens we could enjoy our homefront garden victories.

CHAPTER 9

"I'll Wring Your Neck"

The French philosopher Voltaire advised people, "Tend your garden." My grandparents did that in the summer, but all year round they tended their chickens. No matter how bad the war news, chickens had to be fed, eggs gathered. No matter how well the war front fared, that was no excuse for leaving the poultry uncared for. When it came to chickens, everyone helped out in one way or another. Our family formed a united front in the campaign of raising and processing our small flock.

Grandma—and Grandpa, too, but not as much as Grandma—prized our chickens. She heaped praise on her hens that kept us in eggs and occasionally provided a bird for a chicken and noodle casserole. Maybe this concern reflected her tie to the farm they lost in the Depression. When she didn't compliment them, she complained about them. "They just gobble up feed. They don't lay eggs, they don't put on weight."

As much as she groused about the chickens, she wouldn't be without them. Grandma's hot and cold attitude toward chickens could be compared to her approach to her grandchildren. She showed love and affection to us by being concerned enough to grumble and lay down the law to care for us.

After meals, we saved meat scraps and bones for our dog Fritzi. Anything else left in our kitchen from preparing meals, or what we scraped off our plates before washing, we tossed into the chicken pen. Our pullets welcomed the sight of a dishpan in outstretched hands, and fought among themselves for the choice tidbits. Every few weeks we went to the feed store for cracked corn, and once in a while, oyster shell. Grandma was more practical than sentimental. "Makes the egg shells strong. Chickens need some grit in their gizzards." She wanted eggs and chickens to eat. We fed the chickens. The chickens in turn should feed us.

Grandma liked to gather eggs. She would gently lift a hen from a nest, carefully taking out the egg under it. If she thought one hen consistently did not produce eggs, she would give it a good chewing out. When she came back with the eggs, or at dinner, she'd announce in a loud voice that even the poultry must have heard, "A certain hen had better start laying, or it'll end up in a pot of noodles one of these days." And Grandma did not bluff. She saw no point in paying good money for feed for a hen that didn't lay. She just cooked the chicken for Sunday dinner.

Killing chickens could be divided into two categories: the individual cases, such as the hen that didn't lay, and the group cases, as when we raised a bunch of chickens for fryers. Old hens she cooked with noodles, because they were tough. Young chickens, tender, made good fryers, so as soon as they grew to good size, we processed them.

Grandma would take care of an old hen or two by herself, but mass executions called for help from the whole family. Usually we set aside a weekend day and we all pitched in. Grandma and Grandpa differed in their approach to butchering chickens. Grandpa found a sturdy, heavy board, and carefully hammered two nails about halfway into the board, an inch or so apart. Earlier he had caught the chickens, and either placed them in a crate or tied them by the legs. With his left hand, Grandpa grabbed a chicken by the legs, plopped it down on the board with its neck between the nails and pulled the head back against the nails to stretch the neck. He raised the sharpened hatchet and quickly brought it down, cleanly severing the head. Grandpa could decapitate several dozen chickens in a few minutes.

Grandma wasn't so fussy, and didn't need nails or a hatchet. She got hold of a chicken by the head, jerked it up and broke its neck, then swung it in a circular movement to wring off the head. Grandma's motion mimicked cranking the engine of an old Model T Ford. Her technique differed from Grandpa's, but was just as quick, with the same result. They tossed heads one way, chickens the other way. The headless chickens spurted blood all over the yard, and the chickens flapped and flopped until they pumped out all their blood.

Some childhood experiences are so intense that they stay lodged in memory until awakened by similar events or experiences later in life. Decades after World War II and my time at Grandma's house, I read a literary description that reminded me of the sights and sounds of slaughtering chickens when I was a boy.

In the Japanese novel *Harp of Burma,* Japanese prisoners in postwar 1945 Burma watch chickens being killed. The heads of the chickens were cut off, but their legs were not bound, and they ran about aimlessly with outstretched wings, until they fell lifeless to the ground. The Japanese prisoners, not knowing when, or even *if,* they would be repatriated to Japan, compared themselves to the helpless and hopeless chickens.

I have read the novel a number of times, using it as a text in college courses. The novel is full of vivid imagery, such as the headless chickens wildly running about, but for me this Burmese episode always calls to mind an American scene. Grandpa raising his hatchet and quickly swinging it down like a guillotine against the execution board. Grandma vigorously cranking her arm, not bringing life to a black Ford but death to a white pullet. And chickens flapping their wings and pumping red blood onto the green grass.

At Grandma's house, although we kids tended to be squeamish about all this blood and death, we didn't want to let on that it bothered us. Grandma and Grandpa didn't mind the gore at all. Their only concern was that one of us might get hurt—burned by the boiling water that had been waiting in big tubs for the chickens. When a chicken finally stopped bleeding and gave up the ghost, we had the job of picking it up by the feet, dousing it quickly in the boiling water to scald it, being careful not to get burned, and then plucking the feathers off.

The smell of scalded chickens and wet feathers is worse than anything. Except, perhaps, rotten eggs.

When Grandma and Grandpa had killed all the chickens, they joined Mother and us kids to scald and pluck chickens. My sisters and I didn't have to help gut the chickens. After plucking, the grownups took the birds inside for the final dressing, and the younger set helped clean up the mess. The memory of the dead chickens lingered when we tried to burn the wet feathers in our burning barrel and they smoldered.

The burning barrel calls for explanation. In the 1940s, small towns had no regular garbage pickup. Even before the war, but especially during the war, people saved bits of every kind of material, such as paper, metal, and grease. We threw our wet garbage, such as table scraps, to the chickens. Only items not salvageable or useable in some fashion we placed in a fifty-gallon metal barrel, and once every week or two, burned. Several times a year we hired a man with a pickup truck to empty the burning barrel and take the ashes to the dump across the river.

When we had a bunch of young fryers, we butchered and froze them, storing them in the locker plant. Old hens we reserved for Sunday dinner. Sometimes Grandma found a partially formed egg inside a hen, a special treat. It was like the yolk of an egg, but smaller. When she cooked it in her chicken and noodles, each of us wanted to eat it.

Grandma made her own noodles, flattening out the dough thin like pie crust on the kitchen table, rolling it up in the shape of a long white cigar, and cutting it into noodle strips with a knife.

When Grandma got mad at us, and from time to time when she joked with us, she'd say "You do that again, and I'll wring your neck!" We knew she was only "funning" us, the term she used for her teasing. We were never in danger of physical harm—I don't recall one instance

Getting rid of trash in a burning barrel. ILLUS-TRATION BY JOHN MICHAEL DOWNS.

of her ever spanking me or my sisters. But she knew how to get our attention, because her verbal threat brought to mind the times we had seen her twist off the heads of chickens. In the poultry battle, humans always ended up the winners, the fowl enemy always the losers. My sisters and I didn't want to even think about joining their company on the blood-stained lawn.

If we acted up and Grandma needed to get us to behave, she just warned us with "I'll wring your neck."

CHAPTER 10

Homefront Battles

Our family did not fully understand how we got into the war. We just believed that the Allies represented good and the Axis powers stood for evil. Although we didn't realize it at the time, Grandma's house also presented a site of conflict, a domestic battleground. In our household we had no bullets or bayonets, but plenty of sharp tongues and pointed comments. Living there taught us a valuable lesson in how not only countries, but also families, always engage in a delicate series of power plays.

When the city of Havana celebrated its centennial in 1948, Grandma and Grandpa Haack joined in the festivities by dressing up in nineteenth century costumes. Even wearing a top hat, Grandpa was shorter than Grandma. FAMILY PHOTO.

Grandma dominated Grandpa. She stood a good head taller than him, but height or strength was never the deciding factor. Most of the time Grandma ran the house, minded the kids, and was the one we asked for permission to do something. Usually Grandpa stayed in the background as the silent observer, hidden behind his newspaper. He put up with her being in control of matters, until she did something he strongly objected to, and then they got into a heated argument. Hardly a day passed that Grandma and Grandpa didn't have some minor verbal skirmish, yet I never saw any physical confrontation between them.

Grandma could control any misbehavior on the part of my sisters and me with the threat of wringing our necks, but she had to adopt different tactics when dealing with her spouse. Grandma held the position of matriarch of the house. Grandpa relied on the strategy of creating his own private space that no one else could invade. Occasionally the boundaries of Grandma's domain and Grandpa's refuge came into conflict and had to be redefined. For example, the two often bickered over his use of tobacco. Usually Grandpa smoked a corncob pipe, preferring Prince Albert tobacco. Until he got a new pipe "broken in," it stunk, and Grandma complained about the smell. Then not long after he got it broken in, it would burn out, and Grandpa did the grousing.

Once in a long while Grandpa demonstrated his independence and bought a cigar or accepted one from a friend. When he brought it home, we dreaded the showdown between Grandma and Grandpa. She would say, "You're not going to *light* that thing *in here,* are you?"

The battle lines had been drawn, and he would not back down. "Hell, Ma, I don't smoke one that often." They would argue back and forth for five or ten minutes, and when she saw he wouldn't give in, she'd tell him, "Well, go ahead and smoke it, but I don't have to be in the same room with you."

She'd stomp off to the kitchen. He'd go into the parlor to huff and puff on his cigar, reading the paper and filling the room with blue smoke. Each retreated to their own territory.

Looking back on this conflict, I am impressed that they had incompatible viewpoints about smoking, expressed their opinions quite vigorously, and arrived at an uneasy compromise. They reached a sort of truce, with neither side giving up their position, but also not resorting to nasty threats, swearing, name-calling, or violence.

Grandma's tongue could be sharp as a sword, yet she had a warm and loving heart. She did not hold back her objection to tobacco and cigars, but neither did that prevent her from expressing her affection. When Grandpa read the newspaper while waiting for a meal, she'd lean over and give him a quick peck on the forehead. Never on the lips. Grandpa just kept reading his paper, but his face showed a hint of a smile.

That kind of brutal honesty mixed with genuine love made Grandma Haack the favorite of everyone in the family. We gladly put up with her gruff language, because we knew she was like her dinner rolls, a hard outer crust that covered a soft and warm inside.

We should not minimize the enormity of World War II, but actually, the scene at Grandma's house could be seen as more complicated and delicate than the war. In a black and white contrast, we designated the Japanese and Nazis as unmitigated evil, and America and her Allies as the unqualified good. Propaganda, news reports, government posters, and movies very effectively demonized enemies and sanctified America.

With our grandparents, we could not mark off a clean-cut division of malevolent and benevolent forces. We kids stayed out of their spats, not daring to take sides, realizing we could say nothing, do nothing, that would change the situation. More of life is painted in the shades of gray than in the sharp juxtaposition of black and white.

Grandpa smoked until his last days. Grandma preceded him in death by a few months in 1962, consumed by lung cancer. At the time my mother remarked, "That just goes to show you, how unfair life is. Grandpa smoked all his life and didn't get cancer. Grandma never smoked, and she's the one who got lung cancer."

In those days we didn't know about the effects of secondhand smoke. As with war, sometimes unintended consequences and collateral damage can be worse than intentional violence.

Battles are won and lost on the warfront and on the homefront.

We will see more of Grandpa in Chapter 18, A Make-Believe Sword and Ostrich Feathers.

CHAPTER 11

"Blow Your —"

The war overshadowed the background of our lives, yet life kept us busy and provided a routine to keep our minds off Daddy's absence.

The Illinois Central Railroad running right by Grandma's house provided a daily source of entertainment and excitement. The tremendous size, sound, and flash of the speeding trains fascinated us—the passenger trains short and fast, the freight trains long and lumbering. Even in winter when we were inside, a passing train shook the whole house and rattled the windows. Grandma and Grandpa would comment on whether the passenger trains were on time, and if not, how late. Grandpa checked his trusty pocket watch to announce the exact minute the train arrived.

Standing in the yard watching a locomotive pass by Grandma's house. ILLUS-TRATION BY JOHN MICHAEL DOWNS.

Although we had fun watching the spectacle of trains thundering by, some boundaries and restrictions determined by Grandma limited this activity. Especially in summer, when we played outside, Grandma had clear rules that we seldom disobeyed. Once we heard the train coming, we should be "in the yard." That meant not on the grass between the curb and the sidewalk, but on the grass between the sidewalk and the house. Well, us kids gave these orders a slight difference in interpretation.

We loved the thrill of being part of the speeding train—the locomotive belching acrid coal smoke that stung our noses, steam from its boiler wafting a light mist over us. The rumbling of the iron wheels on the tracks made the ground vibrate and tickle our bare feet. The swirling air brushed against our faces. To gain the greatest sensory impact from this iron monster, we stood at the very edge of the yard, next to or even perched on the concrete curb. When Grandma saw us fudging on the boundaries, she'd yell *Stay in the yard!*

One day we learned that dogs did not always understand human regulations. Our friend Walter Ray visited us with his dog Popeye, a friendly and playful little mutt, mostly white, but with some black markings, including a black ring around one eye. How he got his name I never heard, but his animated spirit made us think of the cartoon character Popeye.

The Havana depot of the Illinois Central Railroad at the corner of Dearborn and Schrader (Railroad Street) was just a few blocks west of our home on South Orange Street. ILLUSTRATION BY JOHN MICHAEL DOWNS.

Walter had ridden to our house on his bicycle, and Popeye tagged along. That summer day, a lot of kids were playing at our house when the train came by. We all stood where we should be, in the yard, but for some reason Popeye ran across the street and underneath the train, a passenger train, with a half dozen khaki green cars, rushing by at a fast clip. When Popeye loped out towards the train, some of us started to chase after him, while Grandma, watching from the back porch, yelled, "Get back in the yard."

It horrified us to see the dog slip right under the passing train cars. Popeye became a blur of black and white, spinning around, turning this way and that, hidden from view by the wheels at the end of a car, then briefly visible, and then hidden again. We thought the only thing the dog could do was stay put, so we yelled *"Stay there! Stay there!"*

Unfortunately, our shouts had the opposite effect. Popeye seemed to hear us, and made a dash from under the train out onto the street and into the yard, without getting so much as a scratch.

Although all of this lasted only a matter of seconds, it scared us enough for a lifetime. Popeye became his playful old self within a few minutes. Grandma found this a good source of moral example to "stay in the yard."

In the long lulls between trains, occasionally we did venture onto the tracks. We never tired of putting pennies on the rails to let the

Popeye under a passing train. ILLUSTRATION BY JOHN MICHAEL DOWNS.

train flatten the coins into roundish and ovalish patterns. Placed just so, the train wheels pancaked the penny into twice its original size. Grandma didn't really like us to be on the railroad tracks, but if we did it long before the train arrived, she considered it safe, and not a cause for scolding. We knew we had to mind Grandma and her rules, but we had other worries.

In our serious moments, we agreed, "It's against the law to destroy the government's money, and if you get caught, they can throw you in jail."

Whenever someone put a penny on the track, one of us would tease, "Here comes the police!"

The exact placement of the penny required a little knowledge of train technology that we soon mastered. Train wheels have a flange on the inside, which is what keeps the train on the rails. When we positioned the penny (or other coin, if someone felt extravagant) just on the inside edge of the rail, it would be flattened out by the bottom of the wheel and then formed into an "L" shape by the flange. If you put the penny too far to the outside or inside of the rail, the first wheel to hit it knocked it off the track before it was flattened. It took a little practice to put the coin in the right location to produce a mini copper pancake.

A train like the ones we knew—coal-fired steam engines—had two major features of interest. The locomotive made for an impressive sight, huffing down the tracks in a cloud of smoke with its drivers glistening. As soon as it passed, we smelled the stench of coal smoke and sulfur. The engineer never even glanced at us, craning his neck out of the cab and scanning the tracks ahead to make sure they were clear. Approaching each street crossing, he gave several sharp blasts of his steam whistle to warn pedestrians and cars to stay out of the way. The powerful steam whistle was a high pitched soprano screech so loud and piercing that it hurt our ears.

Present-day readers may know the fabled history of the Illinois Central, a legendary rail line famous for its Chicago to St. Louis and New Orleans routes, especially on the Panama Limited. Steven Goodman's 1971 "City of New Orleans" memorialized this Illinois Central train of the same name, in a song made famous by artists such as Arlo Guthrie, Willie Nelson, and Johnny Cash. (Their versions are available on Youtube.) My friends and I in the early 1940s knew nothing of the glamor of traveling in luxury from the shores of Lake Michigan to the Gulf of Mexico. The well to do passengers on such trains were as distant to us as the wealthy owners of yachts who motored from Chicago down the Illinois River to the Mississippi River and New Orleans. We could not imagine that the Illinois Central would become known as an iconic rail line. Our limited contact with the rail line was watching locomotives, passenger cars, and freight trains pass through Havana.

We youngsters found the caboose at the end of freight trains more interesting, because when passing through town, a trainman stood on the platform at the end of the caboose, and from time to time we could get him to blow his whistle.

We lined up on the curb, and as soon as the trainman on the caboose came even with us, at a signal we'd all yell as loud as we could, "Blow your whistle." When he obliged, it sounded a longish tooot-tooooot. The trainman's whistle was lower in tone, a mellow alto if compared to the shrill soprano locomotive whistle.

Bad language and swearing were not allowed for me and my sisters. If we so much as said, "poop," Grandma's slow, scolding pronunciation of your name could dampen your spirits for half a day. With her teeth she cut apart each syllable of your name, like a butcher separating the limbs of a chicken.

The only swearing heard in our house was by Grandpa when he got really mad, and even then, his "Goddammit" got softened to a

Waving to the trainman on the caboose of a freight train. ILLUSTRATION BY JOHN MICHAEL DOWNS.

"Hotdammit." The name of the Lord was not to be taken in vain, and we feared punishment from Grandma as much as divine retribution.

The parents of some kids who lived across the street from us did not censor their speech, which they peppered with profanity and potty language. One naughty trick we learned from them was a variation on "Blow your whistle." When these youngsters chimed in, they shouted "Blow your pisshole." And before long, "Blow your whistle" became a thing of the past. Even when the neighbor kids weren't there, as the last trace of the train came by, we would face the trainman and scream out "Blow your pisshole." He couldn't hear us, of course, whatever we said. But when he blew the whistle, we laughed and laughed, to think that we had fooled him.

Even more importantly, we knew that the thundering clatter of the train meant that Grandma couldn't hear us. We had fooled her, too. The din of the passing train canceled out the scolding of Grandma, and even the wrath of God.

The Earhart children standing in front of Grandma's house, 1943. *Left to right*, Byron, Rosemary, and Sylvia. To the left of Byron in the background is the fence in front of the railroad tracks, at the corner of Schrader and Market. FAMILY COLLECTION.

CHAPTER 12

Orphan Annie and Junior Commandos

uring World War II, America presented a unified homefront, from the national and governmental level down to the local scene and the individual. Junior Commandos offer a good illustration of how official policy and popular activities meshed together like cogs in a machine. Civilians and the military, adults and young people, all worked together to defeat the enemy. Everyone had a role in "the war effort," as we called it. Defeat of the enemy could not be achieved just by the men in the service and the war plant employees. Nor did responsibility for achieving victory rest solely with adults. Even children enlisted in the cause. Boys and girls, like the entire civilian population, helped the men in uniform by doing without some things, such as *not* eating sugar and other food items, and *not* using manufactured goods.

Children's role in the war effort went beyond self-denial, because they could be recruited to work positively, especially to collect scrap. Government agencies created many posters to encourage patriotic attitudes and to stimulate activities aiding the production of war materiel. All media—newspapers and

The Office of War Information created and distributed many posters encouraging civilian support for the war effort, in this case to collect scrap metal. IMAGE COURTESY OF NATIONAL ARCHIVES.

general audience magazines, even including advertisements—did their best to promote active participation by civilians in supporting the war effort.

Cartoons, such as *Little Orphan Annie*, offer a prime example of the way print media brought young people into the war. *Little Orphan Annie* debuted in newspapers in 1924. By 1937 it ranked as the number one strip, ahead of other favorites such as *Popeye*, *Dick Tracy*, and *Blondie*. At Grandma's house our daily newspaper, the *Peoria Journal* (later the *Peoria Journal Star*), belonged to Grandpa's domain, and he got to read it first. As soon as he finished with the paper, my sisters and I took turns reading the cartoons.

In prewar years, the cartoonist Harold Gray portrayed Annie as the orphan underdog who successfully battled against corruption and criminals. This strip inspired a radio show, a number of films, and much later, a Broadway musical, *Annie*. During the war, Gray used his pen to encourage patriotism and attack anyone seen as unpatriotic. In one Sunday strip, he sketched a cartoon with a villain who had been making money on the war and said he hoped the war would last another twenty years. In this cartoon, a man who had lost two sons in the war, beat up the war-profiteer. When a policeman came to break up the fight, Annie told the policeman that the matter was being settled by "democratic processes." During the war our family, like Annie, had no sympathy for profiteers and black marketers. We rooted for Orphan Annie and other cartoon characters who supported the war.

In wartime cartoon strips, Annie turned from her outwitting of domestic crooks to participating in the war effort, even blowing up a German submarine. Gray used his curly-headed heroine as a role model to organize groups of children called the Junior Commandos, who collected newspapers, scrap metal, and other recyclable materials. Annie recruited and led her young civilian soldiers not only in daily and Sunday cartoons, but also in separately issued comic books under the title *Little Orphan Annie's Junior Commandos*. Gray, Annie, and her commandos collected tons of scrap material. This effort had a double dividend, because the government needed scrap to produce war goods; then kids used the money they got for their collection to buy savings stamps and bonds. Annie herself, in a June 24, 1942 cartoon, when asked where the money from scrap sales went, said "Every cent goes to buy war stamps and bonds."

These three panels are taken from Harold Gray, *ARF! The Life and Hard Times of Little Orphan Annie 1933–1945* (New Rochelle, NY: Arlington House, 1970).

In the comic strip, Colonel Annie wore a "JC" armband, short for "Junior Commando." These groups of adolescent warriors developed organizations throughout the country. Boston alone had twenty thousand members.

When I lived at Grandma's house in the early 1940s, I attended elementary school, so I was too young to be involved in the Junior Commandos. My sisters, Rosemary and Sylvia, became members. They and their fellow commandos in Havana proudly posed for a group portrait in front of the Junior High School. Their T-shirts served as their civilian uniforms in the battle against the enemy.

An October 16, 1942 article in the *Democrat* details activities of the Junior Commandos in Havana collecting scrap metal:

My sisters were members of the Junior Commandos in junior high school. This 1944 group photo in front of Havana Central Junior High School shows Rosemary (eighth from the left in the third row from the bottom) and Sylvia (third from the right in the same row). FAMILY COLLECTION.

COMMANDOS WILL RAID FOR SCRAP ALL DAY TODAY TO GET ALL AVAILABLE METAL INTO THE WAR EFFORT

It's a raid!

Havana's Junior Commandos are today raiding every scrap pile in town in an effort to get every last piece of metal now so urgently needed in the war effort. Every home, store, shop and property where there is any possibility of metal being found will be visited by these raiders.

For the past two weeks, a large amount of scrap has been collected by students of the grade schools and several tons are already in the junk yard waiting to be shipped. The response of the citizens has been fine, but there is still more scrap to be collected.

. . . Citizens are urged to speed up the work of the Commandos by getting their scrap out where it can be easily gathered up. Plans call for a house to house canvass, but if anyone is overlooked, he is urged to call the office of Supt. Wilbur Trimpe and students will call for the material.

The illustration for this article shows a group of commandos led by a young man holding an American flag, and boys and girls following with baskets and wagons of scrap metal. The local superintendent of schools assisted Colonel Annie and her recruited commandos. In scrap drives, as in war bond drives, schools became effective tools of mobilizing students and citizens.

Annie's Junior Commandos even enlisted in the campaign to save fats. A January 8, 1943 *Democrat* records this work:

Commandos to Pick Up Fats

The Havana Commandos will call at your home on January 14 and 15 in the second pick-up of waste fats since that important work was assigned them.

This group of Central School students will make a house-to-house canvass on the afternoon of the two days designated and will take your waste fat to a salvage depot where it will be turned in and eventually find its way into a shell that will drop on Berlin or Tokyo.

The article reminds readers that, as with scrap metal, people who happen to miss the commandos, can call Central School.

Even preschool children got in the act of supporting the war effort. A February 13, 1942 issue of the *Democrat* includes a picture titled "Youth and Age Unite in Victory Pledge." The caption's leading sentence announces: "Paul Thomas Ramni, eighteen months old, youngest policy-holder of the Manhattan Life Insurance Company, is assisted by Alfred P. McMurtie, seventy-two years old, the company's oldest employee in launching the Victory Pledge Drive calling for the use of renewal premiums to buy Government Bonds." The caption states that in the future, "renewal premiums received from the entire roster of 22,000 policyholders, will be used until further order, exclusively for the purchase of Government Bonds. The move is aimed to assist America and her Allies in winning the war."

Another youth group active during the war was the Junior Victory Army. As the Los Angeles newspaper articles in an earlier chapter illustrate, the Junior Victory Army (shortened to Junior Army) built model airplanes for the Navy, collected scrap, and did their part in Junior

Army Gardens. Newspaper articles reminded these bantam soldiers to be considerate where they played, because defense workers on the night shift needed their sleep. The Junior Army members received "orders" (like true soldiers) to complete their Home Safety Survey, and to carry their registration card with them. Just as Little Orphan Annie had to be careful of spies and saboteurs, the Junior Army had its coded message (in numbers) to communicate with one another. Although I have no recollection of the Junior Victory Army in Havana, this organization conveys the spirit of children's contribution to homefront efforts.

All elements and levels of the country joined together in supporting the armed forces. Official posters advocated national policy. Individual citizens such as the cartoonist Harold Gray improvised and revised peacetime humor and art to promote patriotism and military victory. On the local level, from Boston to Havana and on to Los Angeles, Junior Commando groups organized to carry out national policy while emulating Annie's heroic ideals. The Junior Victory Army represented another dimension of this civilian youth corps.

Children couldn't go to the battlefield with the soldiers. We couldn't work in a munitions factory. But we could participate in scrap drives that provided raw material for weapons and ammunition, joining the forces of Orphan Annie and her Junior Commandos.

From make-believe cartoons to real life, children's organizations and their patriotic activities joined with all elements and levels of the country to reinforce the military.

CHAPTER 13

Savings Stamps and Snake Dances

$\mathcal{S}$avings stamps and bonds made up another important part of the war effort, both for adults and youngsters. Not exactly contributions in the sense of giving money, savings bonds functioned as investments, while they also served as financial support of the war effort. An individual bought a savings bond from the government. In ten years it would mature at a guaranteed rate. The smallest savings bond cost $18.75. After ten years it could be cashed in for $25.00. In today's inflated economy, this may not seem like much, but for the early 1940s, $18.75 or $25.00 amounted to a considerable sum.

Of course, neither I nor any of the kids I knew had that much cash at one time to buy a savings bond. The most likely way a young person would get hold of a bond was to receive one as a gift for an important occasion such as Christmas, birthday, or graduation. A savings bond as a gift counted as doubly patriotic. First, it meant no purchase of goods, so more could be sent overseas. Second, it helped fund the war effort. Uncle Sam had more money to put into war materiel and care of our troops.

In their own small way, children could participate in fund raising, because the government issued savings bonds—we also called them "war bonds"—in kid-sized denominations. We could buy savings stamps at ten cents each, and paste them onto the squares in a savings book until we filled it and reached the goal of $18.75.

Patriotism and children's participation in the savings effort could not be left to passivity or chance, merely making the savings program available and letting young people decide to join in. The government and volunteer groups promoted war bonds in every area of the civilian population (as well as among servicemen!), and the educational setting was no exception. Schools received savings stamps and books to be sold to children. Teachers, from their position of authority and power, urged their students to buy savings stamps.

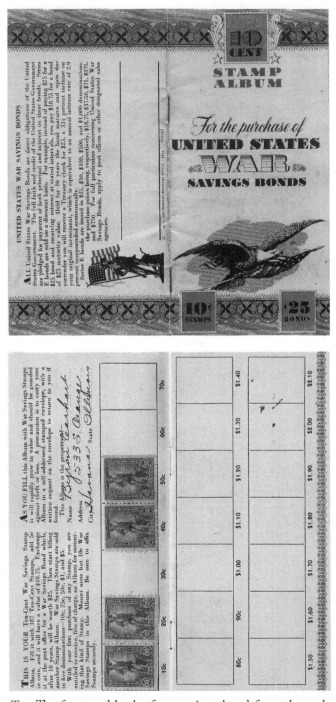

Top, The front and back of my savings bond from the early 1940s. *Above*, The inside of that savings bond, showing ten cent stamps which I pasted in. My name and address are entered in my mother's flowing penmanship. PERSONAL COLLECTION.

Oak Grove School, my first primary school building, on the corner of First and Plum, just one block from our home on South Orange Street. ILLUSTRATION BY JOHN MICHAEL DOWNS.

My most memorable recollection of the savings stamp campaign is still painful and embarrassing to retell. I attended the second grade at Oak Grove School, not long after my father had entered the Navy, and my family still lived on South Orange Street, before we moved in with my mother's parents. For a few months, Mom went to be with Dad where he had been stationed in Bremerton, Washington, and my father's mother, Zoe Earhart, came from nearby Mason City to take care of my sisters and me.

Our paternal grandmother had lived alone for a long time, because our paternal grandfather had died young. My father's mother learned to be quite conservative financially, having had to pinch pennies during the Depression while raising her children without a husband. She reminded us kids she had worked in a five-and-dime store for seventy-five cents a day. We knew better than to ask her for money, because not only would she turn us down, she would tell another story about hard times. She loved us dearly and treated us with kindness and warmth, otherwise, yet her concern for money made her appear to be cold-hearted.

During the time Grandma Earhart took care of us on South Orange Street, the first savings stamp drives at schools really got underway. Our teacher urged us, "Buy as many ten-cent stamps as you can afford."

This photo of Zoe Earhart, son Kenneth and daughter-in-law Mary, with their children Rosemary, Sylvia, and Byron, was taken in Mason City, Illinois in 1937. FAMILY COLLECTION.

Every youngster wanted to look good. Some of the children in my class brought in dimes right away, and slowly others got around to buying stamps.

The teacher began singling out the kids—like me—who still hadn't made a purchase. As a seven-year old I was quite shy, and simply couldn't bring myself to ask Grandma Earhart for money. One day the teacher had me stay after school. "Byron, can't you ask your parents for one dime to buy a savings stamp?"

She had me cornered. "Uh, Dad is in the Navy, and Mom is with him in Seattle."

"Who's taking care of you?"

"My Grandma Earhart."

"Can't you ask her for a little money?"

"Uh, I guess so."

The teacher forced a reluctant promise from me. But when I got home and looked at Grandma, I saw hard times a-coming, and lost my nerve. I don't recall my sisters having this problem, but they were older, and maybe they raided their piggy banks for dimes to buy their stamps.

Eventually my teacher found the solution, sending a note home with me to Grandma Earhart. When she opened the note and read that I was the only one in the class who hadn't bought a stamp, she gave me a much worse scolding than I expected if I had asked for money.

"Byron, why didn't you ask me for some money? Here your dad is in the Navy, and we all need to support the boys in the military. And you made the teacher send a note home. You be sure to tell her that if I had known, I would have sent money with you right away. We may not be rich, we can't afford luxuries, but what we do have we can use to help our boys."

I took my dime to school and got a stamp to paste into my savings book. Finally, our class became "one hundred per cent." Not only the teacher, but the entire class appreciated this achievement. Now our class could be proud of its unanimous and total participation in the war effort.

Not to be one hundred per cent indicated that our class somehow was lacking, even though it might be only a lone holdout. So not only the eyes of the teacher, but the eyes of every student had asked: *When are you going to buy a stamp and make us one hundred per cent?* After that first big mistake, I bought at least one stamp and never ruined the class record. At the end of the war, and for years thereafter, I had a number of savings bonds, which later became part of my college savings fund.

It would be a mistake to remember savings stamps as merely a pressure-driven program. We all felt very proud to be part of the war that everyone so intensely supported. School children had a fun reward for buying stamps. In our elementary school, every month the class that bought the largest amount of stamps got to perform a "snake dance." Students formed a long line, linked by hands on the waist of the person in front. The line "snaked" its way through the school and each classroom, chanting a slogan of their making.

When we learned that another class had won the right to hold that month's snake dance, we groaned, and had to put up with the humiliation of watching the other class weave its way through our room. We always criticized these trespassers. They didn't do as well at their snake dance as us when we had won. They couldn't compare to what we would do the next time we won.

When our teacher gave us the good news that we ranked as the top buyers for that month, we shouted with joy. One of the few times we got really noisy was getting ready for a snake dance. As part of the

A snake dance at Oak Grove School. ILLUSTRATION BY JOHN MICHAEL DOWNS.

preparation we had to pick our own short phrase to chant. The two slogans I recall illustrate well the creative limits of second graders. We debated the merits of "Buy more stamps" over "We buy stamps." It's no wonder I can't recall which of these suggestions won. But the wording wasn't that important. We lined up and invaded the other classrooms, winding our way around each class, up and down the aisles of desks, chanting and laughing at these losers in that month's stamp contest.

While our performance might be strictly amateur, our patriotism was sincere. And we helped the boys over there win the war when we bought savings stamps to defeat other classes and acted out our victorious snake dance.

CHAPTER 14

Convoys and Bivouacs

$\mathcal{S}$ ome incidents of childhood remain so vivid that they never disappear, they just lie dormant in long term memory, waiting to be awakened by similar sights and sounds.

One morning in late summer, 1990, as I came to a green light while driving to work, from the left of the intersection a number of olive drab military vehicles came bearing down on the intersection too fast to heed their red light, so I hit the brakes. The lead military vehicle pulled sharply to the right, hurdled the curb and skidded to a stop. While it still bounced, a khaki-clad man jumped out and ran to the center of the crossroad, signaling cars and trucks from all directions to halt so that his troop carriers and other military units could make a left turn. The President had called up the National Guard to participate in the short-lived Gulf War. Waiting for them to pass, listening to the chorus of roaring diesels and surging gas engines reminded me of similar scenes almost a half century earlier.

In the early 1940s we children learned a new word to describe a long line of military vehicles—a "convoy." At the time I lived on South Orange Street in Havana, state route 97 ran up the steep hill of Dearborn Street just one block away. Troops from Camp Ellis, a half hour to the west, came through Havana, heading east up the hill. Our house stood only a few hundred yards from this highway. When we played outside, we could hear the exhausts groaning as soldiers gunned their engines to make good speed up the incline. The transports drove so close to each other that if one slowed down or stopped, the following truck could plow into the one ahead. The *Camp Ellis News* reported one such incident for May 12, 1944. "Three Ellismen Injured in Convoy Mishap. Three Camp Ellis soldiers who had been with their units on flood duty were injured enroute to Camp Ellis Thursday night when a truck from one unit rammed into the back of the rear truck of the convoy a mile east of Jacksonville. . . ." This kind of daredevil, go-for-broke driving made these vehicles and their soldiers interesting to watch.

When our family still lived on South Orange Street, as soon as we kids heard the commotion of loud exhausts, we all yelled "Convoy!" and ran to Dearborn Street to watch. We liked to be there to count all the units as they passed. The lead vehicle had a large American flag attached to its front bumper. Most of the trucks had stakes and a canvas cover over the top. Soldiers sat on benches behind the cab and on both sides. Many of these recent recruits or draftees had recently graduated from high school. Their khaki uniforms matched the olive drab of their vehicles. They seemed to be having such a good time, laughing and joking.

A major attraction in these caravans was jeeps, usually with one soldier seated next to the driver. In many cases, this passenger had a combat boot resting on the hood, with the windshield folded down. The instant acceptance and popularity of the jeep highlights the enthusiastic patriotism of war years. It may be hard for twenty-first century readers to appreciate the excitement generated by this new device. Today, "Jeep" stands for the name of a car company with a full line of cars. This company's current vehicle that is the direct successor to the military vehicle

A convoy of army vehicles on bivouac driving up Dearborn Hill in Havana.
ILLUSTRATION BY JOHN MICHAEL DOWNS.

still has some of the adventurous aura of its wartime ancestor. But in the early 1940s, we had seen nothing like this innovation.

In 1940, two automobile companies, Ford and Willys, received army contracts to build a reconnaissance and light cargo vehicle. The finished product resulted in a remarkably successful hybrid: useful and durable as a light truck, rugged and versatile with its four-wheel drive and high clearance off-road capability, nimble and maneuverable as a car, and appealing to the eye. In spite of its serviceable specifications, it had a dashing appearance like a stylish but all-terrain convertible. The government shipped hundreds of thousands of jeeps overseas; they came to be relied on by both Americans and our Allies.

General Eisenhower praised the Jeep as one of the three tools that won the war (together with the Dakota military transport airplane, and the landing craft). The Andrews Sisters sang a rousing, humorous 1942 tune, "Six Jerks in a Jeep," that expressed the exuberance for this wartime invention. The YouTube video of this song shows the three Andrews sisters in WAAC uniforms in the back of the jeep, belting out the madcap lyrics. Three soldiers crammed themselves into the front of the jeep, as it bounced across the landscape. Like Rosie the Riveter, the jeep became one of the iconic images of World War II that has endured down to the present.

To me and the neighborhood kids in the early 1940s, the soldiers in the jeeps and the troops in the trucks of caravans seemed to be like a carefree group of young men going to a church picnic. We knew they had set out "on bivouac," but couldn't spell the word or explain what it meant. It might just as well have been a name for fun and games, although somehow we realized they were training for war. My buddies and I wished we could join the party and ride in—maybe even drive—a jeep.

Sometimes tanks participated in this military parade. With huge engines and no mufflers, their treads clattered and chattered against the brick paving as they clambered up the hill. They made so much noise that the smaller children stuck fingers in their ears. We welcomed the big event of these metal monsters lumbering through Havana. The deafening sound of the tanks destroyed our notion of the carefree picnic atmosphere of bivouac, reminding us of the brutal war that awaited these soldiers in training. The nightly radio broadcasts and newsreels in movie theaters taught us that war always involves a life or death struggle.

A tank in the convoy of army vehicles in Havana. ILLUSTRATION BY JOHN MICHAEL DOWNS.

When we moved to the north side of Havana, to Grandma's house, we lived too far away from the main highway to see the military traffic. Only when we drove out of town did we have a chance to view America's army on patrol. The government reminded us that use of a car should be limited to bare necessities, and civilians had no right to drive for pleasure. Convoys owned the road. The appearance of a lead jeep followed by a line of camouflaged vehicles signaled all civilian vehicles to pull off the road and wait until the army passed. As our car swayed from the artificial windstorm whipped up, my sisters and I counted every jeep and transport. Then we compared this convoy to others we had seen.

Gasoline rationing limited civilian car and truck traffic, and tires became scarce. Even if we had ration stamps for gasoline, we tried not to drive too much, because when our tires wore out we might not be able to get new ones. To conserve gas and save on tires, the government ordered civilians to drive no more than 35 miles an hour.

Once when my uncle drove our car from Farmington to Havana, I was sitting in the front and noticed the speedometer go past 35 and then on the open road reach 55. My patriotic duty called, so I told my uncle that he was going much faster than the 35 speed limit. He let me know that he knew the speed limit and how fast we were going, and it was OK. Our 1941 Oldsmobile with a six-cylinder engine could go faster than 55 with safety, but I worried that not just our uncle, but our car and family had become unwilling accomplices in violating the government's rules, wasting both gasoline and tires.

An ironic note on speeding: it became more of a problem after the war than during the war. A friend told me of his experience in 1946 when a neighbor bought one of the first postwar Lincolns, and took him for a ride, quickly pushing the car past 80 miles an hour. After three years of driving at the snail's pace of 35 miles an hour, people overcompensated by driving much too fast. Across the country, the rash of accidents led to a safety campaign, complete with graphic warnings.

The *Democrat* on September 7, 1945 posted its own front page article, titled "Warn Drivers Against Post-War Speed Spree." The first sentence of the article gives the gist of this message of caution: "Drivers of the

This cartoon depicts, in dramatic overstatement, the country's concern with deaths due to speeding after the restrictions on speed limits were to be lifted in postwar times. IMAGE COURTESY OF NATIONAL ARCHIVES/WIKIMEDIA.

nation were warned today that neither they nor their cars are in shape to indulge in a post-war speed spree without piling up the biggest traffic toll in the country's history."

In later years, I have heard the word "convoy" used in various ways. A newspaper picture showing a mother duck leading her ducklings to water may be captioned "a convoy of ducks." Or a number of cars or recreation vehicles traveling together can be described as a convoy. And in war campaigns around the world, even a group of supply trucks might be called a convoy. A fleet of transport ships sailing together also made up a convoy. But for me this term will always be linked to the sights and sounds of the convoys I saw in Havana: a freight train-like procession of brownish-green vehicles. Transports roaring, jeeps whining, and tanks belching and lurching their way up Dearborn hill preparing to vanquish the enemy at some unknown bivouac.

CHAPTER 15

One-Armed Bandits in Little Reno

L iving at Grandma's house framed an ideal, innocent time. From a child's viewpoint, life in Havana seemed safe and good. Danger existed in the foreign world, the war zone. "Over there" our military fought battles against bad people. Enemies lurked outside America, forcing good men like Dad to enlist in order to go overseas and protect America. Havana and America stood for "the land of the free, the home of the brave." If I had continued to live on South Orange Street instead of moving to our grandparents' house, my view of early 1940s Havana would not have been much different. Moving to their residence didn't alter my opinion of this small town, but Havana did change remarkably as a result of the war.

Some of that change came about as a matter of fact, inevitable. For example, when Dad enlisted in the Navy, it made sense for us to live in Grandma's big house, because she had the room. That way, we could rent out our house to an Army family.

In order to train large numbers of recruits, the Army opened Camp Ellis, about twenty miles west of Havana in Fulton County. The government evicted farmers from 17,750 acres of farmland, which they quickly transformed into one of the country's major training facilities. Camp Ellis holds a fascinating story in its own right, told in later chapters.

My knowledge of this nearby camp and its impact on Havana is limited and indirect, some based on personal experience, other information gained from the local newspaper and historical accounts. We rented our house to the family of an officer who helped train soldiers at Camp Ellis. Naturally, this officer's family wanted to be near him. The government urged Havanans to be patriotic and make housing available to those who needed it, both military personnel and civilian war workers.

An article in the October 16, 1942 *Democrat* outlines the local housing situation:

NEW ARMY CAMP MAKES HOUSING PROBLEM HERE
800 WAR WORKERS ARE EXPECTED TO LIVE IN HAVANA

Construction work at the new army camp in Fulton county known at present as the Spoon River Project, is under way following the letting of practically all the contracts and already Havana is facing a housing problem.

Mayor Keith, acting upon the suggestion of officials, conducted a survey of housing space here this week in an effort to make facilities available to an estimated 750 persons who will live here while employed on construction work. . . .

This kind of change came about naturally, and didn't have a negative effect on Havana. Other change turned out to be not so beneficial and universally appreciated. Take a large number of draftees, young and facing the possibility of death overseas, who have been training hard all week, give them weekend passes, and watch out! What money they had they gladly spent on a good time before they went into battle and would have no chance for fun. Wartime Havana experienced scarcity of goods, but never a shortage of people eager to entertain soldiers and take their money. In short, Havana became one of the weekend pass hot spots for Camp Ellis soldiers.

They drank in Havana, and they also liked the bars on Havana's two "beaches," Quiver Beach to the north and Matanzas Beach to the south. Both beaches had their taverns, which long outlasted the war. But soldiers needed something more than liquor to attract them and relieve them of their money. Gambling of various kinds provided that added attraction. My childhood memories associate the rise of gambling with the war, and yet the war did not create, it only nourished, the games of chance already in place.

Early Havana's reputation as a gambling site earned it the title of "little Reno." The great fishing and hunting opportunities (especially for ducks and geese) drew many well-to-do sportsmen. As far back as 1889, United States President Harrison came to Havana to hunt ducks, an event that locals memorialized in a picture postcard showing the president on the bank of the Illinois River at the foot of Main Street. In the twentieth century, wealthy sportsmen came to Havana loaded not only with guns and fishing equipment, but also with money. Drinking and gambling alternated with fishing and hunting. Local legend has it that Al Capone came to Havana from Chicago (and nearby Cicero) both for recreation and to help set up casinos. Havana existed as an "R & R" destination long before the war started.

What the soldiers and their money did to gambling had the same effect as water and summer sun on a field of young corn. Card games and crap tables provided the big draw for late night carousing, but many soldiers favored slot machines as their game of choice. A "memory" by Irene Dudley Neteler (in Bordner's book on Camp Ellis) noted that the military hierarchy even extended to Havana and to off-duty activities. Camp rules for enlisted soldiers limited them only to play the slots in The Evergreens, a Neteler family nightclub on the south edge of Havana. "Gambling was prevalent in the area at that time. The officers were the only ones allowed to go to the Casino. Enlisted men were allowed to play the five and ten cent slot machines only. Of course, they often would sneak a few quarters or half-dollars into the slots. They also would give a few dollars to an officer to bet for them in the Casino."

Neteler wrote that the influx of soldiers from Eastern states also brought a change in the menu. Shrimp did not appear as a common item in Midwestern restaurants, but the preferences of Camp Ellis patrons soon made this an ordinary feature. Neteler offered a humorous anecdote: the first time a waitress received an order for "shrimp cocktail," she went to the bar for this unknown drink, and had to be rerouted to the kitchen. This nightclub survived the war, known more for its steaks than its shrimp. As a teenager, I delivered steaks that this restaurant ordered from Earhart Food Locker. Like the change in menu to include shrimp, the increased gambling activity continued after the war.

Slot machines had advantages for both gambler and owner. The gambler needed no knowledge or skill to play one, could afford to get into the action with only a handful of coins, and could begin or quit any time. On the owner's side, the slots had an advantage over card games and crap tables because they required no human labor (like a dealer in poker or a croupier for crap tables). Slot machines only asked for a few square feet of space. They didn't need a late night "gambling den" setting, and could be installed in regular businesses to take in money any time the business was open.

People seemed to have a peculiar perception of slot machines. They could tell themselves that slot machines did not "really" involve gambling,

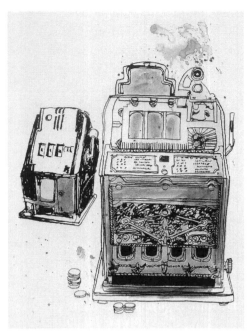

Two examples of slot machines with their right-handed levers. ILLUSTRATION BY JOHN MICHAEL DOWNS.

because you played them in ordinary businesses, in daytime. People, especially women and children, who felt constrained by social mores or were prevented by law from entering a nighttime drinking/gambling place, felt more free to go into a store during the day, make some purchase, and then drop a few coins in a slot machine.

It took no skill or reason to play the slots. People relied on luck pure and simple. Some regular players, like several of my junior high buddies, claimed they could beat the slots. Kenny, one of my best friends said, "Just wait, and watch someone feed a machine, and lose a lot of money. Then, after the loser walks away, you can drop in a few coins and 'milk' it of winnings."

This crudely constructed theory claimed that every so often the machine had to pay off, in order to keep the sucker playing. You just had to catch the machine when it was ready to pay off. While in elementary school I never noticed these devices. As a junior high student, I took over my older sister's newspaper route, which meant that every Saturday I had a payday, a percentage of the money I collected that day. Nevertheless, I seldom played the slots, being too stingy with my hard-earned money. After losing a few "buffalo heads," I hated, as my paternal grandmother liked to say, to "send good money after bad."

The cynical view of slot machines earned the devices the nickname of "one-armed bandits," because they robbed the gambler with that single arm (handle) the people pulled to play it. As a boy I never saw the card tables or crap tables, but during the war, slot machines appeared in so many businesses you could not avoid them. I really noticed them after the war, when as a teenager I hung around the drug stores (all of which had soda fountains). Every drug store had several slots, and even the tiny newsstand out of which I carried newspapers had one.

I saw women come into that small newsstand, buy a newspaper or magazine, but hardly glance at it, then walk to the cashier and hand over two dollar bills. "Give me two rolls of nickels." Each roll wrapped in paper contained twenty nickels. Then they hurried over to the slot machine, tore the paper off the coins, and began to feed nickels in, one at a time, winning a few and losing more, until all those nickels were gone. Then they bought another roll, and another, and another. . . . After these women got hooked on playing the slots, they didn't even pretend to be interested in buying any reading material. They just walked right up to the register and got what they came for—nickels to feed the machine.

Most of my friends in junior high played the slots. This form of mechanical gambling had no minimum age. I saw old wooden cases for Coke bottles placed in front of slot machines for children to stand on so they could reach high enough to drop their coins in the slot. The war came, the government built Camp Ellis, Army recruits flooded the town, and gambling prospered. The war ended, the government dismantled Camp Ellis and sold its buildings as surplus, and then auctioned off the camp to farmers for their corn fields. The Army recruits who survived the war had long since returned to their homes. But the slot machines outlived the war, and received no discharge, honorable or dishonorable. For years after the war, Havana had the reputation of a "wide-open" town for gambling, especially slot machines.

Even people who didn't play the slots and frequent the gambling places knew who owned them. They drove fancy new cars immediately after the war when such cars were expensive and hard to come by. They had no other income except for gambling, wore flashy clothes, and flaunted their wealth. We looked down on these ne'er do wells who didn't really work for a living, but took the hard earned money of others. No one in our family gambled.

Thanks to two-fisted gamblers from Camp Ellis, Havana lived up to its reputation as a haven for one-armed bandits in Little Reno, especially during, and even after, the war.

In the postwar period, religious and political forces eradicated gambling. Most churches and many citizens attacked the immorality of betting. The Baptist church I attended helped lead this battle. America had vanquished evil in Europe and Japan, so now we had to stamp out vice in our very midst. Members of my church could be outspoken.

"Gambling has no place in Heaven." "You're right, it doesn't do any good, and just gives our town a bad reputation."

Eventually the state government enforced a ban on gambling, and the slot machines disappeared. On Halloween Night in 1953, Illinois State Troopers raided and closed down more than a dozen Mason County casinos.

Excerpts from the November 5, 1953 *Democrat* give the gist of this Halloween night trick-without-treat:

STATE COPS SEIZE GAMING EQUIPMENT, MONEY IN RAID HERE

Surprise Visit Here Nets Two Truckloads Equipment, Over $4,000

Mason County's gambling activities were again in the limelight nationwide, after more than 50 state troopers staged a lightning-like raid on 14 taverns and restaurants in this area Saturday evening at about 10 o'clock. . . .

ORDERLY IN HAVANA

The state troopers operated in a most efficient, orderly and swift manner in Havana. . . .

It was estimated that the officers picked up more than $4,000 in cash from crap tables, roulette wheels and poker tables in the county and value of equipment seized would run into several thousands of dollars. Two trucks were necessary to haul away the equipment. . . .

Havana, like America of the 1940s and 1950s, in my memory, was steeped in righteous, even self-righteous attitudes. America had stepped up to the challenge and defeated Japan and Germany overseas. Some considered the elimination of gambling in America the defeat of an internal enemy.

In retrospect, some Havana people lament the loss of gambling, especially because of its heavy toll on Havana's economy. The city lost many jobs, fewer tourists and gamblers came to Havana, and restaurants as well as other businesses suffered. A 2014 interview with local residents Don and Jean Blessman reveals the unintended consequences of the ban on gambling. Jean Blessman's father, Louis Becker, owned and ran several businesses that featured gambling. The reporter who interviewed this couple summed up their assessment of post-gambling Havana: "Gambling had been a big draw that brought in visitors, and those visitors brought in entertainers, and it all added up to a very busy downtown scene, especially on weekends. Now Havana's downtown looks more like a silent Norman Rockwell picture postcard. . . . While the realities of a declining economy and how it affects a city like Havana are too numerous to peg solely on the loss of gambling, it sure was a harsh blow." (This information is taken from "The lost city of Little Reno: How a Halloween raid changed Havana's luck," by Ken Harris, *Pekin Daily Times,* Friday, April 18, 2014, page C5.)

This article corrects several misconceptions. Although local lore and legend claim that Capone had been behind the rise of casinos in Havana, several of the older men who owned gambling establishments deny any Mafia or racket connections. According to them, gambling in Havana developed as a local, home-grown industry. This article also touches on the irony of the fact that, only several decades after the Halloween night raid, gambling became legal statewide. In 1974, the state established the Illinois lottery, and in 1990 the state legislature approved riverboat gaming.

From the 1980s and 1990s, gambling assumed a respectable reputation with its high tech form of state lotteries. The revenues (allegedly) help fill depleted state coffers. One of the arguments against gambling had been that it was immoral and promoted crime. In recent times the supposedly crooked small-town gangsters have been replaced by the friendly cashiers at the grocery or convenience store. Two other differences between slot machines and state lotteries are the local/personal character of slots over against the centralized/impersonal handling of lotteries.

The old fashioned slot machine might have been mechanical, but when you shook hands with a one-armed bandit, you knew what was robbing or rewarding you. The loss or win came directly and immediately. Today when buying a mega-prize lottery ticket, your destiny lies in the electronic memory of the wholly impersonal (and thereby holy?) computer, whose mysterious decision is communicated over the mass media of television, radio, and newspaper.

The more personalized forms of gambling have been revived in the romantic setting of riverboat casinos on the Illinois and Mississippi Rivers. The curious logic in the lobbying campaign for legalized gambling on riverboats maintained that confining gaming to the rivers and boats would thereby keep the cities free and pure. However one views this twisted reasoning, surely we cannot conclude that the people who board the modern riverboats do so with the intention of cleaning up the cities. No, by entering one of these floating casinos, a person escapes the humdrum routine of the here and now, going back to the exciting times of the nineteenth century riverboats and venturing out into the gambler's dream of making that one big win. Gamblers look far beyond logic and statistics, to that time and place where lady luck smiles on them.

Old style gambling with card games, crap tables, and slots long ago disappeared from Havana, but its reputation as a fast town lived on for many years. During the mid-1950s, when I attended Knox College in Galesburg, more than an hour's drive away, fraternities that wanted to "tie one on," knew Havana as the place to go for a good time. They would get away from the college's eyes, drive to one of the bars on Havana's beaches, and not worry about being underage. The fraternity guys razzed me about coming from such a rough town.

However, the attraction for fraternities was just easy access to liquor. The 1953 Halloween night raid had eliminated the one-armed bandits.

CHAPTER 16

Cornfield Soldiers, Happy Civilians, and Singing POWs

When we lived at Grandma's house, we saw the war on two very different levels. First and foremost, we worried about Dad and other members of the military we knew, fearing that they might be wounded or killed, hoping that they would return safely. We considered as less important information about events in faraway lands, news of warfare broadcast on the radio and projected in newsreels. After Pearl Harbor, the Pacific Coast shifted to high alert for Japanese planes and submarines. The East Coast became the scene of many ships sunk by German U-boats. The mid-continent location of the Midwest insulated it from the threat of invasions and attacks.

War made its presence known in central Illinois by the construction of Camp Ellis, a major training center, twenty miles west of Havana, near the towns of Ipava and Table Grove. The planning and development of the camp had to overcome a number of difficulties. First, farmers had to be evicted from 17,750 acres of farmland, and their homes razed. Some of these families had pioneer ties to the earliest American settlers in the region. Although some owners grumbled, especially about the amount of money the government determined each family would receive for their property, the eviction resulted in no sustained resistance.

Central to the plan for creating Camp Ellis had been the assumption that the government could hire enough workers, secure and transport enough material, and then in a matter of months erect an elaborate military facility that ordinarily would take several years. The Illinois residents who lived around this area, at first skeptical that the camp could be completed so quickly, did everything they could to make the plan succeed.

Construction began in September, 1942 and ended six months later, in spite of nightmarish conditions of an early winter and then spring

Postcard images of the barracks where trainees slept, and the mess hall where they ate, during their time at Camp Ellis. IMAGES COURTESY OF MARION COR-NELIUS, EASLEY PIONEER MUSEUM.

thaws that turned the ground into deep mud. During this frantic time, contractors built "a streamlined military city of one-story barracks, complete water and drainage system, fire department, modern hospital, warehouses, recreational facilities, and a prisoner of war camp" (*The Story of Camp Ellis*, p. 11). The camp had its own railroad and 2,200 buildings. One example of the incredible speed of construction: the completion in one day of a metal-grid landing strip 5,800 feet long and 150 feet wide. Partly because Camp Ellis became a training site for medics, they constructed a vast hospital occupying 140 acres. The camp also had its own chapel. At its peak this facility eventually housed 40,000 trainees and civilians, and 5,000 prisoners of war. The camp trained 125,000 men before it closed in 1945. The rapid and efficient creation of a major training camp and POW camp in itself stands as a minor victory in the larger battle of World War II.

Two postcard images of Camp Ellis: a row of barracks, and a chapel for religious services. IMAGES COURTESY OF MARION CORNELIUS, EASLEY PIONEER MUSEUM.

Two postcard images of Camp Ellis facilities: above, the theater, and below, the recreation building. IMAGES COURTESY OF MARION CORNELIUS, EASLEY PIONEER MUSEUM.

Local historian Marjorie Rich Bordner titled her record of this transformation of farmland into military camp: *From Cornfields to Marching Feet: Camp Ellis, Illinois.* This book is actually two works in one, the first 128 pages being a reprint of *The Story of Camp Ellis,* compiled by the military staff of the camp. Those interested in the camp itself can read the first half of Bordner's book. Those who live in, or travel to,

Illinois may go to the Easley Pioneer Museum in Ipava, Illinois, which preserves a wealth of photos, documents, and memorabilia on Camp Ellis. The museum even has one link from the metal-grid landing strip. The second half of Bordner's book, individual "memories" of the camp, will be quoted and summarized later.

The role of African-Americans at this training facility remains an unwritten chapter of the record of Camp Ellis. The official account, *The Story of Camp Ellis,* does not mention the presence of this minority, nor does it indicate that they were segregated from the White majority. Only one of Bordner's "memories," by David G. Johnson, touches on the subject of segregation: "Camp Ellis was segregated at the time with a black section and a white section as well as the fenced in place for German Prisoners of War." Ironically, *The Story of Camp Ellis* devotes a number of pages (36–40) to prisoners of war, but none to Black soldiers.

Another memory from Bordner's book, by Helen E. Everitt, a teacher who was hired to teach illiterate inductees to read, mentions Black soldiers. Some men entered the army with very little education. Everitt taught them to read and write. She remembers about her students that "They were so eager to learn and proud of their successes, and so appreciative of what they were accomplishing." She recalls "the courtesy and respect shown by the students, especially the blacks." She also mentions "the class where there were blacks, whites, Mexicans, and one Indian, who couldn't speak English." Everitt does not deal with segregation and the fact that her students were of different ethnic background. These soldier-students were lumped together as the "Work or Fight" men, who were given the alternative to find defense work or to serve in the military.

Two pieces from the November 12, 1943 *Democrat* open a window to the question of race at Camp Ellis. Each piece is quoted in full. The first is a news item:

CAMP ELLIS NEGRO KILLED BY FULTON COUNTY FARM MEN

MAN TRAPPED IN HOME WHERE FARMER'S WIFE WAS ASSAULTED

A negro soldier stationed at Camp Ellis was shot and killed last Monday night in the vicinity of the camp by a group of farmers of the community. The negro was trapped in the farm home of George Quigley after several telephone calls to women of the community had been traced to the home.

The Quigley home was the scene of a rape attack Thursday night, November 4, and when several women on a party line received telephone calls and insulting remarks were made to them, a group of farmers rushed to the Quigley home and found a negro soldier at the telephone. They ordered him to come out and assured him he would be turned over to the military authorities without harm. He extinguished the light in the room and refused to come out until several shots had been fired into the building. When he did come out he was swinging a club which he threw at one of the men. As he made his way to an out building he was confronted by another of the posse. He was armed with a fruit jar which he threw at the man who ordered him to stop, and as he did so the man fired a shot gun charge into his chest. He died in the farm yard fifteen minutes later.

Following the shooting, another negro soldier, under questioning admitted that he had committed the attack in the Quigley home last week.

The Quigleys were not at home at the time of the shooting. Following the attack on Mrs. Quigley while her husband was forced at the point of a gun to stand by a window while the crime was committed, they had moved from their farm home which borders the camp.

The negro who admitted the attack has been turned over to the civilian authorities for prosecution.

A coroner's jury, inquiring into the death of the negro, exonerated the man who did the shooting. The verdict was justifiable homicide.

The second article from the same issue of the *Democrat* is an editorial about this incident.

A SERIOUS PROBLEM

The military and the civilian authorities in the communities surrounding Camp Ellis are confronted with a serious problem. The problem was brought into the headlines this week when announcement was made that a negro soldier had been shot and killed in a farm home in Fulton County, following an attack by a negro soldier on the wife of a prominent farmer in the vicinity of the camp.

Rumblings of dissension between negro soldiers and white soldiers and between different factions of the negroes at the camp have been heard for some time. It is rumored that more blood-shed is likely unless something is done in the near future to relieve a tension that appears to be growing.

That a situation such as this exists is deplorable. The negroes stationed at Camp Ellis are pretty well isolated from their own people. They are forced to seek recreation under a severe handicap, and in some of the larger communities the report is that their presence is resented.

It is not just that all negro soldiers at Camp Ellis be condemned by the act of one or two soldiers who fail to respect the uniform they wear. A large percentage of these men are doing a commendable job of soldiering and they performed a valuable service to the community last spring when floods threatened to destroy valuable property.

However, the fact that they wear the uniform of the United States Army does not license them to commit such atrocities as have been credited to them. Unless swift justice is administered, more serious trouble may be expected.

This news article and editorial are quoted in full here because I have no other information to offer to place this incident in context. A paragraph from a 2014 exhibit on Camp Ellis prepared by the Dickson Mounds State Museum, (now housed at the Easley Pioneer Museum), throws some light on this situation in the region.

In the 1940s the African-American population of Western Illinois was almost nonexistent, and area communities were perplexed by the sudden arrival of numbers of African-American soldiers. While the Fulton County State's Attorney expressed pride in the fact that his home town, Lewistown—an all-white community—opened its restaurants, taverns, theaters, and other public places to African-American servicemen, this was the exception, and not the rule. Separate USO centers were established in Peoria, Galesburg, and Macomb; and many facilities were segregated in most towns. The War experience itself would bring many issues of segregation to national attention.

Although the situation at Camp Ellis is unclear, at other military facilities and at war factories across the country, African-Americans resented their treatment in separate and often inferior quarters. Some incidents led to violence, shootings, riots, and deaths. A fortunate aspect of Camp Ellis is that no race riots occurred here. At least, I found none reported in the *Democrat*, the 1944 issues of the *Camp Ellis News*, or in Bordner's book.

The second half of Bordner's book contains a valuable set of 173 recollections or "memories" of people who had close ties to Camp Ellis as army personnel, civilian employees, or visitors, and even one account by a prisoner of war. Bordner solicited and edited these accounts, recollections arranged alphabetically by last name. In her preface to these "Memories," Bordner sums up the gist of this collection: "whether one was in uniform or was a civilian; all were doing their bit for the War Cause" (p. 132).

These memories, from a few paragraphs to a few pages in length, make for fascinating reading. Her book provides a good starting point for anyone who wants to relive the experience of the war years in situations such as Camp Ellis.

As a boy, I never visited this training site. My mother and grandparents were preoccupied with running the Earhart Food Locker, and with raising three children. My sisters and I kept busy with school work and the company of playmates. Having no direct memories of the camp myself, I quote and summarize some of the accounts from Bordner's book to provide the reader a glimpse into the atmosphere and activities of this training facility.

Bordner's own "memory" within this collection captures the dominant attitude and major motivation of all the people who wrote accounts for her: "Patriotism was at the top of everybody's list all of the time." This theme appears in the recollections of veterans who had trained there. Emil C. Evancich wrote about a reunion of Camp Ellis veterans: "all praised their mothers and wives for displaying the Blue Star Banner in a window for all to see during the War, showing that they had someone serving their country. Schools and churches also displayed their banners in praise of their members in service."

In *The Story of Camp Ellis*, soldiers who underwent training here gave high marks to their military instructors for providing valuable lessons that proved highly useful when they shipped overseas to active duty. High-ranking officers gave credit to the Camp Ellis-trained engineers, medics, quartermasters, and other supply personnel who served under their command on the warfront. We quote a few of these favorable comments. A major general stated that "A grand job of training was done." A Lieutenant Col. wrote that "the best units I have seen in this whole area always seem to come from Ellis. The last does not only include QM units, but Medical and Engineer Units as well."

Becoming a soldier and fighting a war was serious business, and these young men served their country well. But, being young men, they also lived at the prime age for finding a mate. Many of these soldiers, as well as young women from the area, remember fondly their mixture of patriotic duty with romantic courting and early marriage. As one soldier put it, "Camp Ellis changed my future, and for the better."

They also became deeply involved in sports and recreation. *The Story of Camp Ellis* boasts that "The soldiers of Camp Ellis were never lacking for entertainment whether they were training in the camp proper or whether they were miles away fighting floods or making their bivouac encampments. Dances, band concerts, USO shows, all-soldier camp productions, company parties, roller skating and service club games provided those fun-seeking soldiers with a menu as appetizing as any to be found in the Sixth Service Command" (p. 113). Big name sports figures such as the fighter Joe Louis and the pitcher Bob Feller, as well as many Hollywood actors and actresses, made their appearance at the camp.

I looked through a complete run of the 1944 *Camp Ellis News,* full of articles on sports and entertainment. People in surrounding towns welcomed the soldiers and their musical performances. These men were serious about their military training, but just as intent on having a good time.

The large contingent of civilians who built and maintained Camp Ellis shared a similar attitude toward country and life in general: they were patriotic and proud of being a part of the war effort, yet they also had a lot of fun during and after their workday. Central Illinois in the early 1940s, still recovering from the Depression, knew unemployment and underemployment, with low wages. Social life and entertainment were rather limited. The construction of Camp Ellis created many jobs, with better pay, so people could be patriotic while earning a decent wage.

Kathryn Evans Turner summed up the economic fortune of her father, who first worked to construct the camp, then served as a civilian guard. "This was welcome employment when the country was emerging from the Depression of the 1930s and the country was at War." Bill Ulmer wrote about his father, who also served as a guard, sometimes guarding POWs: "He started at 60 cents an hour, working up to $1.15. This was the most money he had ever made." To a twenty-first century reader this wage may seem incredibly low, yet it indicates how bad the economy was in the mid-twentieth century.

A large number of women ran the day to day affairs of this Camp. Bordner worked as secretary to an officer in charge of Civilian Personnel. The memories of many young women related how easily they applied and secured employment, how grateful they were for the generous pay, and how much they enjoyed the work and the fringe benefits of good food and being able to take part in the social and entertainment life of the camp.

Lee Ann Ziener sums up her own personal combination of patriotism, pay, and pleasure. "Pearl Harbor mobilized every American citizen to some type of service to augment the war effort and to end the giant international conflict." Unemployed at the time Camp Ellis was erected, she found a job at the Officers' Club, and worked her way up to a position as a stenographer at an annual salary of $1,200, "far more than most other stenographic jobs." On lunch hours, she and her friend played ping pong and pool.

Some young women graduated from high school one day, and began working at Camp Ellis the next day, making money instead of paying out for college tuition. Mary Alma Radosevich Haney wrote enthusiastically about her Camp Ellis experience. "It was such fun at the prime of Camp Ellis to be able to enjoy all Special Service facilities and not be considered as active military." She liked attending the big name band performances and seeing the Hollywood entertainers, and even competing in sports against the WACS. "I can truly say that the experience and education I received at Camp Ellis was more than equivalent to what I would have received in college, as I had planned to attend." The men and women who worked on base were happy civilians.

In addition to the army trainees and non-military workers, Camp Ellis included a third group of people, the prisoners of war (POWs), some Italians, but most of them Germans captured in the ill-fated African campaign of Rommel. A strange aspect of these prisoners is that, although they did not share the patriotism of the American soldiers and civilians, they did have in common with these Americans the quest for a good time during their unintentional stay in mid-America.

In fact, rather than being patriotic in the sense of belief in and loyalty to the Nazi rationale of the superior Aryan race, these prisoners had become reluctant participants in the war. Because the hard-core Nazis had been separated from most of the prisoners confined at Camp Ellis, these POWs were used for various labor assignments on and off the camp. With Camp Ellis soldiers, they helped sandbag levies against floods, and assisted farmers in the surrounding region.

An odd turn of events on both the American and (mostly) German sides was a reversal of propaganda perceptions. Americans, who had been told by the government about Nazi plans to rule the world and destroy democracy, feared these POWs. Don Jobe, the son of a farmer who had hired POWs from the camp to hand-pick corn, "was shocked and frightened of the thought that German POWs would be helping. I was sure they would all look like and act like Hitler. I had formed an opinion that all Germans must be like Hitler." As the prisoners worked, this fearful young American remarked that, "They seemed to be happy in what they were doing, laughing, joking in their language." The MP who accompanied the prisoners told the local farmers not to worry: "the POWs were no threat to us. He also expressed how happy they were not to be in the War."

Harvey S. Bubb, Sr., who worked at the Post Engineer's Fiscal Office, got to know POWs rather well, and relays one German prisoner's experience. "He said his father gave him 3 musts when he went off to war. His father told him he must enlist, not wait to be drafted. He must enlist in the African Campaign. He must get to the front lines as soon as he could, and surrender. So he became a quick POW for the Allies."

A number of the personal accounts from the camp tell the same story of initial fear of prisoners, but with time came trust and pity, even kind treatment. Allen Blount relates one such anecdote about POWs who were brought to his home to dig a ditch. "My mother was scared to pieces and was going to take us kids to our grandparents' home in Canton but she didn't, and after a while she felt sorry for them and was sending garden produce and milk out to them. My father reasoned that these men were made to fight and wouldn't she be thankful, if one of us were there, that someone would show us compassion."

Harry M. Underwood tells a similar story. "They enjoyed our cigarettes so much and would do anything to get some. Theirs were terrible. We were not supposed to give them any tobacco or anything else, but we did for they were just men like ourselves, far from home and families." The camp restricted interaction with prisoners, but a crude form of exchange developed, with prisoners making rings out of silver dollars and receiving cigarettes or food.

The prisoners had heard German propaganda about the terrible conditions in America and the bad people there. Soon they saw through this false propaganda, and they appreciated the good food and adequate accommodations. Many of them conveyed the information that after the war they would like to return to live here.

Bordner includes a memory from one prisoner of war, Kurt G. Pechmann, which she wrote down for him. Drafted into the German army, he first suffered through the Russian Front and then later was captured in Italy, and shipped to the United States and Camp Ellis. When he arrived, he weighed 128 pounds. After eating the good food at Ellis, he left for Germany in 1945 weighing 185 pounds. "Many tears were shed by the POWs as they passed the Statue of Liberty to return to Germany for they had fallen in love with America."

After returning to Poland (former German territory), Pechmann married and was able to come back to America, setting up his own granite cutting business. Bordner sums up his experience: "Mr. Pechmann has spent his life doing so much 'giving back' to America, for America has been so good to him." Among his many good deeds was the repair of a vandalized Veteran's Memorial. He and his sons built the Vietnam Veterans' Memorial in Milwaukee, Wisconsin. President Reagan wrote him a letter of appreciation.

Mr. Pechmann's journey from enemy soldier to prisoner of war to immigrant and on to decorated patriot is a remarkable tale of how personal contact can reverse impersonal propaganda. Both on the German and the American side, this reversal of attitudes is amazing. A number of the memories in Bordner's book tell of Americans' initial fear of enemy prisoners in the heart of America's Midwest; when these people came into contact with the prisoners, the fear disappeared.

While I was preparing this book, and looking for other memories, Wilma Bishop Hardesty wrote me about her experiences in rural Mason County during the war. She saw the complexion of Havana change on weekends as khaki-clad soldiers filled the streets, and she even was able to visit with some soldiers on bivouac near their farm. She felt very uneasy about going to Camp Ellis and getting close to the German soldiers, but "when I saw these blonde very young men, I thought they couldn't possibly be dangerous." (Personal communication.)

Bordner relates an experience similar to that of Hardesty: initial ambivalence toward Germans who had been painted in propaganda as Nazis. Her job included fingerprinting prisoners. At first she had been "scared to death to fingerprint any Germans because U.S. propaganda had convinced her that all were Nazis." However, once she interacted with them, she found that they turned out to be "mostly decent people."

An unusual aspect of the German prisoners mentioned in many memories is that they sang so well, even when marching. Gene Edwards wrote of his father, "My father who is 83 now, still remembers how beautiful the POWs sang." William Harrison Kraemer wrote of his experience guarding German POWs on their way through Havana to work on farms. "As we went through Havana they sang German songs, songs used as international friendship. . . . They enjoyed the truck drives traveling through Havana so they could see the town and Havana people looked forward each day to the two army 6x6s with the POWs singing German songs."

The singing of German POWs in Illinois reminds me of a novel about Japanese POWs in Burma during and after World War II. Michio Takeyama's *Harp of Burma* tells about Japanese POWs who kept up their spirits by singing. Americans, both those who worked at Camp Ellis, and those who came into contact with prisoners outside the camp, were surprised at the high morale of these German prisoners. And one American heard the songs as an appeal for international friendship. During the 1960s and the counter-culture "flower power" movement, a popular phrase was "make love, not war." A lesson from the songs of the German POWs seems to be "make music, not war."

When I was growing up in Havana, I gained my indirect impression of Camp Ellis especially from watching the convoys of young American trainees on their way to bivouacs. I could hardly comprehend that the happy-go-lucky young recruits in drab Army vehicles were the same ones fighting the war and giving their lives on the battlefield. Reading about the actual experiences of the people at Camp Ellis taught me that their lives bore similarities to my wartime experiences, juggling serious patriotism and fear of battle with the pursuit of everyday pleasures.

The human dynamics of Camp Ellis form a complex tale difficult to sum up in a few words, but the main players in this drama were cornfield soldiers, happy civilians, and singing POWs.

CHAPTER 17

Red Ryder

War always involves guns, but guns are not always involved in war. My first experience with guns took place during World War II, but had nothing to do with the military or warfare. My earliest connection with a gun contrasted sharply with the small arms training of soldiers at nearby Camp Ellis. The story of my first BB gun had more to do with being a boy and growing up in the Midwest, where to be a boy meant to have a BB gun.

In every boy's or girl's life there comes a time when the desire for something totally consumes him or her. A time when nothing else in the world matters. The thing that you absolutely must have, without which you cannot live, and occupies your thoughts every waking minute, even appearing in dreams.

In the play *A Christmas Story*, the main character, a boy, desperately wants a BB gun, but his parents say that gift is out of the question. As the story unfolds, finally it is Christmas day, and the boy unwraps every present, but does not find his longed-for gift. Then the father looks around, and lo and behold, a long, thin package contains the air rifle.

Our grandsons, professional actors, have played roles in a number of performances of *A Christmas Story*. Every time I view the drama, or hear about it, the scenes of my childhood at Grandma Haack's house reappear.

Like the leading character in *A Christmas Story*, I wanted a BB gun more than anything else. I don't recall the brand name, but later I owned a Red Ryder BB gun, so let's call it a Red Ryder. *Wanting* a BB gun didn't really have anything to do with living at Grandma's house. It was just that point in a boy's life, when to live meant to have, to hold, to shoot a BB gun. Without that gun life didn't seem worthwhile. Every red-blooded Midwestern boy wanted his own BB gun.

But *getting* a BB gun. That's where living at Grandma's had a lot to do with it. Or maybe I should say *not* getting it. I mentioned my heart's

A 1940 ad for a Red Ryder BB gun. In addition to the description of the features of the "carbine," the ad includes the option of ordering a "reminder kit" to help a youngster remind parents he wants a Red Ryder for Christmas. PHOTO COURTESY OF THE DAISY AIRGUN MUSEUM, WWW.DAISYMUSEUM.COM.

deepest wish to my mother, who gave me a non-committal "We'll see." I didn't realize that she would have to clear the matter with Grandma and Grandpa. This was part of the problem of living in a three-generation house. I thought that if Mom okayed it, that settled the matter, but it didn't.

Objections to the gun came not from Grandma but from Grandpa. In this case, Grandpa would not let Mom and Grandma make a family decision. I don't know when or how they first discussed the matter, but I heard some of the worst arguments among the three seniors in the household. Grandpa had never been warm with us children. He acknowledged our presence, but did not interact much with us. He would never be mean to us, but then again he didn't too much notice his grandchildren. So long as we left him alone, he would leave us alone.

The discussion about the BB gun was altogether different. He opposed it and would not change his mind. When he got very mad he would swear in front of us children, and his "Goddammit" became accentuated to a "Hotdammit." I will never forget him saying to Grandma in the thick of one of these arguments, "Hotdammit, Ma, he's too *young* for a gun!"

Granted, I was young, yet I couldn't comprehend Grandpa's objection. To me, boys and BB guns went together. After all, I wasn't asking for a rifle or a shotgun with live ammunition. That would be too much. Sure, I might be too young for a real gun. But a puny air-powered BB gun?

One of the famous lines in *A Christmas Story* is the objection, "You'll shoot your eye out, kid!" Grandpa never saw the play, which appeared four decades after the war, but he knew that line and spoke it like a veteran trouper.

From time to time Mom and my grandparents discussed me getting a gun. Mom and Grandma never said absolutely, positively "No," but I didn't see how Grandpa would ever give in. And he seemed to hold the veto power in the decision.

I didn't recognize the family politics at work behind the scenes. Mom and Grandma used the tactics of squeezing Grandpa between them. Eventually these three reached a compromise.

Mom gave me the good news. "Alright, you can have your BB gun. But Grandpa has to teach you how to shoot it."

I couldn't refuse this arrangement, although I wasn't too happy with it. Grandpa didn't do much of anything with my sisters or me, so how could he teach me to shoot? Sure enough, when I got the gun (it must have been a prewar model left in stock), and Grandpa "taught" me to shoot, it turned out to be a disappointing lesson. First came all the obvious "don'ts." "Don't point the gun at anyone." "Don't shoot near the house." Grandpa went on and on with his don'ts.

Finally we went out in the back yard by the sheds and he set up a tin can about twenty feet away. I loaded the gun and was able to aim and hit the can easily. After about ten shots, Grandpa called an end to the lesson. Grandpa and I went back in the house with the gun. He had fulfilled his obligation of teaching me to shoot the gun. After that, I could use the gun, usually taking it out of the house when Grandpa was not around.

It may have been a good thing that neither Grandpa nor I ever visited Camp Ellis during the war, because they had a very sophisticated rifle range. It featured many targets, which could be fired at from high and low positions, from angles right and left. While these fledgling soldiers practiced their marksmanship, other soldiers shot live ammunition over their heads. Some civilians who witnessed trainees shooting their weapons when they were literally, "under fire," came away frightened by the sights and sounds of simulated warfare.

If Grandpa had seen this perilous situation, he would have repeated even more forcefully his, "Hotdammit, Ma, he's too young for a gun!" Maybe if I had viewed this rifle range in action, I would have conceded more readily his point about my being too young for a real gun. But I don't think it would have destroyed my boyhood dream of having an air-powered BB gun.

My "basic training" in safety and accuracy with Grandpa was much more simple and brief than Army procedures, and also quite unsatisfying. If all I could do with Red Ryder was occasionally, under Grandpa's supervision, put a dozen dents in a tin can, what was the point of having it?

I thought that the fun of having a BB gun would be ruined by such limitations. But this was just Grandpa's way of making good on the compromise. Or at least saving face with his wife and daughter. After that first lesson, the gun became mine to use as I pleased. I took the gun out of the house and brought it back in when Grandpa wasn't around, just to avoid any problems. But he had made good on the terms of the agreement, he had taught me how to shoot. From that point on he had no responsibility for the gun.

The road to the compromise taught me a good lesson in diplomacy. Often, in family squabbles, business disagreements, or even international conflicts, it is not direct confrontation, but indirect communication and backdoor diplomacy that brings the achieved result. If I had thrown a fit with my mother, she probably would have refused to seek out Grandma as an ally. If I had objected to the compromise of Grandpa training me to shoot, he would have refused to let me have the gun. And if I had voiced my dissatisfaction about the brief shooting practice with a tin can, Grandpa might have taken the gun and kept it. Although I was too naive to understand the subtleties of human interaction in this tense negotiation, fortunately I was just smart enough to keep my mouth shut. All I cared about was that I had my BB gun!

Having a BB gun made the vacant lot behind the sheds more fun than ever. If I had owned the BB gun when we found the egg on the old combine, we would have used the egg for target practice. My main game was sparrows, which everyone considered a nuisance, and I did my best to reduce their numbers.

This BB gun, as I recall it, similar to the later Red Ryders, was not very powerful. It held a lot of BBs, loaded in a long tube under the barrel itself. The copper-clad BBs were cheap at the hardware store. After loading the gun with fifty or a hundred BBs, you pulled down on the lever that depressed a spring and at the same time put a BB in the barrel and cocked the gun. The trigger released the spring and fired the BB with air pressure. After about fifty feet the BB lost most of its power, and its trajectory sagged so much it was hard to aim. I had difficulty sneaking up on a sparrow close enough to kill it.

Reminiscing about my Red Ryder, I think the strangest part of this childhood experience during the war is that my friends and I always considered shooting it a sport, part of the growing up in America as a small town boy. Not once did we consider it a military weapon. Never did we pretend to attack and shoot Germans and Japanese, or march with it over our shoulder like soldiers. We were just having fun.

In those days many boys had BB guns, and we even carried them up and down the streets and alleys. So long as we didn't shoot near a house, no one complained about us. The worst thing I ever did with the gun was to take it to my elementary school, Rockwell School. One of my buddies named Junior liked to shoot it with me, and he was much more daring than I was.

I couldn't always get the gun out of the house without Grandpa seeing me, but Junior had an idea. "We can just to take it to school and we can shoot it on the way to and from school."

I said, "No, I don't think we should."

Junior insisted, "Oh, come on, it'll be fun."

I objected, "Yeah, it would be fun, but what will we do with it when we get to school? We can't take it in the school."

Junior said, "Don't worry about that, we can find a place to hide it before we get on the playground."

So one day after lunch I did sneak the gun out of the house, and we had fun shooting it on the way to school. We spied an open garage in an alley about a half block from Rockwell School, where I hid the gun before entering the playground. All afternoon I worried about the gun, and it surprised me to find it when school got out. I felt so relieved that I didn't take it to school again.

If the teachers knew I had brought the gun to school, and especially if Grandpa found out about it, that would have been the end of Red Ryder.

CHAPTER 18

A Make-Believe Sword and Ostrich Feathers

We called our home Grandma's house, but where did that leave Grandpa? Although my grandfather was present, he was more like a shadow. Grandpa's past held two mysteries. One was how he and his wife got together in the first place. Grandma's photos from the time of her late teens and early twenties showed her to be a beautiful young woman. And yet she didn't marry until her late twenties. Grandma never told the family about any suitors before Grandpa, yet given her striking appearance, it would be strange if some young men did not find her attractive. For some reason she didn't find the right man, and, apparently, marrying Grandpa meant settling for the consolation prize.

The other mystery, talked about but never fully revealed, was how this couple lost their farm after World War I. They never recovered financially, and the resentment that festered between the two, particularly from Grandma toward her husband, seemed to be rooted in this disastrous event. As I grew older I realized that Grandpa never

This portrait shows Ruth Eaton (Haack), whom we knew just as Grandma Haack, as a beautiful young woman in a fine gown at the time of her high school graduation. FAMILY COLLECTION.

127

> the largest hotel in Frisco.
> After some time we returned to our
> rooms and retired. The next day,
> August 18, was the "Naval Parade." Aug-
> ust 19, was the "Grand Parade," which
> was very grand, and lasted for
> several hours. In the parade, Illinois
> took the lead. In the evening, we
> went to Chinatown. There we visited
> a Chinese Tailor Shop. The shop
> was long and narrow with the
> workmen along the sides. Each one
> had a certain part to do, and
> when it was done, the garment
> was passed to the next one. So
> every one had a hand in every
> garment that was made. From
> here we went to a "Chinese Theatre."
> The Orchestra, which was made up
> of what sounded like tin pans,
> played most of the time. The men

Grandma Haack (then Ruth Eaton) wrote "A Trip to California" after her 1903 train trip with four other ladies and five gentlemen to the 1903 encampment of the G.A.R (Grand Army of the Republic) in San Francisco. This page of the diary includes mention of the day for the "Naval Parade" and the day for the "Grand Parade." It is interesting that she began this trip on the Illinois Central Railroad, and that the only major trans-continental journey of her life was to commemorate a war. A copy of this 30-page diary in her handwriting is deposited with the Havana Public Library. The cursive lettering of "At Grandma's House" on the cover of this book is patterned after her handwriting in the diary. FAMILY COLLECTION.

escaped from this failure. I always wondered what he had been like before they lost the farm. If they had not lost the farm, or if he had not traded the paint store for a farm, how would their life have been different? Would they have owned a house and a car? Would their relationship have been more harmonious? These two Illinois natives, like many of their peers, just accepted their lot and made the best of their lives.

My sisters and cousins never tried to reach out to Grandpa. He was present but not really accessible. As in the case of the BB gun, most of the time Grandpa seemed to be a wet blanket. He objected to almost anything, it seemed.

Only two things really brought Grandpa to life—pinochle, and the Masonic Lodge. From an early age my sisters and I learned to play pinochle, usually double pinochle, played by combining two regular pinochle decks. Once the cards hit the table, Grandpa became transformed into a ruthless card player. When he got poor cards, he groused about how bad his cards were. "One card. Just one more card, and I would have had a double run. Then you wouldn't have gotten the bid."

When he got a good hand, he would bid and bid, often higher than he could possibly bid and make it. "Well, I went down, but at least I won the bid. I couldn't let you have the bid. I knew what you were coming in, hearts, wasn't it?"

When his opponents won the bid, he could be equally tough. He especially liked to trump a key trick, raising his card dramatically above his head, and with a quick flip of his wrist slapping the trump onto the table. "Take that one, if you can!"

Pinochle was the only game he seemed to enjoy. When Grandma reminisced about living on the farm, she recalled the good times they had when other couples would hitch up a team of horses to come over and they'd play cards.

Grandpa's other passion was the Masonic Lodge. He completely tuned out religion, but became a diehard Mason. In all the years I knew him, I can only recall a few times when he attended church, all of those occasions for funerals and weddings. This was a subject past argument. Grandma went to church on her own, taking us kids, but never asked Grandpa to join us.

On the other hand, Grandpa loved the pomp and ceremony of the Masonic Lodge, and wouldn't miss a lodge meeting. It was all supposed to be hush-hush secret, and we children didn't know much about it. But when Grandpa socialized with other Masons, he came alive, transformed into a different person. He boasted about how perfect their part of the ceremony was. The Masonic Lodge had its distinctive uniform, a military-style suit featuring scabbard and sword, topped off by a Napoleon-like curved hat covered with real ostrich plumes.

I learned about this not by seeing the lodge ceremonies, but by going into our upstairs storage room where he kept the whole outfit

This portrait of Charles F. Haack shows him proudly sporting his lodge pin from his vest pocket. FAMILY COLLECTION.

in an elaborate case filled with mothballs. The suit was much too big for me, but I could put on my head the hat for which an ostrich had sacrificed some of its plumage, and swagger with the sword and scabbard. There was no danger in removing the make-believe sword and playing with it because it was completely decorative, with no sharp edges.

Much sharper than the Masonic sword was Grandpa's tongue when he found out I had been playing with his precious secret outfit. In this case, at least, Grandma and Grandpa stood together. They were both lodge members, I had committed sacrilege, and had to pay the consequences and bear his wrath. "How many times have I told you, don't play with my lodge outfit. It's not a toy, and it cost a lot of money."

He didn't spank me, but he got so furious I wished he would spank me so he would stop scolding.

When I grew older, Grandpa wanted me to join the junior side of the Masonic order, called DeMolay. For the first time I went to the meetings and saw the old people marching around "the hall" in their formal dresses and monkey suits. By that time the swords and Napoleon hats had lost their charm. I wanted nothing more than to escape this kooky atmosphere.

It was okay for kids to dress up and play games with mock uniforms and fake swords, but what were these *adults* doing, acting out children's games? Masks and weird hats were fine for Halloween or a costume party, yet I couldn't understand why grownups played make-believe in funny outfits.

Women seem to be attracted to a man in a military uniform. Grandpa found a mystique in the Masonic regalia and an enthrallment in their pageantry that far out-trumped any religious ritual.

Not until years later, when Grandma and Grandpa died in 1962, did I discover something of what the Masonic Lodge (and for my grandmother, the Order of the Eastern Star) had meant to them. I remember from my grandmother's funeral, conducted by a Baptist minister, at the graveside after the minister finished speaking, one of the lodge members stood up. I recognized him as a postman who had carried mail in Havana for many years.

To my astonishment, he recited without a single note a lengthy litany, talking about the stars in heaven, and asking the stars to take back this sister of theirs. It impressed me as the most beautiful part of the whole funeral.

After all, the Masonic Lodge and the Order of the Eastern Star amounted to more than just a pseudo-sword and ostrich feathers.

CHAPTER 19

"Just a Stone's Throw from Church"

Grandma's house—especially Grandma—provided my real introduction to religion, in other words, the Baptist Church. Grandpa went to church only when absolutely necessary, to mark the union of marriage or the separation of death. The Masonic Lodge dictated his sense of the sacred. Where others said, "I'm going to church," Grandpa would say "I'm going to the hall," meaning the Masonic Lodge Hall, one very large undivided room above a clothing store on Main Street.

Grandma enjoyed the lodge, too, which for her meant the Order of the Eastern Star. Today Grandma would be called a double-dipper. She went to church on Sunday, and to the lodge on weekdays several times a month. My parents had been lukewarm Methodists—they called themselves Methodists, but I don't ever recall their going to church before we lived at Grandma's house.

After we moved in with grandparents, it became second nature to go to Sunday School at the Baptist Church. Saturday night we reserved for bath night, so that the next morning we could quickly get ready for church. Sunday A.M. began pleasant, then got ugly, and later turned peaceful again.

We slept in late and had a leisurely breakfast, maybe pancakes, because grownups didn't have to work. After we ate, we rushed to get out and put on our Sunday best clothes, and spruce up a little. We never allowed enough time between breakfast and dressing for Sunday School, which started at 9:30. As the hands of the clock moved past 9:00 toward 9:30, Grandma got irritated and began to snap at our heels. She would hurry my sisters and me, and finally when she got really mad, she announced to all of us: "What a shame! We're just a stone's throw from church! Just a *stone's throw away!* And we can't be on time."

She sounded this declaration like the conductor's "All Aboard" on a train. Ready or not, we headed out the door and walked as fast as we could the three blocks to the Baptist Church. Grandma was right. We did live "just a stone's throw from church."

Grandma focused on the fact that we couldn't be on time. Looking back, what impressed me was the transmogrification of Grandma while covering those three short blocks. It takes a caterpillar a long time to be transformed from an ugly worm into a beautiful butterfly, but in the space of three blocks, less than ten minutes, we saw an angry devil reincarnated as a benevolent angel. Leaving the house, Grandma played the role of Lucifer's apprentice herding her tardy sinners. But by the time we had hurried two blocks and turned north on Plum Street with the church in sight, her anger cooled and her frown faded away. Then, entering the church, she became miraculously reborn a winged saint guiding her little cherubs, making sure they had money for the offering.

The Havana Baptist Church, located in a typical small-town Protestant building, had a white clapboard exterior with a modest steeple that served as a bell tower. We seldom achieved our goal of stepping into the church before the bell announced the 9:30 beginning of Sunday school. Children who arrived early might get a chance to pull the heavy braided rope that swung the bell into action. The building's architecture followed a simple twofold function: they designated for Sunday School the downstairs, a half-basement with windows at ground level; the upper level they reserved for "church," what we called the formal service and sermon.

Neither floor had any subdivisions, except that one end of the lower level was partitioned off as a kitchen, and one corner of the church under the belfry had a small separate room on each floor. At 9:30, two Sunday School services started, one for children downstairs, and one for adults upstairs. On the lower level, they arranged chairs in circles for children, and in the upper level, they designated certain pews for different adult groups. Makeshift curtains separated the various groups downstairs. They age-graded children by circle. Adults taught lessons for part of the hour, and then the girls and boys all joined for some hymns and a talk by the church school superintendent and a closing prayer shortly before 10:30.

Sunday School could be a noisy time. Only children who came with their parents stayed for "church," the longer service lasting from 10:30 to just before noon. "Church" presented a sharp contrast to Sunday School, much more serious, with no talking or squirming allowed. During the time we lived with Grandma, I seldom stayed for church.

My sisters and I walked the few blocks home and Grandma returned by herself after the church service, about noon.

The upper story, reserved for the church service, featured a larger than life-size picture of long-haired Jesus in a robe, painted on the wall behind the pulpit and organ. An American flag had a prominent place at one side of the pulpit. During the war, piety and patriotism became inseparable. In sermons and in prayers the minister and the congregation joined in both general petitions for protection of "our boys over there," and for individual consideration of named family members serving in the armed forces.

In the early 1940s, churches served both as dividing and unifying forces. Our Baptist Church saw itself set apart as the bastion of Christian truth and ethical propriety, with serious questions about the authenticity of other denominations, and especially Catholics. But when it came to support for the war, all Christian organizations closed ranks, seeing America and God working together for the good of the world and the Kingdom of God. This theme of Christian unity and support of the war will be seen later in Chapter 29 and the description of Memorial Day ceremonies.

On the side wall hung an armed services flag, a grim reminder of the human cost of the war. Each blue star stood for a church member in the military. When we learned of a death in action, we honored the fallen hero in a special part of the Sunday church service, replacing his blue star with a gold star. In this way, our Baptist Church memorialized

This poster shows the single gold star flag in a home setting, with the family pet expressing the emotion of sadness for the dead sailor, indicated by part of a navy uniform. The phrase "because somebody talked" reinforces the constant concern about "loose lips" regarding troop locations, movements, and activities. The consequence of talking or writing about military information might result in the death of a loved one and the replacement of a blue star with a gold star. IMAGE COURTESY OF NATIONAL ARCHIVES/WIKIMEDIA.

and sanctified the military death, seen as a sacrifice for country and religion.

In every church gathering, the preacher offered prayers for the protection of loved ones, including general petitions for all of our military personnel, and even naming individuals from our church in the armed forces. The preacher and the congregation assumed that "our boys" were risking, and even sacrificing, their lives for the good of the country and the work of God.

A March 19, 1943 article in the *Democrat* reports on the dedication service for a flag in this Baptist Church:

FORTY STARS IN BAPTIST CHURCH SERVICE FLAG
LEGION POST WILL CONDUCT
DEDICATION SERVICES SUNDAY

A service flag bearing 39 blue stars and one gold star will be dedicated at the Baptist church Sunday morning. Havana Post No 138, The American Legion, will have charge of the dedication services.

Each star in the flag represents a boy in the service who attended church or Sunday school at the Baptist church. . . .

Quite different from casual Sunday School, we set aside "Church" as a contemplative place, with no joking possible. The minister might venture into mild humor during a sermon, resulting in no more than a weak smile. A hearty laugh would have been as out of place here as a sermon in a saloon. The holiest of holies, the solemnest of solemnities, took place at the monthly communion service. On communion Sunday, the silvery communion set rested in its place on the table in front of the pulpit: a circular aluminum tray with many round holes for the thimble-size communion glasses, and an aluminum plate with a cover. The tiny glasses had been filled with grape juice, and bread had been sliced into small cubes.

After the sermon on communion Sunday, the minister called forward the deacons to pass the "wine" (Welch's grape juice) and bread from one pew to the next. The deacons, usually middle-aged men, might be burly and overweight, but under the burden of this great responsibility of distributing the body and blood of Our Lord, they became as unassuming as possible, shrinking in size. With eyes on the floor and hands folded, they showed they were unworthy of this honor. Each church member sipped the grape juice and ate the bread as they were passed down the pew; like the deacons, they did not raise their eyes. This symbolized the body and blood of the savior who was looking down at us from the mural on the wall behind the pulpit.

For Baptists the only practice that might compete for sanctity with communion was baptism. Ironically, it had to be held in the "basement," because Baptists take very literally the New Testament accounts of baptizing *in water*, and when our church had been built, it was not feasible to put a baptism tank in the second story. The front of the Sunday School area in the basement had a trap door in the floor, like the ones used in old houses for steps to the basement. Raising this trap door revealed a large metal-lined tank that could be filled with water. Steps led down into it from one end.

During baptism services the minister first explained the symbolism: this rite, patterned after the example of John the Baptist baptizing Jesus, followed the baptism ceremony of the early church. Going into and under the water, we die; rising up from the water, we are reborn in Christ. The minister walked down the stairs into the water and turned around. The ones to be baptized had dressed in white and waited for this signal in the kitchen. As they came forward, one by one, joining the minister in the water, death and resurrection were reenacted for—and by—each white-clad initiate. I think all people are afraid of water, and the utter helplessness of the actual baptism experience heightens this fear.

The new member-to-be walked down the steps into the three-feet deep water, turned around, and as the minister put one hand in the small of the back and the other hand behind the person's neck, the sinner used both hands to cover the nose and, taking a deep breath, leaned back into the minister's arms. Giving up control of body to the minister and surrendering to the Lord, the baptismal candidate had to fight all the ordinary instincts for self-survival by falling backwards and being submerged in the water. Not once. Not twice. But three times. Once for the Father, once for the Son, and once more for the Holy Ghost. After the first two submersions (Baptists call it immersion) the minister raised the person back to vertical, allowed time for catching a breath, and then plunged the initiate beneath the water for a third time. In Baptist teaching, the triple immersion symbolizes dying to the old self, the third emersion marks being reborn to the new (saved) self.

Some children panicked or burst into tears during or after baptism. For adults, the problem could prove more practical. The minister might not have the strength to lift up a two hundred-pound man in an almost prone position underwater and unable to raise himself. I recall a few cases where the minister had to enlist the aid of another member to assist in the baptism of a large person.

Baptists, like most American Protestant groups of the time, were very clear about their respective denomination's centrality to the Christian faith. We viewed Catholics as not really Christian because of their mechanical, magical dependence on ritual. One of their worst sins was infant baptism. Church members' complaints against the Catholic Church were very clear about this: "How can a baby confess its sins and profess Jesus as Christ and Lord?"

We considered being baptized and becoming a member of the church a serious act. Many times I heard that "Only when a person reaches the age of reason can he or she ask for baptism."

We had no hard and fast rule on the minimal age for this, but 12 or 13 years old was the generally accepted threshold for "the age of reason." For Catholics to practice infant baptism, and then to mechanically go through confession and the mass for the rest of their lives amounted to a denial of Christ's death on the cross. Or so Baptists thought.

We saw Catholics as the prime examples of the mistake of infant baptism; but even when other churches admitted adult members, they practiced the anemic form of baptism by sprinkling water over the head of the new member, using a baptismal font. We considered this not as bad as infant baptism, yet it still deviated from the New Testament model.

We looked down on the Protestant groups who got carried away with their emotions, calling them Holy Rollers. Across the street from Grandma's house, a "basement church" had been built. At that time, some people had "basement houses." A family could only afford to excavate a basement (with cement blocks for the walls), roof it over and tarpaper it. They lived in this basement until they had the money to complete the first story of the house and move themselves and their belongings to the ground level. These houses looked funny because they had a sloping covered stairway that emerged from one corner of the below ground house for the doorway.

The church opposite Grandma's house had been built this way, by a group of Holy Rollers, whose services could be viewed by young eyes looking down the basement windows of their church. On Sunday evenings when we had nothing else to do, we would peek at these people and laugh at them for being so "funny." Several decades later as a

Looking at a Holy Rollers' service through basement windows. ILLUSTRATION
BY JOHN MICHAEL DOWNS.

doctoral student, I went to Japan and conducted field work on Japanese
religious practices. I conducted my first amateur field work in Havana
looking through a basement window at Holy Rollers.

Baptists generally remained critical of these emotionalists. At the
time, members of my church did not view with favor such outlandish
behavior as speaking in tongues, being sanctified, or being filled with
the holy spirit. Nevertheless, over the years, some members left our
Baptist church and joined other churches in order to participate in and
experience "tongues" and other "gifts." Baptists followed Jesus and the
New Testament. They made their own profession of faith and were
baptized in water the same as Jesus. Baptists found their own salvation
with Jesus. They didn't depend on priests or mechanical ritual or fanatic
emotionalism.

And they didn't use swords and ostrich feathers!

I wasn't baptized until the age of twelve, but I was a Baptist long
before that. After watching a number of baptisms, this drama of life-
death-and-resurrection impressed a young person like me.

An incident from my teenage years illustrates our seriousness, and
the certainty of our righteousness. High school boys and girls belonged
to the Baptist Young People's Union, which we called just the BYPU.
We welcomed the name change to the Baptist Youth Fellowship, with
the acronym BYF, dropping the "PU."

Almost all the members of the BYF had been baptized, and considered it their religious duty to bring all people in the world to saving faith in Christ. We also felt compelled to rid the land of immorality and injustice. The religious no-no's included refraining from smoking, drinking, and premarital sex. At the time, our Baptist Church joined the local movement to eliminate gambling and erase the stain on Havana's reputation as "Little Reno."

As dedicated Christians who had been baptized, we assumed responsibility to maintain personal morality and to improve social morality. It was not enough just to *believe* that all people were the children of God, we should act to make sure that all people were treated fairly. While discussing what our BYF should do to improve social life in Havana, the topic of racial equality came up. This took place about 1950, when Havana was lily white, with no minority residents. We had heard about a local ordinance to make sure Havana stayed all White, at least after dark. No Negroes (to use the language of the day) were allowed in Havana after dark. We considered this at least one social injustice that we, as dedicated Christians, should challenge.

Finally, we gathered up enough courage to walk the two blocks to the Havana Police Station and confront the officers. With wavering voices, we stated our position that as Christians, we believed that all people were equal in the eyes of God, and that it was wrong to have a law that banned Negroes from being in town after dark.

The policemen patiently and politely listened to our impassioned statements. Then they told us that Havana had no such law.

That marked our first and final march for social justice.

Social activism like our verbal protest at the police station may have been, in part, a feature of teenage assertion of independence and adult responsibility. But religious identity, in my case, had been established in my pre-teen years.

While I was still in elementary school, a teacher asked our class what is today an unaskable question: "How many of you are Christians? Raise your hand if you are a Christian." Not a native of Havana, the teacher didn't understand why only a few hands were raised. She was unbelieving (as in incredulous) and confronted me directly: "Are *you* a Christian?" I said, "No, I'm a *Baptist.*"

She countered that I was still a Christian, and that confused me. In our town, the term "Christians" referred to the members of the "Christian Church," more widely known today as the Disciples of Christ

Church. But after I stated proudly that I was Baptist, others took that as their cue to insist they were Catholic, Methodist, and so on.

From Grandma's perspective, we lived "a stone's throw away from church."

Looking back at the rock-solid position that our Baptist viewpoint was the only correct faith, and all other forms of Christianity were suspect, maybe we resided more than a stone's throw away from church.

CHAPTER 20

By the River

nly three blocks separated Grandma's house and the Baptist Church. But "the river," the Illinois River, lay closer, just a block or so, less than a stone's throw away. The railroad in front of our house snaked around the edge of the town down the center of Railroad Street, which on the north side of town hugged the bluff overlooking the stream. We couldn't see this waterway from our house because an old factory building to the west of the railroad tracks blocked our view. But by crossing the railroad tracks we could view the river just below us. A brief walk brought us down the hill and to the water's edge.

Market Street ran west past the front of Grandma's house over the railroad tracks and descended the slope of the bluff, forming a gentle curve to the south along the bank and then circling east up the hill that became Main Street. The horseshoe-shaped area from the edge of the bluff to the water's edge marked off Riverfront Park. The hillside of the bluff, covered with trees and bushes, made a pleasant place for boys to run and hide, chase and hunt. The flat ground from the bottom of the hill to the circling road offered space for a picnic area with tables. Towering cottonwood trees shaded the park, in early summer powdering the whole neighborhood with fluffy white seeds.

Riverfront Park also had its miniature history lesson. A wood sign in the park commemorated Abraham Lincoln's 1832 "stop" on his way back from the Black Hawk War, many years before he became president. When my buddies and I got tired running up and down the bluffs, we sometimes lingered by this sign, rereading its historic message, and trying to recreate in our minds the 1832 scene of the tall, lanky Lincoln beaching his canoe. Was this the spot where he landed, and did he stand here looking out over this area that later became our park?

When we moved to Grandma's house and new friends asked me where I lived, I said, "By the river," because our home was so close to

Illinois prides itself as the "Land of Lincoln." This stone, replacing the earlier wood sign, commemorates Lincoln's 1832 trip down the Illinois River and stop in Havana at the time of the Black Hawk War. AUTHOR'S PHOTO.

it. Actually, this waterway flanked the whole town, and my parents' house on Orange Street was only about four blocks from it, but we had no convenient and scenic access to the banks. At Grandma's house, the river and the riverfront formed an extension of our living space. As a boy, I enjoyed being near this scenic and welcoming site.

When we're young we sense and take for granted the subtle shadings of space without ever being taught formally the reasons why. For example, "by the river" indicated a completely different world from "on the river." We considered Railroad Street "by the river," as we did streets in the south end of town along the bluff overlooking the water. But the area below the bluffs, subject to spring flooding (today it would be called the flood plain) we thought of as "on the river." People who couldn't afford other land or housing put up makeshift buildings on this marginal ground. These people had little money, and they just threw up a building without bothering to buy the land. So in those days before political correctness, we called them "squatters" when we wanted to pretend politeness, "river rats" when we didn't bother to pretend.

Floods and flooding made their appearance almost as regularly as the annual passage from winter to spring. And then came the Big Flood of

1943. In spring of that year the water began rising as usual, but never stopped. The Illinois River climbed the banks and spilled over the arc of the curving road enclosing the park, as it did many years. Then the water kept rising, until it covered the entire park area and began to creep up the bluff. The unfortunate people who lived "on the river" saw their houses "in the river," and finally "under the river." They would have needed submarines to go home. Of course, most of these flimsy houses got swept away in the swirling flood waters.

The whole city of Havana, situated above the bluff, faced no danger from the high water. West of Havana, what had been "across the river," became a vast sea. Flood waters overflowed the banks, crept up the levees until they spilled over, or rose high enough to find a weak spot and punched gaping holes through it. By 1943, Camp Ellis had become operational, and many recruits fought their first battles against our local version of "Old Man River." They tried to sandbag the levees and hold the flood waters back, but this fluid foe would not be defeated.

When we crossed the bridge over the Illinois River, we traveled west on the roadway high above the low-lying farmland, thousands of acres. In the Big Flood of 1943, this road became a tiny ribbon separating a vast sea on either side. Viewing this watery transformation of the landscape, and watching the flood waters surge through a hole in the dike, we felt glad we lived on the bluff. Safe and comfortable, we learned to respect the force of the waters.

Living by the river meant we could be near it and appreciate it without being tagged river rats. A boy needed no invitation or organized activity to have fun at the water's edge, because it presented an ever changing, endless source of amusement. We found it interesting just to walk along the bank to see what had washed up since the last time we were there. Or we'd throw a rock as far as we could, watching the waterspout mark its entrance into the waves. We loved to skip rocks: search for a flat, thin rock, get right next to the shoreline and lean as low as we could, then throw it so the flat side of the rock missed a wave and hit the surface of the river. We tried to see how many times and how far our rock would skip.

Moving large rocks along the shoreline sometimes revealed the hiding place of crayfish, which we called crawdads. Large crawdads could hurt you or even draw blood with their big claws, but we let the small ones try out their weaponry on our fingers. They made good bait for fishing. The small ones we used whole, and the tails of the large ones

ILLUSTRATION BY JOHN MICHAEL DOWNS.

were good for catfish. But when we played along the river we usually just threw the crawdads back after we were through teasing them.

Traffic up and down the river provided unending entertainment. Havana was a major shipping terminal for grain and coal, and some gravel. Just north of town lay the coal docks, where the Illinois Central railroad transported trainloads of coal from southern Illinois. The coal, dumped out of cars and carried by conveyors to empty barges on the river, got shipped in long "tows" down the Illinois and Mississippi River to New Orleans for export. A number of grain elevators rose from the bluff on the west side of town, extending the spindly legs of their grain conveyors out over the water and the pilings for tying up barges. Tow-boats with powerful twin diesel engines maneuvered barges between the banks in long double lines. These boats spotted empty barges at the water's edge, waiting to be ferried into place at an elevator and filled with tens of thousands of bushels of grain.

My buddies and I never tired of watching the boats and barges move upstream and downstream, plowing aside furrows of water that angled their way to shore, crashing over the rocks and making the rowboats along the riverbank dance back and forth to the rhythm of the waves. Usually commercial fisherman tied up several floating fish markets along the riverfront. These fishermen caught fish in nets and sold them

Havana was, and still is, an important grain terminal for the surrounding area. Farmers truck their crops (corn, wheat, soybeans) to these elevators, where they are stored and offloaded onto barges for shipping down the Illinois and Mississippi Rivers to New Orleans. This earlier picture shows the stern wheeler Columbia (which later sank) against the background of an elevator. The bridge at the left was later removed. PHOTO COURTESY OF NANCY GLICK AND THE HA-VANA PUBLIC LIBRARY.

fresh, also leaving some of their catch in large wooden traps in the water next to their boats, so they could kill and clean fish on order. The wake from barges shoved the houseboat affairs this way and that.

Even at night, when we lived at Grandma's house, the stream kept us company. Barges ran twenty-four hours a day, announcing their approach by both sight and sound, probing the sky with their carbon arc searchlights, splitting the air with their powerful horns. Especially when we sat in the west parlor at night, the boats made their presence known; the first person to notice one would say, "Boat on the river."

River traffic wasn't just barges. During the summer there might be fancy motor boats from Chicago, because they could travel from Chicago down the Illinois and then by way of the Mississippi to New Orleans. We marveled especially at the Chris Craft "yachts." I learned later, from local people who fought against the pollution and sewage coming down the Illinois River from Chicago, a name for these

Havana was a major source of fresh water fish, as the abundance of fish markets indicates, in this early picture with a stern wheeler in the background. PHOTO COURTESY OF NANCY GLICK AND THE HAVANA PUBLIC LIBRARY.

Chicagoans, "sons of the beaches." In wartime, even the wealthy had no gasoline for their pleasure boats.

During the war, the government floated new naval vessels down the Illinois River. For mid-continent Havanans, it was a major event to stand at the riverfront and watch these huge grayish ships pass. They had a strange appearance, only half-built, without superstructures, to make sure they would clear all the low bridges along the way. We understood they traveled to New Orleans and then became completed and fitted out for war service. To people of central Illinois, these vessels seemed huge, because most of us had never seen ocean-going ships.

Even Midwesterners far removed from major waterways and the oceans came into contact with these marine vessels. While reading Mary Watters' *Illinois in the Second World War*, I discovered a local and family connection to these ships and their destination of New Orleans. "In January, 1943, students from Mason City, Hoopeston, and Lake City journeyed to New Orleans, where JoAnne Bloh, aged eight, of the Pleasant Valley School of Mason City, christened the good ship *Blackhawk* with a bottle of ginger ale." JoAnne Bloh (Jackson) is a distant cousin on my father's side. She wrote me that she still remembers the trip to New Orleans and the christening, a highlight of her life.

Boats, ships, vessels, yachts, rowboats—all kinds of water transportation. And yet the stern wheelers stood out as the most romantic and interesting of all. Living in the Midwest, no person can escape knowledge of Mark Twain, Huck Finn, Tom Sawyer, and the whole river mystique. For those of us who lived close to, by, or on the Illinois River, such literary images took a back seat to the real thing. Occasionally the U.S. Corps of Army Engineers would send its stern wheel vessel to Havana, and it became an immediate attraction. Strictly a working boat, no one was allowed on it, but they couldn't keep us from lining the bank and gawking.

Some ten years later, after the boat was decommissioned by the Army and put into service as a commercial towboat transporting gravel to Chicago (which earned the sternwheeler the name "Gravel Gertie") I landed a summer job on her. But that's another story.

The other stern wheelers making an annual stop at Havana were the old-time excursion boats, twin funnels standing proudly above a glistening white double-decked boat. A steam calliope musically foretold their coming by playing old fashioned tunes. If the townspeople had not read the advance flyers, the calliope made a special appeal to one and all. Kids usually took the afternoon excursion, a trip upstream and downstream, with some refreshments thrown in. This outing featured the same river, the same sights, that most of us had seen many times. But being on the stern wheeler somehow made it more exciting. Adults might go on the moonlight excursion, which included music and dancing.

A pleasure trip on a stern wheeler counted as one instance when being "on the river" was better than being "by the river.

CHAPTER 21

Gone Fishin'

*E*ven before we moved in with Grandma, I had heard her talk about fishing, and wanted to be introduced to the mystery of how people could pull fish out of water. When we moved to her house, living so close to the river, I asked Mother, "Can I go fishing with Grandma?"

Mother agreed to anything that Grandma did with us kids, knowing she would take care of us, and we would mind her. Grandma liked the idea. "Sure, let's go catch some fish."

I promised to do anything she said.

I didn't dare ask Grandpa about fishing, figuring that he would be against it. He had a good reason to fear the river, because when he was young, his brother had drowned in the Illinois River. As with the BB gun, he objected, but this time he didn't veto the venture. He refused to row the boat to take us fishing, so Grandma asked our neighbor Doc to take us. My first fishing experience with Grandma and Doc in the Illinois River, we caught nothing, didn't even get a bite.

Our bad luck that day may have been an omen not to fish in the river. Grandma preferred to fish in the shallow water of ponds beside the highway, across the river. The next time we went fishing, in what we called a "ditch," I caught my first fish, a sunfish.

West of Havana across the river lay "the bottoms," low-lying ground rich and black, the deposit of thousands of years of spring floods. Several miles separate the eastern bluff at Havana and the hills forming the western bluff. This expansive depression defines the limits within which the Illinois River has meandered over the millennia. In 1943 during the Big Flood, the waterway temporarily reclaimed its ancient territory. Even today the bottoms are prone to flooding, except where the U.S. Corps of Engineers has thrown up a levee to protect the farmland (and hem in the stream, causing problems elsewhere).

The road west of Havana formed a kind of levee, a high ground some thirty feet above the bottom land. Alongside much of this road lay the ditches, which may have been the source for the fill dirt that made up the roadbed. Whatever the origin of those ditches, they provided many enjoyable hours of fishing for Grandma and me.

Grandma taught me the first step in fishing, getting the bait. She hated to buy worms, although hot weather sometimes forced us to go to the bait shop. She preferred to keep her own worm bed, throwing out coffee grounds and even dish water on the bed to keep it wet and inviting for earthworms. The first time I saw her carry her dish pan out on the back porch and empty it into a spaded patch of dirt, I asked her what she was doing. She laughed, "I'm feedin' the worms."

Every week or two we dug worms from the bed, keeping a large coffee can of worms handy for when we could go fishing. Other times we drove across the river to the bottoms. The water table close to the surface, and shade from tall trees, made the ground moist. We dug for worms in the soil under piles of dead leaves.

Usually we settled for these earthworms. Sometimes we stayed up after sundown and hunted night crawlers, "dew worms," with a flashlight. In late evening these oversize worms made their appearance, sticking their heads out of the ground. We had to walk very softly, slowly moving the light around the grass to spot the "crawler," then deftly grabbing its head between forefinger and thumb. All too often, just as you leaned down to get one, it sprang back into its hole, like a stretched rubber band returning to its original size. And even if you were quick enough to grab one, it could slip right through your fingers. Caught and pulled too quickly, the worm snapped in two, and would die, so we threw it away. You had to clamp your forefinger and thumb on the head of the dew worm and slowly, patiently ease it out of its hole. Catching crawlers took quicker eyes and hands than fishing!

We also dug redworms out of the corn cob pile by the grain elevators. Elevators in those days took mostly ear corn from farmers, and then shelled it before shipping. This created huge piles of corn cobs at the side of the elevators. These were the same corn cobs Doc hauled in his cart to Grandma's house, and I carried into the kitchen for kindling in the cast iron range and the parlor stove. The cob pile, dry on top, moist a few inches down, gradually changed from half decomposed cobs to humus. When we couldn't find worms anywhere else, even in hot, dry weather, we could always manage to locate redworms under the corn cobs. We just had to dig a little deeper. Grandma and I didn't like to fish with redworms, because they were skinny and very wiggly, hard to thread onto a hook. Some people swore by them and insisted on fishing with them, saying they attracted fish with their constant wriggling.

Other people used minnows for bait, but they were a pain to net, expensive to buy, and then had to be thrown away at the end of the day. Small crawdads or crawdad tails we used for catfish. We sometimes cooked doughballs, boiling corn meal in water with a little sweetener, until very thick, and rolled into balls about the size of a nickel. We used them as bait for catching carp. In later years I also collected grass-hoppers, and even scouted out catalpa trees to gather catalpa worms for bait.

Mostly we just fished with bamboo poles—Grandma called them "cane poles." We tied one end of a line to the tip of the bamboo pole, attached a

hook to the other end, weighted it with a sinker, and topped it with a bobber that we adjusted for the desired depth. Fishing from shore, we'd swing our line out, wait for a bite signaled by a movement of the bobber, and then try to hook and catch the fish. From a sporting vantage point, we were poor sportsmen—no artificial flies, no lures. Just bait, hook, and catch.

Mostly we caught sunfish, with a few catfish and carp thrown in. Sun-fish come in many varieties with a host of local names, like bluegill and pump-kin seed. Crappie, similar to sunfish, have a silvery and charcoal speckled body. "Catfish," too, is a general family name for a number of relatives. In the Illinois River, and also in the nearby Spoon River, channel cat could be found. Channel cat are silvery-gray and rather slim. A rare form of cat-fish, known as the spoonbill, has a "bill" like the bill of a cap extending beyond its head. When commercial

Grandma Haack at the end of a successful day of fishing, proudly holding her stringer of fish. FAMILY COLLECTION.

fishermen netted a spoonbill, they nailed its strange head to the side of their shop near Riverfront Park. Carp are also of several varieties, like buffalo and suckers.

What people eat depends mostly on what they are willing to eat. Some Americans turn up their noses at carp. But after the war, when my dad ran the locker plant again, he smoked some carp I caught, and it tasted as good as smoked salmon. In China, carp is a delicacy. In Japan, the catfish is seen as the monster under the earth (like the Leviathan in the Bible) that causes earthquakes, and usually is not eaten. In central Illinois, and in some other areas of the country, fried catfish—dipped in batter or flour or corn meal and deep fried to a golden brown—is a delicacy. Some prefer "channel cats," others swear by the small bullheads. But all catfish lovers agree that the best "cats" are about a pound and a half or smaller. The "farm catfish" sold today, raised in containment ponds and usually much larger fish cut into individual servings, usually have a muddy taste and give their wild cousins a bad reputation.

Mother had no interest in fishing, but she loved to eat the freshwater fish we caught. I didn't need to apologize for bringing home small sunfish. She said, "I don't care how small they are, they fry up brown and crispy." When we had fish, she ate more than anyone else, and piled high a plate of fish bones in front of her.

Dad, a businessman and meat cutter, also had talent as an excellent cook. In our house he always had the job of frying fish. He taught us, "The secret to good fried fish is to get the grease hot, and keep it hot." When he returned from the war, he went to the local blacksmith and ordered a custom-built fish fryer made out of half-inch thick steel welded into a rectangular pan. Three inches high, and about one foot by a foot and a half, it was large enough to contain a large amount of grease (in those days we used more lard than other oil) and would hold the heat. For convenience, he had the blacksmith fashion a loop handle on the short ends of the fryer. This pan was large enough to fit over several gas burners. Dad scooped in dollops of lard, melting it and heating it until it began to smoke. Fish had been washed and dried, then rolled in corn meal. As the lard started to smoke, Dad would take a pinch of corn meal between thumb and forefinger and drop it into the grease. When it bubbled vigorously, he announced, "Now we're ready to fry." He picked up a fish by the tail, carefully lowering it into the hot oil so as not to splash. We enjoyed watching him lay down lines of fish in an artistic pattern, never letting one fish touch another. "Don't crowd your fish. Putting too many fish in cools down the grease, and that's what makes the fish greasy." Dad's fish never turned out greasy, fried to a perfect golden brown, crispy and tasty.

Some fish we loathed, especially the gar, also known as the alligator gar. A long roundish fish, it has a narrow jaw jutting out and full of teeth like its namesake the alligator. They thrive in warm muddy waters that other fish can barely survive in. Gars like to bask in the sun near the surface of the water, and can be recognized by their cigar-shaped bodies and long snouts. Later I learned to shoot gars with a rifle. When I was young, whenever we caught a gar, we would fling it into the weeds to die. We thought they weren't fit to eat, and didn't like the fact that they preyed on other fish, limiting the numbers of "game fish."

We considered the dogfish another "rough fish." This remarkable creature dates back millions of years, and has the ability to survive on a very low oxygen rate in the water. Its fins and scales show its ancient lineage, because it looks like a cross between a reptile and a fish. Its body shape resembles that of a catfish, but its mouth is like the gar, full of needle sharp teeth. Dogfish, too, we threw in the bushes and left to die. When I was about twelve years old I landed a foot-long dogfish, and hurried so much to throw away this nuisance that I wasn't careful in removing the hook. The dogfish clamped down on my finger and I almost lost the fleshy tip of that finger.

Readers not familiar with gar and dogfish (also known as bowfin) can find images and descriptions online in sources such as:

https://en.m.wikipedia.org/wiki/Bowfin
https://en.m.wikipedia.org/wiki/Gar

I think we had some unconscious association of gars and dogfish with snakes, because we all agreed that we would never eat eel. Northeast of Havana flowed a swift stream called Quiver Creek, and in later years when we fished there, we would occasionally catch eel. We wouldn't even touch it, shaking it off our line. Not until I went to Japan as an adult did I learn to eat eel, one of my favorite Japanese dishes.

Turtles we considered a nuisance, and hard to dehook because of their sharp and powerful jaws. We let the turtles get loose from our hooks. Only once did I catch a large snapping turtle, which we took to a shop at the riverfront and had them clean it for us. Grandma fried the turtle meat and we all had a taste of this strange dish.

Some beautiful fish we caught when I was young seem to have disappeared from the region, apparently because of pollution. In Spoon River we often caught a silvery white perch, which had the local name of "sheepshead." We also caught ring-tailed perch, which I later saw in the Great Lakes. And striped bass were a sight—white with black "stripes" or marks running the length of their body. Grandma called them "streakers." I don't know if these fish are still found in the Havana area, but anglers still catch bass, the most scrappy game fish in our area. We also fished for much smaller rock bass among rocks; we called them goggle eyes because of their large heads and mouths with protruding eyes.

When I was young we listened to a popular song, "Gone Fishin'," and it comes to mind when I think of all those lovely times when we sat on the bank of a ditch and waited for a fish to bite. Many a time during my adult life, especially during long committee meetings, I wished I was back in the days when I had 'gone fishin'.'

CHAPTER 22

The Ball of String

*a*t Grandma's house, almost everything of any use was used. And used. And reused, often in a different, creative fashion. A phrase from the Depression that became a popular wartime slogan, featured in more than 400 magazines, was "Use it up, wear it out, make it do or do without." At Grandma's house, everyone became a true believer in this creed.

An example of this principle has already been seen, because most of the year Grandma dumped her coffee grounds and dish water onto the worm bed, one of the many ways in which she saved by turning ordinary, throwaway items into something other than their ordinary purposes. Dish water was for washing dishes, and coffee grounds were for making coffee, but she transformed them into means of raising earthworms for fishing.

She had two guidelines working in tandem: be as frugal and use as little as possible, and never throw anything away. Both principles have been seen, even in fishing. Don't buy worms or other bait if you can find it or raise it yourself. And don't throw away coffee grounds, use them to feed the worms in the worm bed.

The kitchen can be seen as the heart of the American house, especially with regard to consumption. Today we would call my grandmother's kitchen a recycling center. What I remember most vividly about this reuse mentality was the ball of string in the drawer of the cupboard. In those days, many merchants wrapped a purchase in paper and tied it with string. When Grandma came home from shopping, she first took care of food and merchandise on the kitchen table. She would carefully *untie* packages, hating it when she had to cut a perfectly good length of string. "Get me the ball of string," she'd say, and one of my sisters or I would bring the ball from the cupboard drawer. Most of the time the string had assumed the size of a baseball. When it got much bigger it wouldn't fit in the drawer, and we started a new ball. We found the end of the string on the ball, knotted it to the newly acquired piece of string, and did this again for each purchase. When we needed a piece of string, we took some off the ball. This amounted to a double savings: we saved the string from a purchase when we didn't throw it away, and we saved by not having to buy string.

Much of this saving became almost inbred, instinctual. True, during World War II we wanted to be patriotic: to be frugal, save, and reuse. But this came naturally for people who had lived through the Depression. They didn't need a war or a call to patriotism to do what they had always done. In the cupboard drawer we had not only a ball of string, but also a ball of foil. We saved all foil, wrapped it around the ball and scrunched it to make it stick. We sold foil, or contributed it to a scrap drive.

Our family never discarded newspapers, but saved and sold them for scrap paper. Doc made part of his living collecting and selling paper and cardboard. My mother said that when she gave birth, in her parents' house in the country, they laid down newspapers on the table that served as a delivery bed. We also used newspaper as wrapping paper. When we bought fish at the riverfront fish shops, the owner wrapped the fish in newspaper, and if we happened to give someone extra fish we had, we went to the newspaper pile and got some for wrapping.

Tin became especially precious during wartime. Empty tin cans not in use, such as for storing and transporting worms, had both ends cut out, their paper labels removed, and flattened. Toothpaste tubes were prized in the war effort, too. I remember special bins for depositing empty toothpaste tubes. And later, to even prevent the use of such tubes, the government asked us to switch to tooth powder, which came in cardboard packages. I hated using the tooth powder, which felt gritty, like having sand in your mouth.

Some things that modern people consider simply "waste," such as grease, Grandma and her generation carefully saved. Grease we saved and strained, to remove food particles. When a large amount of grease accumulated, Grandma mixed it with lye to make soap. She used a slaw cutter (for shredding cabbage) to make soap flakes for washing dishes. During the war, housewives saved an amazing amount of household fat and donated it for armaments. On page 262 of *Studies in Food Rationing,* a chart for "Salvaged Household Fats," shows that in late

The Office of War Information created and distributed a number of posters encouraging the collection of scrap metal for the war effort. IMAGE COURTESY OF NATIONAL ARCHIVES/WIKIMEDIA.

1943, households saved nine million pounds of fats, and the following year, due to "Points Allowed for Fats," this number increased to fifteen million, and later reached a high of eighteen million.

The campaign to save fats posed an opportunity too good to pass up to promote negative attitudes toward enemies as positive encouragement for support of the war. The following article appeared in the September 22, 1944 issue of the *Democrat:*

SLAP A JAP WITH OILS AND FATS!

Until those nasty, little, grinning Nipponese, sons-of-banzai are driven back to Tokio this country is going to be short about a billion pounds a year of fats and oils we formerly received from the palms and cocoanut groves of the South Seas.

But—most women seem to think the fats and oil shortage is due to stepped up war production and that as soon as the shooting dies down in Europe the situation will ease up. Even in peacetime, under normal production loads, American industry uses ten billion pounds of fats and oils every year, and imports 20 per cent of it.

Mrs. America, God bless her, has missed that point. She knows, 98 per cent of her, that she should save used kitchen fats for munitions, medicines, etc., and turn them in. Actually a recent survey tells that 74 per cent of housewives have a can of used fat in the refrigerator right now and are adding to it constantly.

The first few words of this diatribe invoke the stereotype of Japanese ("Nipponese") seen in wartime films: the diminutive, inscrutable Asians grinning with buck teeth and small circular eyeglasses—the same ones who carried out the sneak attack on Pearl Harbor. The epithet "sons-of-banzai" is a printable version of "sons-of-bitches," which at the time was unprintable. This phrase is a Midwestern tongue in cheek similar to the downstate Illinois people calling Chicagoans in their fancy yachts "sons of the beaches." This announcement is a clever strategy to persuade housewives to save fats as a way to "slap a Jap."

Wartime frugality continued in the postwar era. Long after the war ended my mother still made soap by mixing grease and lye, pouring it out in the bottom of a cardboard box (obtained for free from a store), and letting it harden before cutting it into squares. If you didn't look closely and smell it, you might mistake it for a cake with off-white cream frosting.

Bacon grease had its own special category, because of its flavoring. During spring and summer, Grandma saved bacon grease to use in a kind of dressing, heating it with vinegar and sugar to pour over leaf lettuce to make "wilted lettuce," similar to spinach or turnip greens. In winter, Grandma used bacon grease to pop popcorn, which gave it a smoky bacon taste.

In Grandma's house we followed a hierarchy in the food chain, starting with self-sufficiency and ending with "store-bought." The first link in the chain dictated: if you can grow it, don't buy it. This was the rationale for the regular garden, expanded into the Victory garden. By preserving food—canning or freezing it—the garden's harvest helped feed us year-round. We raised chickens, and the only things that kept Grandma from raising pigs, and maybe milking a cow, was our location in town and lack of space.

Some foods we did not grow, we could gather. In spring we walked along fencerows and picked wild asparagus and rhubarb, a seasonal outing both fun in the doing and tasty in the eating. Grandma sometimes made salad with dandelion greens, but my own family couldn't get used to the bitterness and didn't take to this dish. In summer we picked wild raspberries and blackberries in the fencerows and woods. We also took advantage of mother nature's generosity by catching fish. Grandpa didn't hunt, so we had no wild game, but sometimes friends gave us a few ducks or rabbits they had killed.

We could also lower the cost of food by providing some of the labor. We didn't have a strawberry bed, but would pay a lower price for strawberries by picking them, what today is called "U-pick." We had yet another consideration before we had to resort to "store-bought." If we had to buy something, we preferred to purchase direct from the producer rather than get it through a retailer.

A woman who worked at the locker plant lived on a farm, milking her own cows and separating the cream. Mother bought a pint of heavy cream from her every week. It was cheaper than from the store, and thicker and better in quality. In the same way, if a farmer or other customer had extra vegetables or fruit and offered them for sale, we could avoid any mark-up by a middleman. In the 1940s we had no discount or wholesale stores.

Some savings combined several of these techniques. For example, when making ketchup we used tomatoes from the garden, but of course Grandma had to buy vinegar, spices, and saccharin from the store.

However, the expense of these ingredients amounted to less than store-bought ketchup. Grandma saved by supplying her own labor.

Grandma also prepared her own hot sauce. She'd buy hot red peppers and stuff them in a small cruet, then fill it with vinegar. This was very tasty sprinkled over meat, and the cruet could be refilled a number of times before the peppers had to be replaced. (At the present moment, while this book is being written, on our kitchen counter is a cruet of red peppers and vinegar—my favorite hot sauce.)

As a last resort, when no other means proved practical, we purchased at retail price from a store. Grandma always bought spices and extracts from the Watkins dealer who visited the house with his sample cases. And of course we had to buy staples—sugar, flour, corn meal, and the like. But we followed the general rule to avoid store and retail purchases by whatever means possible.

Almost any kind of food scrap, even potato peels, could be fed to the chickens, which turned into eggs and fried chicken. We gave table left-overs, such as bones, to the dog or cats. We didn't have much garbage. We had very little left over, which we put in the burning barrel, to be reduced in size, and then every few months we hired someone to haul away the ashes. Doc handled much of our old newspapers and cans, but during the war we had all kinds of "drives" and special places to deposit paper, tin, and other materials.

We never threw away any item of clothing. Old clothes had various categories. In the mending basket we put holey socks, shirts without buttons, pants with the knees out, ripped items. In other words, they could be mended. If not requiring too much fixing up, they would pass for school, and if not good enough for school, they could still be worn after school and for garden work or fishing.

The January 14, 1944 issue of the *Democrat* printed this example of government encouragement to save waste paper for production of war materiel.

In the rag bag went clothes beyond all repair—when the seat wore through on pants, or there was a bad rip. Clothes you grew out of but which were still serviceable would be discreetly offered to relatives first, and if there were no takers, given to a church charity. Only one time did I really object to a hand-me-down, when I was on the receiving end of a few items from an older female cousin. They were too obvious—the shirts buttoned on the wrong side. Clothing items beyond all hope of repair would still be used for cleaning, and at worst they could be sold for rags.

Finally, we had the sock bag. We kept socks separate, because grandma reserved them for making throw rugs. She braided old stockings of all kinds into rugs, being especially fond of oval shaped rugs. Rags of any kind can be used for these braided rugs, cutting the rags into strips. I have even seen "runners" for stairs made out of these rag rugs. Savings came from a twofold strategy: using and reusing whatever we had, and avoiding purchases whenever possible. The recycling of rags into rugs meant we did not have to buy throw rugs.

In wartime, avoiding use of the car became a major goal. When Mother took Grandma and me for a Sunday fishing trip across the river in one of the ditches, only a few miles, she didn't drop us off and agree to come back and pick us up at a certain time. Rather, she brought the Sunday newspaper or other reading with her and spent the afternoon parked under a shade tree, reading. This saved an extra trip, avoiding unnecessary use of gas and tires.

However, avoidance had its limits. One of the disadvantages of frugality for both Grandma and Grandpa is that they hated to use electricity, such as lamps. Each of them would read late into the afternoon or early evening, depending on the season, not wanting to break down and be the one to turn on a light. Usually Grandma would give in and turn on a reading light. If she started making supper and saw Grandpa in the parlor holding the newspaper at arms' length by the window to catch the fading light, she scolded him: "Well, turn on a *light!* We can afford lights." Grandpa would refuse, saying, "I can see." He'd wait five or ten minutes and then, reluctantly, switch on a light. And woe to the one who left a room with a light on. We knew to turn off a light if we weren't using it, and to remember "Waste not, want not."

Today we would call much of this "recycling," but Grandma and Grandpa never heard of such a fancy word. For them it was just matter-of-fact, everyday good sense, like keeping the ball of string.

CHAPTER 23

Bell Bottom Trousers

e enjoyed living at Grandma's house, a pleasant and homey experience, but we knew it wasn't forever. And most of all, we missed Daddy. Before the war he worked long hours, so we saw too little of him when we were small, and yet he made up for it when he was with us, always laughing, joking, and teasing. Several times he took my two sisters and me along on a business trip to Peoria, while mother managed the Locker. Mid-morning when we hit the edge of Peoria, Daddy saw an A & W root beer stand, and asked us, "How about a hot dog and a root beer?"

Three pint-sized voices roared approval of Dad's suggestion. That was the kind of spontaneous, fun-loving father we missed so much during the war. Mother would have vetoed this spur of the moment

ILLUSTRATION BY JOHN MICHAEL DOWNS.

snack, insisting that we wait til noon and "don't spoil your appetite for lunch." Daddy had always been more of a free spirit.

When he first entered the Navy for basic training, I was still too young to realize what was going on. I remember when we took him to another city, either Peoria or Chicago, and a long street car ride that was more interesting to me than the imminent farewell to Dad. The worst part was that my two sisters cried and cried. Old enough to realize that this was not a simple goodby, they knew it meant a long time without our father, and war could mean death.

Only later did I understand what had happened, because that's when we left our own house and moved in with Grandma, changing schools and making new friends, having to mind grandparents as well as Mom. It became a confusing time for us kids. We missed our father terribly, and we feared that he would never come home.

Mom never mentioned the possibility that Daddy might be killed. She kept a stiff upper lift and a brave front. My sisters and I shared Mom's anxieties, but followed her example by hiding our fear and not talking about it.

Kenneth H. Earhart in his Navy uniform; the "C" under the eagle on his shoulder indicates his service as a cook in the galley. FAMILY COLLECTION.

At the same time, we felt very proud that in late 1942 he had volunteered for the service. We told friends, "Our Dad *enlisted.*" Other men waited for the draft to call them up or tried to get a deferment or exemption. Because he was thirty-one years old and had three children, he might easily have sat out the war years, running the locker plant and helping people cope with the food situation. So we tried to be proud, but underneath we were mad that some other country had made it necessary for him to leave us.

When Dad came home on leave, he looked very handsome in his navy blues, and we forgot all about fear and resentment, basking in his presence. He taught us new words, like the nickname "gob" for sailor. And his navy pants had a strange appearance because they flared out at the bottom, without cuffs—bell bottoms. About this time my folks bought me my own navy blue uniform, complete with bell bottom trousers. The suit brought me glances of admiration and friendly comments. I wore it to Sunday School almost every week.

Daddy's leave was great and it was terrible. We loved him being home and yet we knew it would be all too short. We wanted to be with him every minute, and we smothered him. Naturally, he became impatient because he knew better than we did how little time he had. I wanted to show him my new school. I had come home for lunch, so he drove me back, as I gave him directions. Instead of taking him straight east on Market Street for four blocks and then north on Broadway for about six blocks, I had him turning right and left every block,

When my father was in the Navy, I was much too young to enlist, but could wear my Navy uniform that made me a kind of junior sailor. FAMILY COLLECTION.

because that's the way I walked it. I felt disappointed that he just wanted to get there as fast as possible.

While he was home, I went out to play after school and was hitting a tennis ball with a broom stick. It was difficult enough for me just to connect with the narrow broom stick, and I couldn't hit the ball too far. Playing in a vacant lot across Market Street next to the Holy Rollers basement church, I turned towards Grandma's house to hit the ball across the street into our yard. For the first time I really hit the ball square, and I watched it sail up, up, over the street, toward the house, right through the east parlor front window. I came home crying, not worrying so much about getting a spanking as for making trouble while Dad was home.

Dad didn't say much—he just looked at me sadly, telling me it was nothing to worry about. He was getting ready to leave his family for overseas duty, risking his life. A broken window was nothing to get upset about or cry over.

We enjoyed suppers with everyone there. But we weren't supposed to be at Grandma's house when Daddy was home. It wasn't a holiday, like Christmas. It was everyday. And everyday we should be in our own house, on South Orange Street. It wasn't the same. Daddy didn't joke and laugh as much as usual. It made for an uneasy time.

When his leave ended and he returned to the Navy, we missed him all the more. In our young minds, pride got crowded out by fear and anger.

An earlier sentimental and romantic tune that became popular in wartime described this bittersweet farewell—"Now is the hour, when we must say goodbye." It continues with lyrics about soon the loved one will be sailing away, but asks for him to remember people on the homefront, who will be waiting for him. This song expresses very well what our family felt when Dad returned to Seattle. (Now Is the Hour can be heard on YouTube.)

Daddy was stationed at Bremerton, a base near Seattle, and we began to learn about the area in postcards and letters. Because of his background in the locker plant, the Navy assigned him to preparing and cooking food. He taught us more Navy lingo.

FAREWELL FOR KENNETH EARHART, SC2c OF NAVY

Kenneth Harry Earhart SC 2c has been stationed at Sand Point, Washington, for the past year and a half, and left Monday for Seattle after a leave from duty spent with his wife and three children at Havana. Kenneth formerly was manager of a fine meat shop in the A&P store in Mason City before moving to Havana.

Last Friday night, March 24, 1944, a group of 37 relatives and friends gathered at the home of Mr. Earhart's brother-in-law and sister, Mr. and Mrs. Henry Becker, on West Chestnut street, and had a farewell dinner for him. Those who enjoyed the dinner and hospitality included Kenneth Earhart SC 2c, wife and the children, Rosemary, Sylvia and Byron, of Havana; Mr. and Mrs. Elmo Elliott and Dixie, and Mrs. Zoe Earhart, of Farmington, Ill.; Mr. and Mrs. Bent Benscoter and daughter, Mabel, Mr. and Mrs. John Bloh, and Joanne, Mr. and Mrs. Wesley Knoles and Johnnie, Mr. and Mrs. Cecil Benedict, Mr. and Mrs. Roy Hess, Mrs. Mae Hess, Mr. and Mrs. Kenneth Knoles and Kenny Lee, Mr. and Mrs. Will Pottorf, Mr. and Mrs. John Pottorf, Gail Pottorf, Mrs. George Doggett and Nancy Jo, of this city; Mr. and Mrs. Melvin Parr, of Easton; and Mr. and Mrs. Henry Becker, Joy, Jessie and Eldon.

This newspaper clipping reports the farewell dinner for our Father at the end of his leave, before he shipped out on the USS Missouri. FAMILY COLLECTION.

They called chipped beef on toast SOS, "shit on the shingle." Because this was sailor talk, Mom and Grandma did not object to a little off-color language. We heard about the shakedown cruise from Seattle down the coast of California, when everyone hung over the rail and "puked their guts out."

He didn't know how long he would be stationed in Seattle, and he kept writing about how lovely the area was. He could be there for the rest of the war. Eventually Mother left Fred in charge of the store and went to be with him for a few months. She found a small apartment and even got a job in a market, because help was scarce. They

ILLUSTRATION BY JOHN MICHAEL DOWNS.

enjoyed their brief time together in Seattle, like a second honeymoon, and talked about it for years afterward. My sisters and I envied Mom making the cross-country train trip and being with Daddy, but we kept busy with schoolwork. Then Mom returned to Havana when Dad shipped out, to somewhere in the Pacific. The Navy stationed him on the battleship USS Missouri.

From that point our fears increased. It became difficult to get mail to and from the ship, and Daddy couldn't write about where they were. It was bad enough when we were deprived of the presence of our father, but now that he served in a war zone, anything could happen.

Whenever I went to church, I hated to look at the armed services flag, and its field of many blue stars with a few gold stars. I dreaded the ceremony for the death of a military man from our church, replacing a blue star with a gold star, experiencing a mixture of many emotions. I felt very sorry for the poor family suffering the loss. At the same time, I gave a sigh of relief that it was not our father. Then came the realization that I had wished death on someone else's loved one, and a sense of guilt overwhelmed me. The ceremony seemed to last forever,

When our father went overseas, he asked mother to have a family picture taken so he would have one with him. We used precious gas to drive to Springfield, Illinois for this professional photo. FAMILY COLLECTION.

and even when it finally ended, I couldn't get it out of my mind. My fear lingered—the next gold star could be for our father.

War always seems to inspire song writers. One song popular during the war was "Bell Bottom Trousers," which can be heard on Youtube. Its opening lines are:

> "Bell bottom trousers, and a coat of navy blue.
> I love my sailor boy, and he loves me too."

CHAPTER 24

Ink and Blood, Life and Death

*a*s an elementary school pupil, I did not read newspapers. My introduction to journalism came a few years later after entering junior high, when I took over my older sister's paper route. For that morning route I delivered the *Chicago Tribune* and the *Chicago Sun-Times.* Later I delivered the *Peoria Journal-Star* for an afternoon route. The *Canton Ledger, Pekin Times,* and *Springfield Register* tried to make inroads into Havana, but did not gain many readers.

The lifeblood of a small town flows in the ink of its local newspaper. For Havana that meant *The Mason County Democrat,* a weekly serving both Mason County and some of Fulton County. This publication has the distinction of being the oldest operating establishment in the city, dating back to its founding in 1849 and enjoying continuous publication to the present (under several names).

Although as a pre-teen I did not read the *Democrat,* recently I looked through the war year issues of December, 1941 through September, 1945. Scanning the headlines, main articles, editorials, and advertisements allowed me to relive the era from the viewpoint of the local press, and feel the pulse of the citizens during

In the days before computers, newspapers were prepared on linotype machines such as this one. ILLUSTRATION BY JOHN MICHAEL DOWNS.

this critical period. The black ink of newsprint and its accounts of dead and wounded paint the picture of life and death in wartime in my hometown as recorded in the columns of this paper.

My lasting impression from reading these four years of the *Democrat* is how much the war dominated every aspect of life in Havana and Mason County. Previous chapters of this book have quoted or summarized this newspaper's articles reporting on many war-related events, such as the organization of Victory gardens, the collection of scrap and grease, and the announcement of War Bond Drives. During these years, most of the reporting in the *Democrat* directly or indirectly dealt with the war.

Other Illinois and American newspapers shared *The Mason County Democrat*'s preoccupation with the war. Mary Watters in her *Illinois in the Second World War* states that "newspapers had become text-books on war programs: the draft, rationing, civilian defense, Victory gardens, war bonds, income taxes." She quotes a 1943 observation from the *Chicago Daily News:* "'We became in a very real sense the interpreter for a government grown so complex it couldn't explain itself.'" (Watters, Vol. I, p. 479).

Four years of the weekly issues of *The Mason County Democrat* contain more information than can be easily summed up, but for articles directly dealing with the war, two topics stand out. One is news of the national and international events of military campaigns, especially the victories and defeats, the loss and gain of territory, for the Allied and Axis powers. The other topic is accounts detailing the impact of the conflict on the local citizenry, especially the reports about military personnel from Havana and Mason County. The focus of this book is on the Illinois homefront, rather than the overseas warfront, so I only touch briefly on national and international aspects before concentrating at greater length on local and regional dimensions of wartime experience.

The Sunday, December 7, 1941 plane attack on Pearl Harbor by the Japanese filled the airwaves across the country, shocking all Americans. Because the *Democrat* was a weekly paper published on Friday, the local announcement of Pearl Harbor came almost a week later on December 12. The headlines and initial paragraphs of the lead story capture the mood of America, from small towns like Havana to Washington:

**JAPANESE LAUNCH ATTACK FROM AIR ON
HAWAII AND OTHER POSSESSIONS**

CONGRESS ACTS RAPIDLY IN WAR DECLARATION
AFTER PRESIDENT ROOSEVELT CALLS ACT BY
JAPANESE UNPROVOKED AND DASTARDLY

3000 CASUALTIES IN FIRST ATTACK

SURPRISE ATTACK ON PEARL HARBOR AND OTHER
POSSESSIONS OCCURRED SUNDAY, DEC. 7

BULLETIN!

On Thursday morning, December 11, Germany and Italy declared war on the United States. The Congress of the United States immediately accepted the situation and voted unanimously in recognizing that a state of war existed between Germany and Italy as well as with Japan.

Radio reports on Thursday were to the effect that Congress had voted to permit the sending of troops anywhere in the world and that all draftees were to be held for the duration of the war and for six months after hostilities were ended if necessary.

In bold type and capital letters, the black ink of the *Democrat* summed up for residents of Havana and Mason County what they already knew. America had been attacked, the blood of thousands of casualties had been spilled, and we were at war "for the duration" of the hostilities, with no end forecast to the length of service for draftees. The lengthy article that followed these headlines and bulletin included President Roosevelt's famous label of December 7, 1941 as "a date which will live in infamy."

The December 12, 1941 editorial response to this catastrophic event included both reprimand to those who had minimized the Pacific threat, and praise of those who foresaw the danger. Then it bucked up the people of Havana for a long war and many sacrifices:

WE ARE AT WAR!

The people of the United States were rocked from their lethargy Sunday when excited voices came from their loud speakers announcing that Japanese bombers had attacked the Hawaiian islands and other of our possessions in the Pacific ocean.

Some of the listeners were more surprised than others. In that group were those who had been listening to the Wheelers and the Lindbergs of the country for months and had taken seriously their assurance that the international pillagers were afraid to cause trouble for us and if their courage was not sufficiently low, the thousands of miles of water that bounded our shores formed a natural unsurmountable obstacle.

Then there was another group . . . Those who had heard the American Legion insist for the past twenty years that our defense was not sufficient to properly guard our welfare. These attacks were no surprise to that group. Those who know war tactics from actual experience . . . perhaps antiquated tactics as compared with the blitz methods now employed . . . knew that our defense was vulnerable and that the war makers could cause us trouble. And they did.

Now we are at war. And in true American fashion, the Lindberg and Wheeler crowd and the American Legion crowd have joined forces in the common cause. We are advised that we must prepare for a long drawnout war in which we will all be called upon to make sacrifices. America is ready to make these sacrifices to the bitter end. In the words of the President, "We will win the war and we will win the Peace that follows."

Havana and Hawaii lie thousands of miles apart, yet the letter of a former Havana resident living in Hawaii brought these locations much closer together. Her firsthand account of the attack on Pearl Harbor appeared in the December 19, 1941 *Democrat:* "I hope by now that you have heard that we are alright. I was about to say safe, but will never feel safe here again so long as we are at war with Japan. At least we were not killed nor injured, but it is certainly shattering to one's mental being and sense of security."

The letter continues with details of the destruction on the morning of December 7. "At about 3 minutes before eight, I heard the terrible firing and the screech and explosion of bombs. I ran out on the lanai and like a panorama the dreadful scene at Pearl Harbor, in a bright and sunshiny morning, was spread before my view. Great billows of black smoke, many planes flying low over Pearl Harbor, bursts of fire and heavy detonation of anti-aircraft guns and chaos at its worst."

Radio broadcasts, newspaper accounts, and letters such as this made it clear that not only Hawaii, the Philippines, and other Asian sites were attacked. America was attacked. Illinois was attacked. Havana was attacked. And all citizens must unite for an extended conflict. An article in the column next to the letter from Hawaii announced,

"Farmers Urged to Salvage Scrap Iron for Defense." Fear of enemies was overcome by the resolve to vanquish them. All segments of society began to gear up for the war effort.

The details of the warfront are important, as the *Democrat* noted in its regular columns "Week of War" and "The Week in Washington." However, our main concern here is not the war as such, but its impact on the local homefront and the human toll. The January 23, 1942 *Democrat* carried the first of what would be an endless stream of similar announcements:

HAVANA'S FIRST WAR CASUALTY HAS BEEN REPORTED

BOBBY JOE BROWN KILLED WHILE ON DUTY WITH U. S. MARINES

The war was brought closer to us last week with the report of the first Havana boy being killed in action. The boy was Robert Joseph (Bobby-Joe) Brown, son of Harold Brown of this city. Mr. Brown received a telegram from the War Department Thursday evening stating that Bobby-Joe had died of wounds received in line of duty while with the United States Marines. . . .

The telegram stated that conditions necessitated burial in the vicinity where death occurred. This fatality marks the first blood shed by a Havana resident in World War II. The time lag of weeks, or longer, between death and notification of kin, was a condition of war that left all loved ones in an agonizing limbo. The fact that even the location of his interment could not be disclosed made for another obstacle to closure for the family. Months later, the only, and slim consolation, was the notification that this marine had died a hero's death and had been granted an award, as noted in a May 15, 1942 article:

ROBERT J. BROWN GETS POSTHUMOUS SERVICE AWARD

Robert J. Brown, the first Havana boy to give up his life in the war, which now grips the world, has been listed as one of the 224 officers and 160 enlisted men who received decorations for heroism in the Philippine War. Bobby Joe was serving with the fourth regiment of the U.S. Marines, attached to the Navy medical unit when he died from wounds received in action. His award was the distinguished service cross, the highest award made at this time.

[A marine officer wrote the family that] Your son, Robert, died honorably and bravely, while performing duty with a patrol at the front lines of Bataan. As in everything he did, or was called upon to do, he exhibited the finest traditions of American manhood, and in keeping with the high standard of the Marine Corps. The patrol was engaged in forcing the withdrawal of certain enemy snipers who had infiltrated through the front lines. Enemy machine gun fire fatally wounded him.

The award was made posthumously.

The language of this obituary extols the individual marine while presenting a model of "the finest traditions of American manhood," for other young men to follow when they were drafted or enlisted.

The January 30, 1942 issue of the *Democrat* announced, "LONNIE DUKES KILLED IN ACTION WITH U. S. NAVY . . . SO FAR AS IS KNOWN THE FIRST Mason county boy to give his life in the defense of his country in the present conflict . . . killed on December 7, while on duty with the U. S. Navy."

These two initial casualties of Havana and Mason County, unfortunately, were followed by notices of deaths or wounded military in almost every subsequent issue of the local paper for the rest of the war. Hardened combat soldiers have written that on the battlefield, whether it was the Civil War or later wars, when dead bodies cover the ground, one becomes numbed to the victims of the grim reaper, and just walks ahead on the bodies, friend or foe. As I read through four years of the Democrat, it became obvious that I could not mention every fallen soldier, marine, sailor or WAAC.

After reading of the deaths of so many local servicemen, I, too, became numb. Then I happened upon the enlistment news of Fred's son. Fred who had worked at Earhart Food Locker. The picture for Fred's son showed a handsome young officer in the Air Force. While reading through later *Democrat* issues, I anticipated, but dreaded, finding the article a year later recording his death. He had piloted a bomber over Germany, did not return, was presumed lost, then declared dead. This hit home. This was the man whose fishing poles and bat I had wanted to buy from his father. This hurt. This made me feel sorry for Fred, who had tried to drown his sorrows in whiskey.

American bombers over Germany, one shot down. ILLUSTRATION BY JOHN MICHAEL DOWNS.

For every parent, sibling, spouse, son or daughter, no number of other deaths can numb you to the pain of the loss of your loved one. When someone you know, your friend, or family member is killed, it is not a statistic. It is a heartbreaker.

In Bordner's book about Camp Ellis, a businesswoman tells a story about a man who came into her Ipava restaurant. His son had been sent overseas. Every day he put nickels in the juke box to play "There's a Star-Spangled Banner Waving Somewhere," and cried through the entire song. The scene was so heartrending that the owner removed the recording from the juke box.

The *Democrat* printed many articles such as the two previous obituaries that give special, individual recognition

Fred receiving the telegram notifying him of his son's death in action. ILLUSTRATION BY JOHN MICHAEL DOWNS.

to those military men who had not just left the local area, but departed this world when they gave their lives for the country. From early 1942 until the end of the war, the newspaper also published an endless stream of general items about the "boys" departing for the service, hopefully a temporary absence until they could return after the successful conclusion of the battles. These articles announced the dates for registration, regulations for the draft, and induction notices. As with all government bureaucracies, be it rationing or the draft, as the war progressed, the rules and procedures shifted. At first the draft was run as a lottery, then it changed to assignment by date of birth.

The titles of some of these articles, especially from the first year of the war, are quoted here to illustrate the barrage of information people received about how many local men were entering military service.

January 9, 1942: "Men Between Ages of 20 and 44 to Register for Service Feb. 16. Registration to be Conducted in High Schools by Faculties under Supervision of Selective Service Boards; 9,000,000 to Register"

January 16, 1942: "Call 21 for Final Draft Examination. Officials Rule That List of Men May Be Published"

February 6, 1942: "County's Draft Quota Is Listed"

February 13, 1942: "Men to Register for Service on Monday, Feb. 16. 20 to 45 Year Group Not Registered Are Affected"

February 20, 1942: "1095 Registered for Service Here Monday, Feb. 16. Drawing to Determine Order Number to be Held in March"

February 27, 1942: "First War-time Draft Lottery Set for Mar. 17. Order Number of Those Registering Feb. 16 to Be Determined"

March 7, 1942: "Thirty-two on Induction List for Early April. List Includes Several That Have Been Re-examined"

June 26, 1942: "Registration of 18–19 Year Olds to Start Today. Lottery to be eliminated; assign numbers according to births."

October 7, 1942: "October Draft Lists Contain Names of 77. One Group to Report October 14; Second on October 19" (Because this article contains the name of my father, the first paragraph is quoted here.) "Mason county will send 74 men to Peoria for induction into the army at Peoria during the next two weeks to bring the total number inducted to 105 up to and including the

19th. Induction lists include three men who have enlisted and, as a result, will not be in the two groups: Kenneth Earhart, Gordon Wixom and Eugene Krause, all of Havana, who have enlisted in the U.S. navy."

October 29, 1943: "Fathers Included in November Call for Men in Co. Nine Havana Men Are Included in List Receiving Call"

November 6, 1942: "Nine Draftees Listed to Go November 14. Two of Those Named Have Already Enlisted"

The Democrat sought details of men serving in the military. A January 30, 1942 article spells this out:

Information We Want

The Democrat wishes to publish all the news concerning the men from the county who are serving in the armed forces during the war. There are many enlistments that we have no way of knowing about except through the families. There will be some of our boys wounded, some will give their lives, and we particularly want this information.

There are times when pictures are available and in the event of a death we would like to have a picture of the soldier or sailor.

The files of the paper are a permanent record and the account of these incidents should be recorded.

Some of the news forwarded by families of servicemen to the *Democrat* told about the death, injury, "lost," or "missing in action" notification they had received from the government. In this frightening scenario, it was actually good news if a man was reported as a prisoner, because at least the family knew he had not been killed. A February 14, 1944 article confirmed an American pilot as "reported to be German prisoner." His squadron members had seen his bomber hit, the crew bail out, and all parachutes open. A shortwave broadcast from Germany gave his name as a prisoner. This pilot had been more fortunate than Fred's son.

A February 23, 1945 article gave the news of another pilot who had completed 18 missions over Germany before being shot down and captured. In a letter he sent home through the Red Cross, he wrote that "The Red Cross is doing a wonderful bit of work in these camps and deserves a lot of credit. I wish you would donate $50 to them from my bank account, and send them my appreciation."

The extent of patriotism and sacrifice is captured in the title of a March 2, 1945 article: "Three Sons Fight; Fourth Is Prisoner."

Sons and brothers were not the only family members to be singled out for patriotism. A 1942 song by the Andrews Sisters, "Three Little Sisters," tells of how one sister loved a soldier, one loved a sailor, and one loved a lad in the marines. They were the fairest lasses in the land, and they were true to their boyfriends in the service, staying home and reading magazines. (The song is available on Youtube.)

During the war, special columns kept track of the careers of local servicemen, such as their location of training and specific duties, as well as their promotions, and even the dates of their furloughs back home. The titles of these columns changed, but they kept the same function. Two such titles were "Guardians of Our Welfare," and "Our Boys with the Colors."

It was mainly a man's war, but women were also acknowledged, both individually and as a group. An August 14, 1942 article announces "Havana's First W.A.A.C." (The abbreviations for the Woman's Auxiliary Army Corps varied, sometimes W.A.A.C., other times WAAC, or just WAC.) A November 12, 1943 editorial in the Democrat pays tribute to women in uniform:

The Women's Army Corps. ILLUSTRATION BY JOHN MICHAEL DOWNS.

A SALUTE TO THE WACS

With a desperate need for volunteers for the Women's Army Corps, the Army is urging enlistments for this important branch of service. Many thousands of women who can qualify are needed and a concentrated recruiting drive is now in progress.

American soldiers are falling in battle in all parts of the world and men serving in the United States must be moved to the fighting fronts to replace the casualties, and there are many of the jobs these men have been performing that can be efficiently handled by women. That establishes the need for WACS. (The Havana Public District Library has in its files a record of Mason County Women who served in World War I and World War II.)

As was mentioned in the chapter on Rosie the Riveter, during the war the government and the media gave credit to women in the war effort, usually covering a wide spectrum of vocations: female military personnel, "war worker girls," and even "farmerettes" and housewives. An April 20, 1942 photo of "War Worker Girls in Uniform" notes that "Wearing of the uniform is optional, but many girls prefer it because it is practical and military in appearance." This uniform, like the proposal for uniforms for the Women's Farm Army, was not widely adopted. Throughout the war the government made constant adjustments, experimenting with various ideas and practices, whether it was how to run the draft or what to wear.

Reading the wartime issues of the *Democrat* helped me enter the collective consciousness of the local people, as reported and idealized by the paper's editor and reporters. This paper told us both what we wanted to hear, and also about what we hated to learn. The *Democrat* followed the lives and deaths of local servicemen, using its black ink to report on the red blood of Americans shed in the war.

CHAPTER 25

Editorials: I, We, and WE-ALL

n ewspapers report facts, which are often unpleasant. Journalism also goes beyond the facts, to reflect on local and broader issues and to provide some direction to readers. A newspaper's editorial "we" attempts to be the conscience of the community, reminding everyone of what they have left undone and what they ought to do. The "we" of the editorials in wartime papers echoed Rosie the Riveter's statement of "We can do it." A *Democrat* editorial of February 6, 1942 even goes beyond the ordinary sense of "we" to the heightened wartime sense of "we all." This editorial borrows the words of the President of the International Business Machine Corporation, emphasizing that the Japanese attack on the United States instantly changed our thoughts about "I" and "we":

> WE ALL
>
> . . . Before the attack some of us thought in terms of "I," others in terms of "we." Neither of those terms express our feelings today.
>
> "I" represents only one person.
>
> "We" may mean two or a few persons.
>
> Our slogan now is WE-ALL, which means every loyal individual in the United States.
>
> We are facing a long, hard job, but when the United States decides to fight for a cause, it is in terms of WE-ALL, and nothing can or will stop us.
>
> President Roosevelt, our Commander-in-Chief, can be certain that WE-ALL are back of him, determined to protect our country, our form of government and the freedoms which we cherish.

This editorial captures the ideal for the spirit of America during World War II. Not everyone may have conformed one hundred percent in upholding this spirit, but we held it up as the undisputed ideal. In all of the editorials in the *Democrat* during the war years, the "we" really meant "WE-ALL."

The wartime editorials of the *Democrat* let us hear the voice of *we* Americans who overwhelmingly backed the war effort. Some of these editorials have already been quoted, such as the rousing phrases of the call to arms just after the attack on Pearl Harbor. A sampling of later editorials illustrates the deep sense of united patriotism during World War II. The editor uses his position to criticize shortcomings, praise accomplishments, and encourage greater support in the war effort. The dates, titles, and the gist of the editorials in summary and/or quotation are given below.

December 19, 1941 EDITORIAL
Following up on the December 12, 1941 editorial calling for unified support of the war effort, this piece says not only the military, but all civilians need to contribute to the defense industry and buy Defense Bonds and Defense Stamps. "Let's all put our shoulder to the wheel to show that we appreciate a citizenship in the greatest country in the world."

January 2, 1942 A JOB FOR EVERYBODY
Behind the battle lines, people should serve on the committees that will do the difficult work of regulating commodities, and be considerate of others who have this onerous task. We must work harder and "keep busy and devote every effort toward winning the war in the shortest possible time."

January 16, 1942 AN OPPORTUNITY TO SERVE
During a time of scarce commodities and less gas to travel, "the local merchant will be called upon to supply the demands of the community."

January 23, 1942 WAR-TIME CENSORSHIP
The press will balance the recognized need for not publishing information that would be of use to our enemies. Subversives among us should not try to take advantage of our free speech and free press. But—"DON'T TALK! . . . Don't let a careless word endanger some boy's life or your country's safety."

January 30, 1942 OUR RESPONSIBILITY
"One of our responsibilities that is ours as an agricultural community is the production of food. Food is just as essential to the successful prosecution of this war as are guns and ammunition, ships, aircraft and tanks."

February 6, 1942 WAR TIME
Instead of calling the turning ahead of clocks Daylight Saving Time, it will be called War Time, which "tells America that there is no time left for loafing on the production lines, for grumbling about rationing or income taxes, for delaying civilian defense."

February 13, 1942 ALL THIS AND WPA TOO
Although welfare [WPA] once was a valid way for providing food and shelter for the unfortunate, "Now anyone who has any ambition can secure employment through the regular channels of industry at a much better wage than is provided by occupying the WPA rolls."

February 20, 1942 WASTE NOT WANT NOT
"Among the other freedoms we must forego for the duration is waste. We must begin saving our resources, turning them to the best account for victory."

February 27, 1942 HOW LONG?
"With the whole hearted cooperation of every peace-loving American, and we mean by that displaying the same attitude MacArthur and his men are displaying, we can make short work of these sneaking Orientals and their greedy partners in crime and pillage."

March 6, 1942 THE PART DEFENSE BONDS PLAY
"We must equip and maintain an army of far greater proportion than we have ever before imagined. . . . The Defense Bonds and Defense Stamp Program give all of us a way to take a direct part in the program and it is THE AMERICAN WAY of handling an emergency, everyone carrying their part of the load."

April 7, 1942 SUBSTITUTES FOR EVERYTHING . . . EXCEPT FREEDOM
In wartime we must make do with many substitutes, but "There is only one thing for which we have been unable to figure out a substitute. That is our AMERICAN FREEDOM."

April 24, 1942 WE ARE ON OUR WAY!!!

"The announcement of bombs from our bombers falling on principle Japanese cities indicates that we are on our way to retaliation for the attack on Pearl Harbor December 7 . . . the most heartening news that we have received since the war started." [The newspaper did not know details of the attack, later called the Doolittle raid on Tokyo, launched from American aircraft carriers.]

August 14, 1942 THE FATE OF THE SABOTEURS

". . . war being what it is, others who come to kill and destroy can take warning that they will share the fate meted out to the six [saboteurs] who died, not the death of soldiers, but the death of common murderers."

September 4, 1942 LETTERS TO SOLDIERS

Although the USO is "doing an excellent job so far as its services go," it cannot take the place of a letter from home. Writers should avoid "complaining letters, discouraging letters," instead sending "cheerful letters." "Tell him that all his friends are pulling for him and that they are proud of him." "Encourage him to greater effort. . . ."

[The *Democrat* included a regular note, "Drop Us a Line," giving the names and addresses of men in the military to whom letters could be sent.]

September 11, 1942 AFTER THREE YEARS OF WAR

In spite of "a series of almost uninterrupted triumphs for Hitler and his Axis partners" in Europe, and in Asia "a series of almost uninterrupted disasters for the United Nations' forces," we can be proud of the American and other Allied soldiers, and we need to redouble our efforts on the homefront to support our troops.

October 2, 1942 OUR ENEMIES WHAT TYPE PEOPLE?

We underestimated the Japanese as having inferior military equipment and being weak at warfare, and misjudged the Japanese people to be peaceful. But Japanese propaganda against Britain and America has been efficient in persuading the Japanese people to support their war effort and to undergo incredible sacrifices. Defeating Japan "is a gigantic undertaking, and we should plan for a long and arduous engagement."

February 19, 1943 A BOY DIED LAST NIGHT
(Reprint from *The Courier-Journal*, Louisville, Ky., June 2, 1942, by John Hoagland)
This reprinted editorial is an extended contrast of the trivial inconveniences ordinary Americans are experiencing, when compared to the agony and pain of death on the battlefield.

May 14, 1943 BLACK MARKETS!
We should not make our local butcher or grocer part of the black market by cajoling him to sell more of a product than we have stamps for. "So get along with what you can get legally now." When the war is over, we can go back to the usual plenty and variety we are accustomed to.

December 10, 1943 CALLING ALL FATHERS
Congress decided to draft fathers, a move that may seem to threaten the American family. Actually, fathers should not wait to be enlisted in the military, because "Rearing his family is the most important task that enters any man's span of years," and he should be "automatically enlisted" in that fight.

These editorials from the early years of the war express the attitude of "WE-ALL" who need to work hard together to bring about victory. The tone is a mixture of carrot and stick, praising those doing their part, reprimanding those trying to bend or break the rules. A rare moment of bragging is seen in the account of the Doolittle raid. Other comments warn of the excellent preparation and training of our enemies, and the tough job we have of overcoming them.

During the early years of the war, the *Democrat* dutifully reported on two fronts, following the events on the warfront, while at the same time keeping in tune with the activities of the homefront. In the early 1940s, every home had a family member, friend, neighbor, or acquaintance in the military. Awareness of the war dominated our hearts and minds, pumping through our arteries.

The *Democrat* editorials, like the image of Rosie the Riveter, presented both sides of the patriotic coin: advocating greater cooperation in the war effort, while celebrating a new sense of unified spirit to "we" as all the people of the United States, WE-ALL.

CHAPTER 26

Bad News and Good News—Cookies, and Valentines

The *Democrat* spelled out much of the gloom and doom atmosphere that filled the early years of the war, when losses of life and territory in Europe and Asia seemed almost overwhelming. However, the black ink on pages of the *Democrat* did not paint a totally dark picture. Actually, this paper featured a mixture of what we might call "feel bad" and "feel good" articles. We already saw one example of this combination of "sweet and sour." The previous chapter mentioned the December 12, 1941 devastating news of the attack on Pearl Harbor, which made everyone in America feel terrible. On the same page, in the column next to this horrific description, appeared a bland notice, "Farmers Urged to Salvage Scrap Iron for Defense." It may not have made farmers and others happy to save scrap, but at least they could do something that contributed to the war effort, aiding the military and indirectly getting back at the enemy. Although we were not farmers, our family realized that anything anyone could do that helped fight the war made people on the homefront feel better. It made no difference if it was Rosie the Riveter in the defense plant or the local farmer in the field or the young people collecting scrap.

A page from the June 26, 1942 *Democrat* illustrates the mix and match of bad and good news, in articles on opposite edges of the page. On the right is the story of the survival of a local man who escaped from the sinking of the carrier Lexington by a Japanese torpedo and bomb assault. It was bad that we lost a ship and several hundred men. On the other hand, several thousand of the crew were rescued, which was good news. The rescued sailor from Havana told the harrowing tale of the sinking of the ship and his survival. It was remarkable that he lived to tell his story. On the other hand, his account reminded readers of the perils of war and what dangers other military men faced. On the left of this page is notification of reclassification for married men, who

Burial at sea of sailors from an American ship. ILLUSTRATION BY JOHN MICHAEL DOWNS.

eventually might go into service and be subjected to risks like that of the Lexington survivor.

A column on the far right of the same newspaper page includes an article outlining registration for 18–19 year-olds and the elimination of the lottery for the order of the draft. These men, too, would soon face the hazards of war.

Still on the same page appear three other articles on the lighter side. "A Week of the War" had news about changes in price ceilings, the need for substitutes (such as saccharin for sugar), and the desperate shortage of war workers. A long article, "Merchants Are Urged to Push Sale of Stamps," announced that on July 1 all merchants would devote 15 minutes to war savings stamp sales. Yet another article on this page reported, "Rationing Board Announces Change in Sugar Program."

This single page provides a glimpse of the wartime mentality in central Illinois, and the rest of the nation. We lamented the loss of life, territory, ships and planes, and the early defeats. We cheered for the survivors, the regaining of some territory, and minor victories like the early 1942 Doolittle raid bombing Tokyo.

The obligations and possibilities for civilians were straightforward, but far from simple. Complex and ever changing regulations told us what we had to do. Men were required to report for the draft. All families were ordered to sign up for rationing. Everyone was monitored for following the rules, such as observing blackouts.

Then there was what we could and should do, especially working in war plants, collecting scrap, and planting Victory gardens. Here the voluntary "could" and dutiful "should" merged with what we *wanted* to do. For most people, who were patriotic and tried to do everything they could to help the boys over there, the mandatory actions turned into self-motivated actions, and made us feel better. Our family, probably like other households, might grouse about not having sugar and coffee, but if doing without helped Daddy and other servicemen, we made the best of it and took pride in being patriotic.

This doesn't mean there was no grumbling. In the chapter "For the Duration," I touched on the controversy about the draft, and whether farm boys who got deferments for "essential" service were "hiding behind the corn stalks." The Camp Ellis boys I have called "cornfield soldiers." City people critical of farm boys who got deferments for "essential" work might label these young farmers "cornfield draft dodgers."

Grandma and Mom sometimes talked at the dinner table about the snide remarks made to them at the locker plant. Although customers didn't openly accuse Grandma and Mom of stealing meat from them, the customers made catty remarks: "You're lucky, you own the locker plant and handle all that food, so you must eat well . . . not like the rest of us."

The bad, the good, the ambiguous, and the questionable—these were the facts and judgments that everyone during the war had to juggle in order to make sense out of the world. The city of Havana, Mason County, the state of Illinois, and the country at large had difficulty assessing the immensity of the dangers presented by the war, and the measures that ordinary people could take to assure safety and victory.

The woman who lived in Hawaii and saw the terrible destruction of Pearl Harbor serves as a good barometer of the mentality of the people. Her letter, forwarded to Havana a week after the attack, sums up what most people felt. Although her family survived the attack and was safe for the time being, she wrote that they "will never feel safe here again so long as we are at war with Japan. At least we were not killed nor injured, but it is certainly shattering to one's mental being and sense of security." Not only residents of Hawaii, but people throughout the country were rudely awakened from a false sense of safety, and responded immediately with defensive tactics.

Across the nation, people mobilized in air raid drills and observed blackouts. The people of Hawaii took elaborate precautions to prepare for a repeat attack. A December 5, 2016 MSN article, "Children who lived through Pearl Harbor attack remember," gives details of the changes in the lives of Hawaii youngsters. A 1942 class picture shows Hawaiian students posing with their individual gas masks, because "After the Pearl Harbor attack, schools required students to carry gas masks with them at all times." The memory of these children in Hawaii is similar to my recollections of wartime Illinois. In Hawaii, although "an ever-present worry about a Japanese invasion permeated life in their island home," and they had to keep gas masks around the backs of their chairs while in class and close by when playing outside, they still managed to have a good time. One woman from this 1942 Hawaii class says that her "war memories are happy ones," because she remembers "walking and skipping the four blocks or so from her home to the school, meeting friends along the way."

In Havana, in the heart of the Midwest, although as school children we did not have to carry with us government-issued gas masks, the fear of air raids was sufficient to promote all kinds of precautions. A good example is the January 23, 1942 graphic in the *Democrat*, "How to Distinguish Nationality of Aircraft." The illustrations of aircraft insignia are included for American, British, Russian, Mexican, German, Italian, and Japanese military planes.

The lead sentence of the caption for this illustration states, "Civilian air raid spotters will have no difficulty distinguishing Axis planes from those of the United Nations if they memorize the markings illustrated above." From a twenty-first century perspective, this kind of preparation appears to have been overreaction, and even during the war there was skepticism of such drastic measures. The document "Illinois at War, 1941–1945" states that by 1943, "it was becoming difficult to convince [Illinois] civilians that they were in any real danger of being attacked from the skies. Aircraft observers stationed on watchtowers in cities and towns across Illinois were ridiculed from below," and in 1944 such observers were placed on stand-by status.

A November 13, 1942 article in the *Democrat* reported "Test Blackout Held Here Thur. Was Successful. Air Raid Wardens Report Violations Were Few." Those residents who left lights on during the blackout "marred the record somewhat," and the "chief air raid warden for Mason county has again called to the attention of the people in the county that it is imperative that they extinguish the lights in their homes when they leave." He warned that a blackout could be called at any time, and "there is always a possibility that the blackout is called for actual protection."

The article continues that "It is most regrettable that it was necessary to hail one man before the council for willful violation, following the blackout. He refused to cooperate when the warden asked him to extinguish the lights. When questioned he pleaded that he was administering to a sick child. He was released after a severe reprimand for not making such explanation to the warden, and was warned that a repetition of his refusal to cooperate would draw a fine and possibly a jail sentence, both of which may be imposed under the blackout ordinances passed by the city council."

The article concludes with praise of the air raid wardens and their lengthy training "for the protection of the people in their communities." Lack of cooperation and carelessness on the part of citizens "will be punishable by fine or jail sentences." Such provisions, warnings, and penalties may seem harsh and unnecessary from today's perspective, but they reflect the fear and anxiety of the period.

Wartime America was full of contradictions, such as the tug of war between sacrifice and generosity. Only too well I remember the shortage of sugar, and how at breakfast we watched other family members dip a spoon out of the sugar bowl for cereal. Even if no one said anything, we were all conscious of that *one*—never *two*—spoons of sugar, and whether it was level or heaping. The May 8, 1942 *Democrat* reported that "13,939 Register For Sugar During First Three Days." Nobody wanted to be deprived of their quota of sugar.

In spite of the scarcity of sugar, housewives used some of their precious sweetening to make cookies for soldiers. A short article in the March 17, 1944 *Democrat* details both this generosity, and the process by which they channeled their charity.

COOKIES FOR THE CAMP ELLIS HOSPITAL

Last week end the Ladies' Aid Society of the St. Paul's Lutheran Church made and donated twenty dozen cookies to the Hospital at Camp Ellis. The Red Cross is in charge of this work and at stated intervals each local chapter is asked to make this contribution. Karl Dierker, secretary of the Mason County chapter, was notified that last week was the time given this chapter and the Lutheran ladies very kindly furnished the entire amount required.

When these housewives baked and contributed twenty dozen cookies, actually their families were giving up some of their sugar ration. Every American knows that baking and eating cookies is a downhome good feeling.

Another heartwarming exercise in patriotism was acted out in *not* giving, in this case, valentines. A February 27, 1942 *Democrat* article is titled:

No Valentines At Golden Valley

It had been the custom at Golden Valley school in Pennsylvania township where Miss Leitha Jaggers is the teacher to observe St. Valentine's Day with an exchange of valentines. And there was always competition among the youngsters for the distinction of presenting the teacher with the nicest valentine.

Well, there was no exchange of valentines at Golden Valley this year, and the teacher had to be satisfied with verbal greetings from the children. It happened that the custom was dispensed with when the plan was under discussion and one of the youngsters suggested that the money they intended to spend for appropriate greetings be turned over to the Red Cross to swell the funds for War Relief. The result was that Mrs. Cal Singley, Red Cross chairman in Pennsylvania received $3.01 from the children.

A February 12, 1942 ad in the Democrat provides a positive recommendation to Valentine's Day, which is to give Defense Bonds. The graphic shows Cupid with a military helmet and a rifle, and a message below to buy bonds.

The way Valentine's Day became co-opted by the Red Cross and Defense Bonds is a good example of how thoroughly the war dominated people's lives. Even school children gave up their pennies instead of buying valentines. The collection of $3.01 may seem to be a paltry sum today, but it was all these students had, so in effect it amounted to everything.

Life in America during the war was pervaded by fear and tense blackouts and air raid drills, but also was the scene of generosity with cookies that were donated and valentines that were spoken rather than delivered.

CHAPTER 27

Cartoons and Submarines

Some wartime activities engaged the interests of both children and adults. People of all ages read cartoons. Usually cartoons are funny, yet they can also have their serious side. In the discussion of Little Orphan Annie, we saw that in her role as "Colonel Annie" she organized young people to collect scrap for the war drive. In her prewar days she played the underdog who rooted out corruption and crime. During the war she directed her wits and strategies against waste and unpatriotic citizens. In her color coding of houses on a city map, those who donated scrap received a blue mark, those who bought war stamps got a red mark. When Annie's volunteers asked what color they should use for a household that neither donated scrap nor bought war stamps, Annie had the answer. In a June 23, 1942 strip she said, "If they won't even <u>try</u> to help when our country needs th' help o' everyone? Why that's easy—for them we use a <u>yellow</u> mark." In war terminology, yellow meant coward, "chicken," or unpatriotic. Readers of Annie's antics could cheer on her recruits in their collection of scrap and jeer at those who did not pitch in. Vicariously assisting Annie in her patriotic pursuits gave people a sense of satisfaction.

Many examples of patriotism in the form of cartoons could be given, for many regular strips, and also in single images. Two *Democrat* cartoons took an encouraging tack at persuading people to purchase bonds. A June 12, 1942 cartoon depicts a handsome young man in a sport coat and bow tie, legs spread apart in a proud stance, proclaiming to his buxom lady friend, "Look! Li'l Lambpie—I'm buyin' *Defense Bonds* now through the payroll savings plan at the factory—ain't that super?" Her reply is "How darling!" A young girl walks up behind them waving her stamp book over her head, adding, "Look at my Defense Stamp Book."

A July 17, 1942 cartoon shows a tank moving from left to right across the frame. The sign on the side of the tank is "BUY A U.S. WAR

BOND TODAY!" An Indian chief stands in the turret of the tank with his hand raised, saying "C'mon, folks! Hop on um Bond-Wagon!!" Behind him with her hand raised is a young Indian maiden. Although it would be considered politically incorrect today, this is an attempt to show that all segments of society were behind the bond drives. The pun on bandwagon as bond-wagon added humor to a serious program.

A political cartoon on the front page of the September 11, 1942 issue of the *Democrat* is titled "We Can't Equal Their Sacrifices, but We Might Try." The cartoon features five slim panels stacked on top of each other like a layer cake. The uppermost panel shows the world as a globe, labeled "The Weight of the World's Greatest Tragedy," with the globe almost crushing Roosevelt, Churchill, and Stalin. Underneath that panel, the second panel shows a burning ship from which sailors are swimming and piling into a crowded lifeboat. The third panel is the scene of a military airport with soldiers surrounding a four-engine bomber ready to take off and join other bombers in the distance. The fourth panel depicts a battlefield with troops coming under fire. The fifth panel has the caption above it, "Even if we sacrificed EVERY-THING to buy more bonds we couldn't even the score." This final panel shows a line of civilians, young and old, men and women, marching across the scene clad only in wooden barrels. The "sacrificing EVERY-THING" means if all of us (WE-ALL) even gave up our clothes, we couldn't compare our efforts to the actions of those actually waging and directing the war. Instead of griping about our own sacrifices, we should make fun of ourselves and feel better about what we were giving up.

War could even become a kind of hobby, and frame the theme of a contest. The October 23, 1942 *Democrat* announced a "WAR SCRAP BOOK CONTEST," covering the period from "December 7, 1941 (Pearl Harbor) to and including December 7, 1942." All residents of Mason and Fulton Counties were eligible for this contest, with the entries "on exhibition at the Havana Public Library through the Christmas holidays." Three prizes ranged from a $25.00 War Bond to lesser amounts of War Stamps. The first anniversary of Pearl Harbor marked a fitting time to remember the war. The public exhibition was obviously intended to heighten awareness of the ongoing conflict and to promote War Bonds.

Even during the dark days of the war, people knew how to help wage the war and tickle their funny bones, all at the same time. The newspaper description of the "slave auction" held at the movie theatre for the War Bond Drive, quoted previously, is worth repeating here to show that people were aware of the dual purposes of the slave auction. "The people of Havana and surrounding territory will have a chance to help in winning the war, and at the same time enjoy themselves." In my elementary school, the combination of a snake dance with savings stamps celebrated the marriage of patriotism with entertainment.

Submarines in Illinois make for an intriguing topic. While in Havana in 2014, reading the microfilm edition of the *Democrat*, several days in a row I ate lunch at Grandpa's, a local restaurant. The young man behind the register, recognizing me as an out-of-towner, asked what brought me to Havana. I told him I was writing a book about Havana. When he wondered what I found interesting enough about this town to write a book, I said that most current residents did not know what happened here during the war. I asked him, "Did you know that during World War II, submarines came down the Illinois River?" He didn't answer me, the incredulous look on his face expressing his doubts. I told him that earlier in the morning I had found the January 1, 1943 and January 8, 1943 *Democrat* articles announcing a sub was on its way down the Illinois River, and then its passage through Havana.

Thirty submarines were built in Manitowoc, Wisconsin, tested in Lake Michigan, then floated on barges to the Chicago River and down the Illinois River to New Orleans, where they passed through the Panama Canal and on to the Pacific Ocean. Not only in Havana, but also in Chicago, where the subs left Lake Michigan to enter the Chicago River and then the Illinois River, few people today know about these subs. At the time of this writing, a veterans' group in Chicago is raising funds for a commemorative plaque along the Chicago River.

* * *

Submarines, maybe because of their silent and unseen underwater movement, have had a certain mystique about them, stimulating both fear and admiration. The first local mention of submarines during the war came in the January 16, 1942 *Democrat* headlines:

AXIS SUBMARINE ATTACKS TANKER
ONLY 60 MILES OFF EAST COAST

PART OF CREW RESCUED AFTER PANAMANIAN
TANKER "NORNESS" WAS TORPEDOED;
RAID BRINGS WAR NEAR U. S. SHORES

The war was brought perilously close to the shores of the United States Wednesday when Axis submarines attacked the tanker "Norness" 60 miles south of Montauk Point, Long Island. This is the closest approach yet made to the east coast by enemy warcraft since the entrance of the United States into the war, so far as it is known.

The German sub that sank a tanker so close to New York City caused anxiety up and down the East Coast, and sent shudders throughout America. In sharp contrast, the transit of an American sub right past Havana prompted a moment of pride and achievement. Enemy subs posed sinister threats, the objects of our fear and hatred. American subs represented agents of good against the forces of evil.

Although few remember it, a Japanese sub also made a trip across America. Not by water, but by truck. The Japanese attack on Pearl Harbor came mainly from aircraft carrier based fighters and bombers, especially torpedo bombers. Not so well known is the fact that the Japanese used five two-man submarines in the assault of U.S. ships at Pearl Harbor. Larger subs transported these midget subs to Hawaii, then released them near their target.

They have been called suicide subs, because they were "one-way" missions, propelled by electric motors, with battery power only sufficient for approaching enemy ships and shooting their two torpedoes. They carried no device for charging the batteries. Each sub had a scuttling charge for destroying the sub and its crew after the attack, which also might disable an enemy ship. These mini subs may have been responsible for helping sink American warships at Pearl Harbor. Several of the subs were known to be sunk; one was damaged and washed ashore on a reef. It was captured and became one of the first war trophies of World War II. The surviving crew member was one of the first Japanese prisoners.

In 1942 and 1943 the U.S. Treasury used this Japanese midget sub to promote war bond sales. A July 30, 1943 article tells of its coming appearance in Havana:

JAP SUBMARINE TO BE SHOWN HERE AUGUST 20
SUBMARINE CAPTURED AT PEARL
HARBOR ON TOUR OF U. S.

There is one ship of the Japanese Navy that is fighting every day against the warlords of Japan that built it. That is the two-man suicide submarine which will be exhibited in Havana on Friday, August 20, on a War Savings Tour of the 48 states. . . .

[The article briefly mentions the capture of the ship.]

Now the U. S. Treasury has borrowed it from the Navy and is using it to spark War Savings sales across the country, to raise money to buy torpedoes to fire at Tojo and ships to shoot them. The Japanese sneak boat has already become the country's star salesman of War Stamps and Bonds, with millions of dollars worth to its credit since it started on tour at San Francisco last Navy Day, October 27.

An August 6, 1943 article in the *Democrat* followed up on this story, giving more details of the exhibit. "Two very real looking 'Japanese' figures in authentic uniforms are at their battle stations. This trophy in all its ugly and instructive bearing—sneakish symbolic of our foe in the Pacific—has so stirred Americans that War Savings Bond and Stamp sales have averaged more than $22,000 for every hour the submarine has been exhibited. This Submarine in more ways than one has proven itself to be 'suicide' for the Japanese and in a good measure for Japan." This issue also included "a full page advertisement, sponsored by over 100 business and professional men, giving details of the visit of the Jap suicide submarine to Havana on Friday, August 20."

ILLUSTRATION BY JOHN MICHAEL DOWNS.

The sinister character of submarines has an aura of fantasy surrounding facts and reality. For example, the German saboteurs who landed on the East Coast (and later were executed) probably were brought there by submarines who approached land and then were sent ashore in small rubber inflatables. The presence of actual spies and saboteurs amidst us fanned the anxiety and fear that fueled campaigns of "Don't Talk," and "A Slip of the Lip Can Sink a Ship." A 1942 song performed by Duke Ellington reminded civilians that "A Slip of the Lip Might Sink a Ship." (The song is available on Youtube.)

Fear and suspicion haunted our lives and daily experience. My group of childhood friends was sure that the gypsy traveling through Havana had secret spy messages hidden in the horns of the goats pulling his wagon.

Fact and fantasy teamed up in a series of Little Orphan Annie cartoons, which have Annie locating, then blowing up three German submarines, and capturing spies trying to infiltrate America. Cartoon strips from April through July, 1943 portray Annie's victories. The very notion that submarines played a role in the drama of an inland Midwestern region like Havana and Mason County seems like the stuff of fiction. What was very real to the people of 1940s Havana may appear to contemporary residents as unreal, or even surreal.

* * *

Movies and advertisements illustrate two other examples of the tug of war between reality and fiction. Hollywood has been likened to the great American dream factory. During the war, the government recruited Hollywood to serve political purposes. On one hand it featured patriotic movies about the war; on the other hand it provided pure escape.

Close up of gypsy and his goats—we children suspected him of hiding secrets in the horns of the goats. ILLUSTRATION BY JOHN MICHAEL DOWNS.

On the patriotic side, Hollywood supplied films such as the 1943 *Destination Tokyo*, a thriller about an American submarine that managed to sneak into Tokyo Bay and help make the preparations for Doolittle's 1942 bombing of Tokyo. This mostly fictional film starred Cary Grant and earned an Oscar nomination for the writer Steve Fisher. An ad for *Destination Tokyo* shows the two main characters posed beside a huge torpedo. The text is: "John Garfield and Cary Grant in a scene from their new picture, 'Destination Tokyo.' A story of a submarine crew and their secret mission, coming to the Havana Theatre Sunday for four days." The Doolittle raid furnished a morale-boosting event for the Allied forces, who had suffered a long string of defeats. This movie portrayed Americans as outsmarting the Japanese by using the sinister weapon of a submarine.

Another patriotic movie described in a long article in the March 3, 1944 *Democrat* claims to be "the real thing."

HORROR OF WAR SHOWN IN ACTUAL TARAWA FILM

Modern war in all its appalling horror and devastation stalks across the screen of the Lawford Theatre Saturday, Sunday and Monday, for two terrifying reels and leaves you shaken, but exalted. The picture is "With the Marines At Tarawa," that much heralded factual record of the capture of the string of coral islands in the Pacific which the japs had built into a miniature Gibraltar, and which was taken by an American combined operations force late in November, 1943. Fictional war films seem pale beside the real thing in this picture.

Americans who are inclined to be complacent because of the success of the Allied cause during the past year, should be obliged to see "With the Marines at Tarawa." It shows what a gigantic task lies ahead of us to dig the Japs out of the empire they have established in the Pacific.

The article goes on to explain in great detail the weapons (including flame throwers and torpedoes) and armament needed to flush out the Japanese. "Practically all the 4000 Jap defenders were killed. Just under 3500 Marines were killed and wounded." This is not exactly "feel good" entertainment, but the article says we should see it out of duty to our country and expect to be "shaken but exalted."

Hollywood, as usual, turned out comic fare and humor as well as more serious work and documentaries. An ad in the March 17, 1944 *Democrat* features two films of a lighter nature. *Sailor's Holiday* is about "3 sea wolves on leave . . . and on the <u>prowl</u>." The picture of a scantily clad beauty with a heart-shaped hat is flanked by three handsome men in uniform and military caps. *Rookies in Burma* has no descriptive text, but the two smiling men suggests that these "rookies" are having a good time. Love, sex, and humor always sell, in peace and in war. Documentary films capture the reality of war we must face. Humor and romance allow us to temporarily escape from the death and destruction of the battleground.

Advertisements in newspapers and other media aim to inform the public about products and services, and to persuade people to make use of them. Companies and businesses may also spend their money for civic purposes, such as to promote charities. During World War II, advertisers linked civic duty to patriotic motivation in much of their published material. Here are some examples from the *Democrat.*

The full page ad announcing the exhibition of the captured Japanese two-man sub, "sponsored by over 100 business and professional men," illustrates the extent of civic and patriotic duty. The only "payback" one could expect from such an ad was name recognition from the listing of the sponsors. Another previous example is an ad designed primarily to promote a product (gasoline), and only secondarily aid the military and the war effort. This was the advertisement for D-X gasoline, which supposedly "stretches your gasoline coupons." Some ads offered fifty-fifty propositions, promoting a business and its products while advocating patriotism and support for the war (especially War Bonds).

By far the most frequent patriotic ad in the *Democrat* during the war years was the weekly posting by the Havana National Bank, with the same recommendation: "BUY U.S. DEFENSE BONDS AND STAMPS at THE HAVANA NATIONAL BANK." Here the name of the business is directly associated with a patriotic program. In a small town, everyone knew the president of the bank, the head of several bond drive committees; he was a World War I veteran and an active member of the American Legion.

Ads published locally might originate elsewhere. An early 1942 ad portrays Uncle Sam with his raised fingers forming a "V" against a backdrop of soldiers, tanks, and airplanes under construction. The text proclaims "TWO GREAT ARMIES now serving America for <u>Victory</u>. In which great army will You serve your country?" The American Aircraft Institute in Chicago placed this ad for applicants to their training program for "aircraft plants now building the planes necessary to blow Hitlerism and the barbarous Japs off the face of the earth." The ad seeks to recruit workers while voicing a political and military agenda.

Advertisements need not be for immediate sales and promotions, but directed at future prospects. Nationally circulated magazines told an important story about why "for the duration," domestic products were not available, because factories had shifted from household and personal goods to military materiel. Nevertheless, companies wanted to keep their brand alive for the time being, so that after the war, when domestic production resumed, loyal customers would return to them.

This line of explanation was set forth by the Illinois Central System in a May 1, 1942 *Democrat* commercial, "WAR SETS *NEW* TEST FOR RAILROADS." It tells customers that the War Production Board shifted manufacture of railway equipment to military materiel: "It was a choice between guns and transportation." The ad asks for the patience and understanding of people, because "We all realize and agree that the needs of war come first—in transportation, as in everything else."

The "we all" is an important phrase that civic/patriotic announcements and advertisements repeated over and over. We are all pulling together to fight the war. We should not complain about the local committees in charge of regulations and deferments. We should not rail against the regulators and administers of rationing, because "we all" are in this together. We should not hold it against the local merchant who does not have products for sale. We are all in this fight.

In a February 20, 1942 ad, "Reddy Kilowatt, your electrical servant," in effect the mascot of the Central Illinois Public Service Company, tells people "DEFENSE NEEDS YOUR HELP." He urges everyone to "preserve existing appliances—help win the victory." By keeping appliances in tip-top shape, we will be "insuring the continuance of . . . present living standards for the duration." Both nationally and locally, businesses asked customers to be patient "for the duration," and then resume life (and business) as usual after the end of the war.

Even the local newspaper got in this act, especially in a large October 2, 1942 ad:

Every Employee of This Newspaper
Is a Homefront Soldier in the

FIGHT TO WIN—VICTORY

While America's planes, ships and armed forces smash
at the enemy with fighting machines and manpower—
America's men and women employed at turning out your
daily newspaper—smash at the enemy on the homefront
with the machines that bring forth the written word, and
with the power of a Free Press!

YOUR NEWSPAPER GOES ALL
OUT FOR VICTORY.

Every aspect of printed and visual media, from cartoons and movies—both fictional and documentary—to advertising and editorials,
provided a combination of information, propaganda, and entertainment
centered around the war. Even the horrors of war, such as those seen
in the Tarawa documentary, were described as leaving us "shaken but
exalted." The countrywide tour of the captured miniature Japanese sub
was turned into a spectacle that enabled the spectators to vicariously
participate in the attack on Pearl Harbor, to triumph over the capture
of the sub, and then to perform their patriotic duty by buying bonds
to avenge the attack. The events of the war surrounded us and drew
us into its drama, both on the international warfront and on the local
scene of the homefront.

CHAPTER 28

The USO: Coffee, Cookies, and Dancing

The United States did not suffer from the widespread bombing and devastation that World War II brought to much of Europe and Asia. The attack on Pearl Harbor shocked the country, and the Japanese fought a losing battle on several Alaskan islands, but the United States mainland escaped the scars of war. Except for a few shells and balloon bombs on the West Coast, America's homes, factories, stores, civic centers, and religious buildings remained unscathed. In Havana and across the country, people on the homefront kept busy in many programs to support the warfront.

The local newspaper reported in detail these civilian efforts to help "our boys." The journalistic accounts of these patriotic activities offer a series of snapshots of how people in American contributed to the war effort. These articles provide a kind of picture album of the homefront in its varied but united endeavors to back the military.

Of all the wartime activities, events, and programs described in the *Democrat,* the USO ranked as the most unambiguously and whole-heartedly do-good and feel-good affair. Most of the larger cities and even small towns surrounding Camp Ellis designated a building for USO services that supplied recreation, entertainment, and food to soldiers, especially on weekends. The *Camp Ellis News* printed detailed lists of times for "Latest Train And Bus Schedules To And From Camp Ellis, Macomb, Lewistown, Canton, Havana, Peoria, and Chicago."

In Havana the location of the USO was the Riverside Club, which originally had been a private home, and then changed hands serving various civic groups before becoming the USO. The success of this facility is heralded in a September 3, 1943 *Democrat* article:

MORE THAN 1000 VISIT USO HERE IN PAST WEEK
POPULARITY OF SERVICE MEN'S
CENTER IS INCREASING

During the past week more than 1,000 soldiers have called at the local USO and enjoyed the services available there. Starting with only a very small number on week ends when Camp Ellis was first opened, the number of men visiting here has increased steadily. Havana is generally accepted as the favorite place of recreation of the Camp Ellis soldiers and the friendly home-like atmosphere of the USO has drawn many favorable comments from the boys who visit it.

If the number of men who patronize the unit here continues to grow in the same proportion as it has since the camp was opened, the present facilities will soon be outgrown. . . .

Those serving on the committees are doing an excellent work and are deserving of the thanks of the entire community. The way the boys are received at the USO influences their opinion of the community and there is none of us but what want these boys to know we appreciate what they are doing for us.

Even if allowances are made for hometown pride and enthusiastic reporting, the committees and staff at the USO were certain they were doing good, and the "boys" seemed to thoroughly enjoy themselves.

An April 7, 1944 article in the *Democrat* reported "Open House to be Held at USO Here April 14. . . . The people of Havana are invited to visit the old Riverside club building on that date and learn what has been done for the comfort and convenience of the men in uniform who visit the city." Among the services provided were a snack bar and "free cookies and coffee at all times." The article states that "There were times during the past summer when as many as 3000 boys passed through the center in a week. . . ."

The *Camp Ellis News* in an October 27, 1944 article reported:

HALLOWEEN PARTY IN HAVANA TOMORROW

Ellismen are invited to attend a special Halloween party and dance to be held at the Havana USO tomorrow night, announces Beulah M. Hurley, director of the Havana club. Junior hostesses of the club will be on hand to act as dancing partners.

The Havana USO was not just a stationary service, as indicated by this February 23, 1945 short item in the *Democrat:*

Havana USO

The St. Paul's Lutheran church ladies were in charge of the Snack Bar at the local USO on Sunday, February 18.

Sunday afternoon eighteen of the junior hostesses with Mrs. Margarita Harsman and Miss Edith Dieffenbacher visited the convalescents in the hospital at Camp Ellis. Cards and ping-pong were enjoyed until five o'clock when the hostesses were invited to the patients' mess hall for a cafeteria supper.

At six-thirty the government bus transported the girls to the Service Club No. 1 to the tea dance which ended at nine o'clock.

The USO provided free coffee and tea as well as snacks ("for a nominal fee") at its Havana facility, and at Camp Ellis not only hospital visits and recreation, but also hostesses for dancing. And, apparently, a good time was had by all.

The hometown newspaper reports about the Havana USO were bound to be favorably inclined to their own facility, but the *Camp Ellis News* lavished praise for the hospitality found here. An August 18, 1944 issue of the camp paper highlighted Havana in its "Where To Go—What To Do In Camp Ellis Vicinity." The lead sentence of the article begins, "Mrs. Beulah M. Hurley, USO Director in Havana, and mother of two sons in the service, will tell you in her soft, quiet way that the Illinois River misses its sons—the countless hundreds now in service who made a bedlam of the river front. . . ." After a description of the boating and swimming facilities, the article continues that "For many soldiers this river town has been their second home. It has fine eating and dancing spots, excellent boating and fishing and fair swimming. . . ." After describing the various swimming and eating spots, the reporter states that "Lots of soldiers spend Saturday nights in Havana and a great many of them sleep in a dormitory at the city hall which is sponsored by the USO. The dorm can accommodate 75 men and reservations should be made in advance at the USO. Cost is 35 cents. The USO, which is located on a hill overlooking the river right off the main drag, is one of the most home-like servicemen's centers in the camp area." Other overnight facilities, scenic sites such as Chautauqua Wild Life Refuge, and eating places ("A Mecca for Epicures") are mentioned.

This report by the soldiers who actually visited Havana and used the USO confirms the local accounts of its efficiency and popularity.

Wartime Havana also knew pure entertainment and relaxation, with the compliments of Camp Ellis. An October 8, 1943 article in the *Democrat* gives high praise to talented G. I. performers.

CAPACITY AUDIENCE HEARD CAMP ELLIS ARTISTS SEPT. 30

MUSICAL PROGRAM WAS PRESENTED BY THE U. & I. CLUB

A vast and appreciative audience which filled every available space in the auditorium and lecture room of the Methodist Church greeted the musicians from Camp Ellis Thursday evening when the Music Department of the Utility and Interest Club, with Mrs. Henry Wehner, chairman, presented the first program of the club. . . .

Private Albert Gillis, a graduate of the Juilliard School, is a brilliant young violinist. He thrilled his audience in the Corelli and the Brahms Sonatas by his surety of tone and perfect bowing. . . .

It is ironic that Havana, which in the 1940s had almost no exposure to classical music, would be provided with cultural enrichment from a nearby army training facility. Camp Ellis had its own symphony orchestra that played in regional cities, and was the only Army installation in the U.S. with its own radio network. The Ellismen also created and performed their own musicals, much appreciated both by their fellow troops and by the people of the surrounding cities. Bordner wrote in her memory of that time, "I recall a long-running extravaganza called BY THE NUMBERS, and servicemen performed their various talents for shows on the base and also, the show went on weekends to Macomb, Lewistown, Galesburg, Springfield, Peoria, etc." They had talented vocalists and pianists.

From classical sonatas to popular ballads and musicals, Camp Ellis provided great musical entertainment. Bordner wrote, "What a treat it was to just be part of such talent! Some said the military services were just a cross-section of our society; I firmly believe they were the cream of our society, chosen for having passed standards set, both physically and mentally."

It is difficult to sum up the totality of wartime experience in Havana and central Illinois. Many have quoted General William Tecumseh

Sherman of Civil War fame, that "War is Hell." Both my personal memory and the record of the local newspaper confirm the truth of Sherman's judgment. We cannot claim the opposite, that war is fun. Such a statement would trivialize a serious matter. But it is obvious to me that all people who live through war make sure they have fun. Whether in military service or civilian walks of life, or even in prisoner of war camps, people find ways of enjoying themselves. This was true of the trainees, civilians, and even POWs at Camp Ellis.

The USO defined a "feel good" win-win situation. It let local people contribute to the war effort. At the same time, the USO provided downhome comfort to soldiers with its coffee, cookies, and dancing.

CHAPTER 29

A Flag, New Shoes, and Blisters

When we lived at Grandma's house, except for the daily routine of work and school, and eating and sleeping, the single most important thing in our minds was the fact that Daddy had gone off to war. Families who had a member in the armed forces put a small flag in the window with a star on it. Our flag for Daddy hung in a west window of the parlor facing Railroad Street, where it could be seen by passersby. The flag was a display of pride, and a sign of hope, like lighting a candle and leaving it in the window to guide a loved one back home.

This small flag was similar to the large flags in churches. Of course, a gold star meant that the family member would not be returning. "Gold star mothers" were women who had lost a son. Women also served in the military, for example the WAACs in the Army and the WAVEs in the Navy, but women did not serve in combat and few women lost their lives in World War II. Unfortunately, with the succession of military actions since World War II, the deaths of armed forces personnel has created more gold star mothers. At the time of writing this book, the American Gold Star Mothers, Inc. is an active group of women who have lost sons or daughters in service of the country.

Every day of the year the war was in our minds, but one day was dedicated solely to war, the boys in the service, and the ones who had served or died in the military. Memorial Day during World War II counted as one of the key holidays of the year, certainly the highlight of civic and patriotic pride. The entire city, from the mayor to the school children, and all civic groups, participated. The most prominent organization, of course, was the American Legion.

Children from Havana's three outlying elementary schools, Oak Grove, Riverview, and Rockwell, formed long lines and marched to the center of town. Usually we received two items before the march, and acquired another by the end of the march. Our parents, if at all possible, bought us a new pair of shoes for the parade. The school provided each child with a flag to hold during the march. By the end of the day the stiff new shoes had given most of us blisters where they rubbed the back of our heels. We marched in classes with our teachers, to show by our presence that we honored the war dead of the past and supported the boys in the service.

Havana, incorporated as a city, is also the county seat, with a square block of the downtown reserved for county buildings. In the 1940s, majestic Dutch elms made "the square" a lovely cool place in summer. This lovely park setting was the initial gathering place for Memorial Day. Students from the outlying elementary schools, and also the nearby junior high and high school students, assembled on the streets and grass of this public space.

In the square were only several buildings, set back from the street. The main court building stood in the center, reached by diagonal sidewalks from each corner or several other walks from sides of the square. These brick buildings were surrounded by towering trees, their branches stretching out to form a canopy. In summer the ground formed a huge green square cut into a geometric panorama of different shapes and sizes by the intersecting sidewalks. Park benches by the edge of the sidewalk bordered the street on all four sides. The park benches were the old fashioned wrought iron kind with carved backs, painted dark green but showing the scars of many years of scraping and painting.

This tribute to Civil War Soldiers of 1861–1865 highlights the fact that Illinois is the "Land of Lincoln," and that for the Midwest the Civil War is more of a defining period than the Revolutionary War. AUTHOR'S PHOTO.

This memorial honors the veterans of World War I. In the 1930s and 1940s the American Legion was filled with local men who had served in the "Great War." During World War II they were instrumental in heading many committees for the benefit of the war effort and soldiers, from Red Cross to bond drives to scrap drives. AUTHOR'S PHOTO.

On weekdays, people walked in and out of the county and court buildings, and the "old timers" would find a shady park bench to sit on while they smoked and talked. On summer evenings a vendor with a makeshift trailer sold peanuts, popcorn, and even hot tamales.

A number of monuments decorated the lawn. Granite markers and pillars honored the soldiers and sailors of the Civil War, the War of 1812, and World War I. The Revolutionary War might be remembered, and certainly honored in speeches, but Havana had been settled in the early 1800s, so its people did not directly participate in the nation's founding war. What the Revolutionary War is for New England, the Civil War is for the Midwest: the memory of Lincoln overshadows that of Washington.

On Memorial Day, as large groups of students and civic and veterans groups converged on the square, flowers awakened these sleeping monuments which became the temporary center of attention. Cannons and artillery pieces, the unmelted scrap of former battles, provided year-round but silent reminders of America's wars. Volleys fired from the rifles of aging veterans gave these battlefield relics surrogate voices. Never mind that these rifles had no targets and fired blanks: this was a day to remember, commemorate, and memorialize war and its warriors.

Assembled on the square, we school children watched and listened as school and city leaders read the litany of wars, from the Revolutionary War through the Civil War and the Great War down to the present, "our boys over there in Europe and in the Pacific." These speakers devoted more time to the greatest of America's fallen heroes,

Lincoln, who paid the supreme sacrifice to unite the country. Then the heads of various civic groups laid wreaths and flowers at each of the monuments to honor the men who had served in the armed forces to protect the union that Lincoln gave his life to hold together.

This ceremony climaxed as the American Legion members pointed their World War I vintage rifles at the sky and fired, saluting not only the troops of the first and second world wars, but also the forces in the Civil War and the American Revolution.

We children, lined up near the rifle squad, knew the shots were coming, but couldn't help flinching. Although I was used to the "tunk" sound of my BB gun, I couldn't brace myself for the multiple firings, a deafening roar that assaulted our eardrums. Some boys and girls put their hands over their ears. I loved my BB gun, which was fun. But I

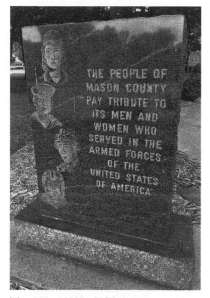

This World War II Tribute commemorates all who served in the war, even honoring a woman as one of the faces of the military. The monument is at the northwest corner of the courthouse square. AUTHOR'S PHOTO.

Americans did not honor veterans of the Korean and Vietnam conflicts as they did the servicemen of the two world wars. Havana and Mason County, like other parts of the country, have come to commemorate these veterans alongside those of earlier wars. AUTHOR'S PHOTO.

hated the American Legion volley, which seemed to tear through my heart and foretell the death of my father.

The first few paragraphs of the May 28, 1943 *Democrat* preview of the Memorial Day program give the gist of this solemn occasion:

CO. HONOR ROLL TO BE DEDICATED MEMORIAL DAY

The Mason County Honor Roll, located at the south entrance of the court house, that was erected a short time ago, will be dedicated Sunday in connection with the Memorial Day program. This attractive panel, constructed to hold 1,500 names, is a project of the Business and Professional Women's club of Havana, and a committee of that organization has worked with a committee of Havana Post, the American Legion, in arranging the program.

The dedication of the Honor Roll which contains approximately 1,000 names at the present time, will be handled by Havana post with Herb Borgelt delivering the address.

MEMORIAL DAY SERVICES

The Memorial Day services will be conducted along the same lines as has been followed in the past. A parade led by the Havana School Band will mark the beginning of the services. Marching will be members of the American Legion Post, The American Legion Auxiliary, the Relief Corps, the school children, members of the Business and Professional Women's club, Boy Scouts and other patriotic and civic groups.

After the ceremonies in the town square, some of the people went by car to Laurel Hill Cemetery. There, members of civic groups put new flags on the graves of veterans. The older graves were for World War I soldiers, but an increasing number of new graves kept company with the fallen martyrs of World War II. The sight of the new flags on these graves made me think of the lines of the poem about French burial grounds we memorized in school:

> "In Flanders fields the poppies blow,
> Between the crosses, row on row."

I didn't know it at the time, but some of that Memorial Day crowd must have gone to the Catholic Cemetery at the south end of town. In my teen years, I took my rifle with friends and went "plinking" in the countryside, walking past this other cemetery. As an elementary school

Harry Tarvin, a Vietnam veteran who owns and runs an appliance business in Havana, has devoted the storefronts of his several buildings as a tribute to veterans. He began with honoring Vietnam veterans, but then expanded the exhibition to photos of all who had served their country in other wars. The location of these buildings is on North Plum Street, facing the west side of the courthouse and the Civil War Tribute. AUTHOR'S PHOTO.

child I only knew of the Laurel Hill Cemetery, and wasn't aware of a religious separation of the dead, Protestant and Catholic.

Havana was not racially, religiously, or economically diverse. In the early 1940s it was all White, although a Chinese family had run a laundry there until the late 1930s. Havana was divided religiously mainly as Protestant and Catholic. I knew of just one Jewish family. Economically the only gap was between manual laborers and clerks at the lower end, farmers and small businessmen in the middle, and

Harry Tarvin, standing next to the side of his storefront honoring veterans other than from Vietnam; Kenneth Earhart's photo in Navy uniform is one of the pictures in this display. The opposite side honors Vietnam veterans. AUTHOR'S PHOTO.

a small number of professionals. Memorial Day unified these various divisions as a unified patriotic force.

Ordinarily, Catholics and Protestants didn't venture into each other's churches, even for weddings and funerals. My own Baptist Church wasn't sure about the Christian status of Catholics, and looked down on the Holy Rollers. However, on Memorial Day, religious groups set aside all differences, because on that day we linked our living spirits with the dead spirits of American wars, in support of the thousand servicemen in the military whose names were listed on the recently erected panel.

My childhood memories of Memorial Day are filtered through the Protestant perceptions of our Baptist Grandmother and Methodist parents, at a time when Laurel Hill Cemetery also included gravesites for Catholics. To supplement my limited viewpoint, on a recent trip to Havana, I visited several other cemeteries. The Catholic cemetery, known as St. Charles' Cemetery for St. Patrick's Catholic Church, is located on the south edge of town, next to the Neteler Cemetery. Both sites included graves for civil war veterans. One grave honored two civil war men and a woman. Each man was identified by his Illinois infantry unit. The inscription for the woman announced "their wife." From the dates on the tombstone, it appears that the woman married one ex-infantryman, and when he passed away, married another ex-infantryman. She is credited with membership in W.R.C., the Womans Relief Corps, the female auxiliary to the Grand Army of the Republic, a veterans group for military on the union side. A nearby grave had a bronze marker, "Womans Relief Corps," the same local unit as for the woman identified as "their wife." In the *Mason County Democrat* article reporting on Memorial Day, this group is called simply "the Relief Corps." These markers are permanent reminders that women have been supporters of men in the military in earlier times. My mother was a longtime member of the American Legion Auxiliary. She and my father sold poppies for the American Legion every Memorial Day until they were in their nineties.

I also visited Fullerton Cemetery, on North Promenade in Havana. This cemetery, active from 1835 to 1893, was also known as Old Soldiers Cemetery. There I located one gravestone from a civil war veteran which had a circular blue badge on it, "U.S. Veteran." These cemeteries attest to the fact that in Havana and central Illinois, the military, religion, and country have stood united over the ages.

Some scholars have interpreted Memorial Day as a celebration of America's cult of the dead, honoring all who served in the nation's military conflicts. As a boy during wartime, I experienced it more concretely as a flag, new shoes, and blisters.

CHAPTER 30

1,760,000 Baskets of Dirt

Memories of summer evenings when we lived at Grandma's house remind me of the fun and games and playing around that make childhood something precious to look back to. Because nightfall came so late with Daylight Saving Time (renamed as War Time), giving us several hours between supper and bedtime, we could make a real excursion. It was almost as if we had another day for playing with friends.

Riverfront Park, nearby and handy, ranked as one of our favorite places, because we could be there and back in a few minutes. On long summer evenings we had time to walk the eight blocks to Rockwell School. We liked the school because it had good playground equipment. We were supposed to be home by dark.

I remember receiving an impromptu English lesson from a girl some years older than me while we played on the swings at Rockwell Park. I told her it would soon be getting dark, and my sisters and I should be heading home. For me there was day and there was night, and that was that. But this wise girl corrected me: no, first came dusk, and then twilight. Dusk is the light at the end of the day, and twilight is the faint afterglow.

I can't recall her exact definitions, but will never forget being introduced to those two lovely words, dusk and twilight. She taught me spiritual terms opening up new realities. Even today, when I listen to Mendelssohn's "A Midsummer Night's Dream," the vision that floats into my mind is that glorious summer day when I first became aware of the magical thresholds that usher us from day to night.

On some of those wonderful, seemingly endless summer evenings, a group of us would agree to meet in Rockwell Park. From Grandma's house we could either follow Railroad Street north along the river and enter at the west side of Rockwell Park, or go one block east on Market

Street and then five blocks due north on Orange Street, arriving at the formal entrance of the park, marked by a stone wall and a set of concrete steps leading up a slight hill to an open-air pavilion. The park was a gently rounded hill with level areas to the west and north for picnic grounds and some playground equipment.

When we went to Rockwell Park, we enjoyed most making up games, not using the playground equipment. The pavilion had stairs up the south and north, the long sides of the rectangular building. A wooden bench extended around the inside perimeter. Above the benches was a wide railing interrupted by posts supporting the roof. We played all kinds of tag in this building, jumping up on the benches. The more daring walked on the railing from post to post, risking a fall on the concrete sidewalk around the pavilion. We joked with each other. "Watch out, you'll break your neck." It became a natural place for a kind of "king of the hill" game, being at the top of the hill, above the floor of the pavilion.

A recent trip to the site invoked recollections of Rockwell Park. When I parked my car along the curb in front of the south entrance, an older woman sweeping her sidewalk on Orange Street paused and stood up straight to eye me suspiciously. She may have seen my out-of-state license plates, and with no kids accompanying me, must have wondered what I was doing at the park. I had stopped to read a historical marker donated and erected by the local Church of the Latter Day Saints (Mormons). One reason I wanted to revisit this childhood playground was because I had heard that this was not simply a park, and the hill was not really a *natural* hill, it was in fact a Native American mound.

The site had been surveyed by digging test holes, and although not completely excavated, was shown to have been constructed

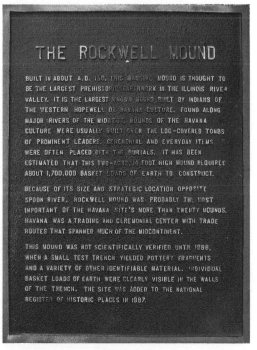

This sign commemorates the building of a Native American mound with 1,700,000 baskets of dirt. AUTHOR'S PHOTO.

as an artificial mound. Archaeologists even found the imprints of the baskets of dirt the Native Americans had used to build the mound. By measuring the approximate contents of one basket, and estimating the total volume of the mound, they concluded it took 1,760,000 baskets of dirt to heap up this mound, with mud from the nearby riverbank. The mound contained some burials, but its main purpose had probably been to serve as a ceremonial meeting ground. Rockwell Park is on the north side of Havana, opposite the mouth of Spoon River. Apparently, Native Americans converged here from north and south by way of the Illinois River, and from the west via Spoon River.

It is inspiring and humbling to think that hundreds of years ago many Native Americans toiled long and hard to carry almost two million baskets of dirt from the bank of the Illinois River to form this mound. Reflecting on this enormous achievement makes me feel ambiguous about Rockwell Park and its pavilion. It gives me a sense of historic connection to have been on this hill that had been of such momentous significance to the Native Americans of the surrounding area.

It also makes me sad and ashamed that we treated it simply as a playground for king of the hill, but it was once a ceremonial and burial mound. In our own Memorial Day services in Havana we honored the military dead with solemnity. At Laurel Hill Cemetery on Memorial Day or on other visits, Mom and Grandma always said, "Never walk on a grave—it's not showing respect for the dead." At Rockwell Park we had not just walked over the Native American dead, we played games, and ran all over them. Of course, we didn't know it at the time, so we weren't intentionally disrespectful. But all the same, we trod on the sacred ground of others.

An irony of this story is that just a few miles west and north of Rockwell Park across the Illinois River, is a famous mound that everyone in the region knows, Dickson Mound. In the early part of the twentieth century a family of chiropractors by the name of Dickson bought land known to be burial grounds, and began to systematically excavate the mound, eventually opening the site to the public, later selling it to the State of Illinois.

Hilly areas surround Dickson Mound; some of this land, the western bluffs of the Illinois River Valley, was planted in apples. Every fall our family drove there to buy apples and cider. During the summer we often picnicked on the grounds of the Dickson Mounds State Park, and went to see the Native American skeletons. School trips also went there. (The

Dickson family that owned the land and excavated the burials called the site "Dickson Mound"; later when it became a state park, it was named Dickson Mounds.)

In the 1990s, a number of Native American groups protested this public display of their ancestors' bones and burial objects, as offensive and even sacrilegious. After all, what would White people think if Native Americans dug up the bones of White people and put them in a public exhibition? How would the people of Havana react if this happened to Laurel Hill Cemetery and the Catholic Cemetery?

Having studied some Native American culture and religion, I can appreciate the fact that these first Americans have too long been exploited, and rightfully wish to reclaim their own past. But as I think back over the many times during the half century that I visited this burial mound, not once can I recall an instance of disrespect. For me, and for the people I knew who visited the mound, this was a rare chance to come into contact with the earliest Americans, the ones who farmed and fished here long before the coming of the white man and the "discovery" of America.

In the late 1940s I camped with Boy Scouts at Dickson Mound. Dr. Dickson, son of the Dickson who opened the site, gave us a guided tour. He even accepted my invitation

DICKSON MOUND

Looking north to Mound Building
from new road

◄ • ◉ • ►

Greatest Display
of
STONE AGE MAN
in
THE WORLD
230 Skeletons
Left in Original Positions

This image is a photo of the front of a brochure given to us when the author and his family visited the private "Dickson Mound" in the 1970s, and viewed the open burial. An inside page of the brochure includes a photo of the open burial from this time period; it is not reproduced here because at the present time it is considered disrespectful to show photos of remains. THANKS TO DAVID C. EARHART FOR PERMISSION TO REPRODUCE THIS PHOTO.

to eat a meal I cooked for him at our campsite on a neighboring hill. We Boy Scouts considered it an honor to be guided and taught about Native Americans by the famous excavator. In our more serious moments as scouts we saw ourselves borrowing from the ways and wisdom of the first Americans.

In the 1980s and 1990s when Native Americans stepped up their protest of the public exhibition of burials at Dickson Mounds, first the governor of Illinois closed the site. Then the people of Fulton County protested, because Dickson Mounds had become an anchor site for local tourism in the Spoon River Drive, a combination of fall colors, local crafts and produce, the charm of Edgar Lee Masters (of *Spoon River Anthology* fame), and the romantic mystery of the ancient inhabitants of Illinois. So the governor reopened the site. The final compromise was for the archaeologists and anthropologists to make their last photographic records, and then to carefully rebury—in place—these bones and artifacts. Illinois newspapers reported this issue at length. (Those who wish to see earlier photographs of the open burial can Google "Dickson Mounds" and go to "images of Dickson Mounds." Pictures of the museum, and a scene of Dr. Dickson removing dirt from a skeleton are on the Dickson Mounds Museum website, at the time of this writing.)

This site, buried for centuries, partially unearthed and exposed for more than a half century, is now reburied for who knows how long. We must honor these people's wish for their ancestors to be treated with respect. And yet I wonder what is the best way to introduce the people of Havana and Fulton County, and the rest of the country, to these ancient Americans.

At Rockwell Park the historical marker mentions not only the pre-Columbian formation of the mound, but also its most important post-Columbian event, a debate held there between Stephen Douglas and Abraham Lincoln on August 13 and 14, 1858 during the campaign for a U.S. senate seat. Abraham Lincoln lost that election, but later became president.

This political debate was not a religious ritual, but certainly qualified as a more proper activity than fun and games on the site of a Native American ceremonial center created by 1,760,000 baskets of dirt.

CHAPTER 31

"Turn the Lights Out!"

During the war, when Daddy was in Seattle, we were proud that he was being patriotic and protecting his country. After he shipped out of Bremerton, Washington, on the battleship USS Missouri, mail from him became sporadic. Our pride turned to fear when he served on a huge ship somewhere in the Pacific, risking his life fighting the Japanese. No one in the military could give details of their location or activities. The government warned civilians to be suspicious of spies, saboteurs, and sabotage. Every child knew the famous motto: "A slip of the lip can sink a ship."

What little we knew of our father's whereabouts and activities, did not satisfy our hunger for more information. He could only give us the bare facts of his duty, that he was in charge of the galley for his ship. As Midwesterners, we had no conception of a galley on a ship. He explained it was the kitchen for the whole ship, preparing huge amounts of food for the crew, and they cooked in large vats. Such information was interesting but unimportant. We wanted to know if he was safe, and if he would survive the war.

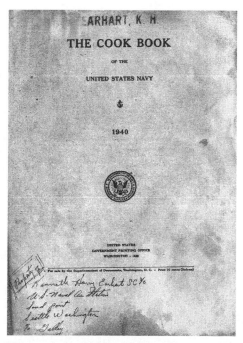

This is the title page of the 1940 navy cook book our father used while on the USS Missouri. His handwriting is in the lower left corner. FAMILY COLLECTION.

Not until 2004 was I able to take my elderly mother and father on a tour of the USS Midway, which had been converted to a floating museum in San Diego. Dad was confined to a wheelchair, but insisted that we help Mom down a flight of stairs to the galley so that she could see the kind of place where he had served. We were impressed with the huge mixers that stood more than five feet high, as well as the enormous vats heated with steam. Dad was pleased that finally his wife could see what he had told her about many times. We ate on the fantail of the ship and consumed the USS Midway's version of SOS (shit on the shingle, chipped beef on toast).

A souvenir of that trip was the book *Beef Stew for 2500: Feeding Our Navy from the Revolutionary War to the Present.* This historical survey of Navy cuisine includes many photos of the modern galleys. Their monumental vats are eye-openers for landlubbers who have never been on Navy ships. The recipes are mind-boggling. The recipe for "Beef Stew for 2500" calls for 630 lbs. beef, 8.5 lbs. salt, 11.25 oz. pepper, 33.75 lbs. flour, 33.75 lbs. fat, plus enormous amounts of other ingredients.

In 2008, after my parents had passed away, my wife and I visited Pearl Harbor, going to the USS Arizona memorial, and then boarding

General MacArthur signing the surrender on the deck of the USS Missouri.
IMAGE COURTESY OF NATIONAL ARCHIVES (DEPARTMENT OF DEFENSE, DEPART-
MENT OF THE NAVY, NAVAL PHOTOGRAPHIC CENTER).

This local newspaper clipping highlights the USS Missouri and the surrender, adding a final paragraph about Kenneth H. Earhart being present at this historic event. FAMILY COLLECTION.

the USS Missouri. The most historic site on the Missouri is the location on deck where the Japanese signed the surrender on September 2, 1945. For me, two other points of interest stood out. On deck, a bent railing marked the spot where a Japanese plane, a kamikaze, struck the ship, but for some reason did not explode. If it had blown up, the whole ship could have gone down, my father with it. Dad received a card authenticating

his being stationed on the USS Missouri at the time of the surrender.

The main interest for me was the galley area below deck. It was a great experience to walk around the huge vats and other food preparation and cooking equipment, realizing that during the war, my father had managed this operation.

Facsimile of the card Dad received for being stationed on the USS Missouri at the time of surrender. FAMILY COLLECTION.

Some of Dad's reminiscences were not so pleasant. He told us that the flour was always infested with bugs. When sailors ate bread, they routinely held a slice up toward a light, to pick out the insect protein before taking a bite of the bread.

The most interesting anecdote my father told us had nothing directly to do with the war or cooking. He supervised food preparation and the sailors who had their specific jobs in handling food and serving meals. Few people today know about the wartime race riots, both in cities such as Detroit and within the military. Minorities, especially African-Americans, were treated as second-class citizens, but during the war they gradually gained more access to meaningful jobs.

My father supervised the galley workers who were a mix of White and African-American men. In line with the general pattern in 1940s America, the "colored" (to use the contemporary term) were designated as porters and servers in Navy galleys. The White sailors were assigned to specific tasks such as baking and cooking. From time to time there was friction between the two races.

On one occasion, to resolve this untenable situation, my father called everyone in the galley together for an announcement. When all his subordinates were assembled, he turned to the man near the light switch, and ordered, "Turn the lights out!" This man objected, saying if he

"Turn the lights out!" ILLUSTRATION BY JOHN MICHAEL DOWNS.

did, it would be pitch black, because there were no portholes in this below deck area. Dad insisted that the lights be doused, so the man complied, flipping the switch. There was silence in the dark before my father spoke again.

"Now. Who's White, and who's colored?"

The men grumbled, "We can't tell in the dark."

Then Dad commanded, "Turn the lights on!"

When the lights came on, he told them, "In this galley we're going to work together all the time as if the lights are out." This set the tone for harmonious relations, and after Dad's impromptu conference, he never had any problem. If men—whatever their race—had their work done, they could go to their bunk or on deck. Their job, not their race, was important. Everyone worked together.

What is remarkable to me is that my father did this on his own, without any government directive from Washington, without any command from a Navy superior. He could not change the Navy and make all people equal, but he could manage his corner of the world in a more humane fashion.

My dad was a self-made man, not graduating from high school until long after the war when he got his GED the same year I received my high school diploma. He grew up in Mason County, Illinois in a time when it was lily white, with no "colored" people living there. He had participated in no sensitivity training seminars or diversity classes. He just did what was right.

The war changed the status of minorities and women for the better, bit by bit, slowly. Although most people did not fully realize it at the time, both women and minorities gained independence and confidence while employed in jobs needed for defense. The freedom they experienced during wartime gave them a new sense of destiny after the war. A book discussing *Rosie the Riveter Revisited* quotes the oral history of an African-American woman who felt that wartime defense work and decent pay liberated her from menial servants' work: "The war made me live better, it really did. My sister always said that Hitler was the one that got us out of the white folks kitchen." (p. 23)

My father harbored no ambitious plans for social and racial equality. Nevertheless, I think he was one of the behind-the-scenes facilitators of the expansion of American democracy. Historians usually write about major racial incidents and dramatic confrontations, momentous turning points of legislation. In order for the major breakthroughs in society to take place, many people behind the scenes, such as Dad in the darkness below the deck of the USS Missouri, had to take initiative on their own. Dad did his small part in working against racial discrimination.

Martin Luther King, Jr. dreamed of a color-blind America. My father had a simple solution for realizing this dream: "Turn the lights out!"

CHAPTER 32

A Japanese Sword and a Panama Hat

We feared that Daddy might be killed in action and never return to us. We did not know, until after he returned home in 1945, that he had several close calls with the grim reaper. While stationed in Bremerton, Washington, he received orders to be in command of a galley on an aircraft carrier. At the last minute, the Navy changed his orders from that ship to the Missouri. When the aircraft carrier he was originally assigned to left Bremerton, it went to the South Pacific where it received a direct hit from a kamikaze plane. The suicide plane and its bomb went through the deck and into the galley where every member of the galley was killed instantly. If Dad had not received a change in orders for the Missouri, he most likely would have died in

A kamikaze attacking the USS Missouri. ILLUSTRATION BY JOHN MICHAEL DOWNS.

that attack. The Missouri, too, got hit by a kamikaze, but it did not explode. Fortunately, we only heard about these near misses for our father after the war.

Throughout World War II we did not have the instant communication and overload of battlefield scenes that have been with us since the Vietnam War and subsequent conflicts. In a pre-television era, the only action of the war we could "see" were the short film clips in the newsreels at the movies. And most of the newsreels showed incidents that took place weeks or months before—U.S. victories, landings, invasions, surrenders of enemy armed forces. Nevertheless, we could imagine terrible scenarios without any visual aids.

Our nightly ritual was listening to the radio commentator Gabriel Heatter. If we heard, "There's good news tonight," as he opened his program, we all repeated his "good news," realizing that our side had won a major victory or breakthrough. When he began the program with "There's bad news tonight," we sat silently as our spirits sank, knowing he would be telling us about high casualties or a major setback.

This is the type of radio we listened to during World War II, learning the news of the warfront in Europe and Asia. ILLUSTRATION BY JOHN MICHAEL DOWNS.

My sisters and I sat close to the radio, as if being next to it would bring us closer to the news. We worried about all American troops, especially for Dad. But we didn't say anything out loud. Mother must have been worried, too, but she didn't mention it, complain, or cry. She was tough, and if she could handle the stress, then us kids had to be just as brave as her.

The radio episodes I remember most vividly announced the remarkable reversal of the Battle of the Bulge in late 1944 and early 1945. By that time, with the successful invasion of Europe on D-Day, and the advance of Allied forces, Americans had become confident that victory was close at hand. Nat King Cole sang a peppy, upbeat song, "D-Day," in which he assured us that our boys would soon be comin' back, because now "they're on a solid track." (This song is available on Youtube.)

The mood of the country was that the end of the war was near. We did not understand exactly what the "bulge" meant. We worried that this counterattack might signal defeat for the Allies in Europe. Gabriel Heatter's reports of loss of territory and heavy casualties made us sad.

We didn't know exactly what was happening in the Pacific, especially the desperate kamikaze suicide attacks by Japanese airplanes on Allied ships. If there had been television in World War II and we had seen the actual footage of kamikaze attacks, diving from the clouds, or skimming the waves, intent on burying their planes, bombs, and bodies in American ships, I doubt if we could have slept as peacefully as we did.

An optimistic view of war in the Pacific received musical support from a 1943 song, "Johnny Got a Zero." The lyrics of this tune played with the fact that in school Johnny was day-dreaming and looking out the window at the sky, so he got a zero as a grade. But when he became an air force pilot and shot down a Japanese plane—"Johnny got a Zero"—he became a hero. (This song is available on Youtube.)

Since the war I have seen plenty of film footage on the kamikaze. Their relentless pursuit of a ship, flying into the face of many thousands of rounds of ammunition, is hypnotically fascinating. Many were blown to bits before reaching their target. Some fulfilled their death wish by diving into the American (or British) ship they chose as their naval coffin. Not many Americans know the Japanese also had suicide submarines, called kaiten.

I have read books about these suicide missions and their pilots, but nothing can ever really "explain" to me this dreadfully fascinating subject. I can't really hate the kamikaze pilots today, knowing that they were living out their ideals, and were not drugged or coerced or tricked into their one-way missions. But neither can I admire them, because I remember all too well the nagging fear of World War II, and cannot cheer, even retroactively and posthumously, for the men who might have attacked the USS Missouri and wounded or killed my father.

The topics of kamikaze and the wider discussion of suicide bombers are quite controversial. The Japanese kamikaze pilots who flew their planes into Allied ships have been labeled "suicide bombers" and "terrorists." The Japanese pilots who trained to be kamikaze attackers, but whose lives were spared by the end of the war, have objected to them being compared to the suicide bombers of the Middle East in recent times, who strap explosives to their bodies and blow themselves up. These Japanese pilots have pointed out that kamikaze were always directed at military targets, never at civilians. This distinction is important, but for sailors on a World War II ship or for guards at a checkpoint and shoppers in the Middle East, the nuances of the differences are not significant. Death, no matter how it is labeled, is still death. The end of life is final. Period.

Even though we never saw or knew the full extent of the bitter warfare in the Pacific, we had viewed enough of the propaganda films to be convinced that these slant-eyed yellow "Japs," with their sneak attack on Pearl Harbor, could never be trusted, and were a formidable enemy. Some newsreels showed that they never gave up, and had to be flushed out of their rocky caves on Pacific islands with flame throwers. We thought we hated the Germans and Japanese equally, but in actual fact our racism was more intense toward the Japanese. My friends and I could use bathroom humor with one another (but never to our parents!) that when we used the toilet we "shit on the Germans and pissed on the Japs." Reserving urine for Japanese probably was an unconscious matching of the yellow peril with yellow pee.

A poll of students taken at Havana Community High School in 1943 documents the more negative view of Japanese. The *Democrat* in a March 12, 1943 article reports that to the question "Is Japan or Germany our most dangerous enemy," 74% of students answered Japan, 24% answered Germany, and 2% did not know. When teachers were asked the same question, "They agreed with the students that Japan was more dangerous than Germany. . . ." This local survey corresponds to the results of a 1942 Gallup poll ranking nationalities in three categories: good as we are, not as good as we are, or definitely inferior. Of seventeen nationalities, Japanese ranked last. Those who want to revisit the racism of World War II may turn to John Dower's book, *War Without Mercy,* which documents greater prejudice toward the Japanese than the Germans.

The defeat of Germany merited a special V-E EDITION of the *Democrat:*

V-E EDITION

This Victory-in-Europe edition of The Mason County Democrat is presented to its more than 3,000 subscribers in thankful celebration of the close of half of World War II—but also with the realization that the Mighty 7th War Loan success will shorten the road to Tokyo.

Partially planned last September, actual work on this 16-page newspaper was started a few minutes after President Truman's official announcement Tuesday morning that German forces had surrendered. Without the rapid and patriotic response of all citizens this edition would not have been possible, and their aid is deeply appreciated.

Following closely after publication of an extra after the death of President Roosevelt, we believe this V-E Day edition is another progressive step in weekly newspaper publication.

The collapse of Germany had been anticipated for some time, as Frank Sinatra predicted in the 1943 tune, "There'll Be a Hot Time in the Town of Berlin," recorded also by Bing Crosby and the Andrews Sisters. A song commemorating the victory was "V-Day Stomp," sung by The Four Cleffs. (These songs are available on Youtube.)

With Germany defeated, all attention turned to the war in the Pacific. Not until after Dad came home did we learn many details of his participation in the last few days of the war. He was handed a rifle, clambered down the netting on the side of the Missouri, and helped occupy Yokohama. He was still officially stationed on the Missouri, but in Yokohama at the time of the surrender. Shortly thereafter he returned to the U.S. by ship.

After the war ended, Americans quickly changed their attitudes toward their former enemy, Japan. All at once the yellow peril perished, replaced by the yellow puzzle.

The mood of Havana, and across the country, was a celebration of victory with a plea for an enduring peace. The headline of the August 17, 1945 Democrat proclaimed, "Great Victory Celebration Held Here. City is Scene of Joy As War in Pacific Ends."

The next issue of the *Democrat*, on August 24, 1945, contained a large number of ads marking the victorious end of war and the beginning of peace. Almost every business and store was represented with its own graphic. In the *Democrat* image "A Righteous Victory," the woman holds a scroll listing the islands and locations of major military engagements in the Pacific, from Pearl Harbor to Japan. In the ad "Victory for Peace" the emphasis is on Victory in War leading to Victory for Peace.

MEET THE GUMBATSU

YOU'LL LEARN SOMETHING!

If you think Germany's Nazis tough, take a good look at Japan's Gumbatsu.

They are the SS, the Gestapo all over again. But the acceptance of their fanatical rule has been far more deeply ingrained in their 70-odd million slaves.

The Gumbatsu is an unholy alliance of high-ranking soldiers, industrialists, wealthy land holders and the members of the Imperial Household.

It controls Japan absolutely. Diabolically clever and ruthless, it has managed to get control of 400 million others—nearly a quarter of the earth's population.

The Gumbatsu has taught its slaves well.

The Japanese soldiers would far rather die than submit to capture. Death is, in his own mind, his passport to Heaven. If he were lying on the battlefield badly wounded, and a soldier in strange uniform offered him water, he would use his last ounce of strength to kill the stranger. He would then be dying for an allegiance the Gumbatsu had taught him. The American soldier would likewise have died. Because of the Gumbatsu.

Read the statistics. A hundred thousand Japs killed. A handful of prisoners. The civilians on a captured Japanese island committing suicide *en masse*.

All right. If you can neither capture a Jap nor succor him, you must kill him. But that costs many more American lives. And many, many times more American bullets, guns and planes. And more ships to transport more ammunition over more miles.

It's a gigantic job to lick the Gumbatsu.

If it is to be done in any reasonable time, it will take all of us to do it.

We must stick by our war jobs.

We must keep buying Bonds and giving blood.

We must get to realize, every one of us, what we're up against in the Gumbatsu. That's the quickest way of getting the Gumbatsu to realize what they're up against in us.

How you can help

1 Keep that war job!
2 Keep buying bonds!
3 Keep doing all your country asks!

IT'S A TOUGH ROAD TO TOKYO

This space contributed in the interest of the MIGHTY 7th WAR LOAN by a Patriotic Citizen of Havana and Mason County

During World War II the leaders of Axis powers, especially Tojo for Japan, Hitler for Germany, and Mussolini for Italy, were criticized in writing and lampooned in cartoons. Early in the war, a decision was made to ease up on earlier critiques of the Japanese emperor, because he was revered by the Japanese people, and criticism of him would backfire. Instead, the official government policy was to blame the gumbatsu, the "unholy alliance of high-ranking soldiers, industrialists, wealthy land holders and the members of the Imperial Household," who had enslaved 70 million Japanese people and gained control over 400 million people. The three-headed rattlesnake features the militarist, industrialist, and landowner. This June 22, 1945 article from the *Mason County Democrat* appears after the defeat of Germany, warning citizens of the dangerous Japanese and encouraging them to carry on with war work and buying bonds.

Large ads trumpeted the same double message of victory and peace in large capital letters:

PEACE

MISSION ACCOMPLISHED

A NEW DAWN OF PEACE

DEMOCRACY LIVES

THANK GOD FOR VICTORY

FREEDOM

THE STARS AND STRIPES FOREVER

WELCOME HOME

ENDURING PEACE.

When Daddy landed in Yokohama, he met no resistance; two souvenirs of war he brought home were a Japanese military sword and rifle. In order to fit the sword in a suitcase he had to remove it from the scabbard and fold it in half, which collectors say significantly reduced its value. Of course my father would never think of selling it. He hung it on our family room wall above the fireplace. To me the rifle was no more interesting than any other rifle. I liked to work its bolt action, but I had seen many rifles, and its only special feature was its Japanese markings. However, the rifle was nothing next to the Japanese sword. While living at Grandma's house I had played with Grandpa's make-believe Masonic sword. It was make-believe because it was as harmless as a butter knife with its rounded edges. Grandpa got mad at me for playing with it because it was *his* plaything—part of his costume that was crowned with the Napoleon hat and its ostrich feather.

But the Japanese sword Daddy brought back was *real*—it was part of the war we had been living and breathing for years. It was probably a Japanese officer's sword, and could have been used by the officer to commit suicide. Of all the Japanese souvenirs Daddy brought home, the Japanese sword stood out. For years after we moved back to the house on Orange Street, I would go up to the attic and rummage through all that "Japanese stuff." I played with the rifle, which had an interesting sight, apparently for sniping from great distances. And I looked through the Japanese military decorations and books with strange writing. But always I came back to the sword, which for me somehow held the secret and spirit of the Japanese.

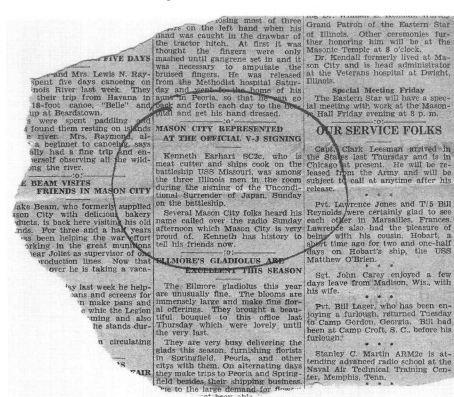

This article from *The Mason County Democrat* gives credit to Kenneth Harry Earhart for being stationed on the USS Missouri at the time of surrender, and acknowledges his wife Mary Earhart for "being in charge of the local locker plant." This scrap of newspaper with the article circled and torn out is an example of how people on the homefront treasured bits and pieces of information about their loved ones. FAMILY COLLECTION.

When people ask me how I happened to spend my life studying Japanese religions, I know there was no single factor, no one decisive moment, nor a particular individual that pushed or persuaded me. A number of influences seemed to come together, some of which were my interest in religion and fascination with language. Also influential were a Japanese student in college who again showed me the strange Japanese script, and several Japanese professors in graduate school.

Historians who write about the war claim that the millions of men and women who served in the war overseas had life-changing experiences. They returned to America as different people, more aware of the world outside the United States. Unknown to me at the time, my adolescence was shaped by this greater concern for the world at large.

Somewhere, behind and below all these other considerations, was Daddy's naval service against the Japanese in the Pacific. And the Japanese sword. My fascination for things Japanese somehow goes back to these first Japanese things I touched and handled.

Daddy's war souvenirs, oddly enough, came from two widely separated countries—Japan and Panama. His ship returned to the U.S. by way of the Panama Canal, so in addition to the mementoes he picked up in Japan, he bought some items in the Canal Zone. He purchased a small silver spoon and fork set which we got out for company, to serve preserves and pickles. And for me he brought home a large floppy woven hat, because he knew I loved to fish, and used a hat to keep the sun out of my eyes. Like the Japanese sword, the big hat had to be folded, but it bounced back into shape better than the sword. We called it the "Panama hat." I used it for many years when I went fishing.

Of all Daddy's souvenirs the most important for me were a Panama hat and a Japanese sword.

CHAPTER 33

The Empty Rocking Chair

avana marked the end of the war with a great celebration. We went downtown, where people had gathered and cars were driving around, horns honking, people waving their arms at each other. Grownups were acting silly, almost like us kids when we did our snake dance in school. It was a happy time for everyone. I felt like the rest of our family, relieved that our dad had survived the war and soon would be coming home.

As a youngster, my buddies and I could not understand the atomic bomb that seemed to bring about the Japanese surrender. We repeated to one another a rumor that, "The atomic bomb was so bright, even a blind man asked what it was." We only knew it was something incredibly powerful.

Our father was one of the fortunate servicemen who was discharged shortly after the end of the war. He mustered out on the east coast and took a train to Chicago. Mother traveled to Chicago to spend a few days with him before they returned to Havana. Their brief stay in the Edgewater Beach Hotel was marred by a meal of bad shrimp that made Mother sick for a few days. By the time they arrived in Havana, our family was glad to see them, but no big reunion or event marked Dad's return. The war was over, and the celebrating lay in the past. It was time to get on with our lives. My sisters and I had started school. Dad just went back to work, picking up where he left off before joining the Navy. He traded in his bell bottom trousers and Navy uniform for a meat cutter's apron. Fred, who had helped Mother keep the locker plant running during the war, retired.

One day in the fall of 1945, I walked to the house where our family had lived until 1943, before we moved to Grandma's house. Daddy was coming home from the war, the officer's family renting our house had left, and we were going "back home." We never knew when the duration would end, and now that the war was over, the duration simply disappeared as if it had never existed.

I was walking on South Orange Street with my buddy Eddie who lived just one house east of us. Our family dog Fritzi went with us, getting reacquainted with the neighborhood smells, but not excited about returning to his former haunts. It seemed strange to me, explaining to Eddie that we were coming back, and would be living there, like before. Permanently. "For the duration" was no more! When we got to 533 South Orange, for a moment it was unreal, seeing the house that had once been our home, and would be again. Unreal, because for so long Grandma's house had been home.

Not long after that Grandma and Grandpa moved out of the big house that had sheltered so many experiences and memories. They rented a smaller house on South Railroad Street, only a few blocks from us on South Orange. However, closeness is measured not just in blocks. The bond that developed over the years I lived with them never disappeared. When I got my driver's license, I drove Grandma and me fishing.

Later, when my future wife and I were dating, some evenings we would call up Grandma and Grandpa to see if they were busy, which

This recent photo shows our former family home much the same as it was in the 1940s and 1950s. Our address was 533 South Orange; later the city renumbered it to 633 South Orange. AUTHOR'S PHOTO.

This casual photo of Grandpa and me partnering in pinochle against my wife, Virginia (who took the picture), and Grandma shows only the serious side of the game, sorting cards and bidding. During play there was a great deal of bantering, joking, threatening, and good-natured outbursts of victory and defeat. FAMILY PHOTO.

they rarely were. We might take some dessert with us, but usually Grandma would say never mind, she had something. When we got there, we'd talk for a while, and then we put together a double deck of cards for pinochle.

When we became adults, Grandpa was much more talkative. He didn't relate well to kids, but accepted grownups, people on his own level. We had an awkward moment before playing pinochle, whether it would be the women against the men, or the young folks against the old folks. We played cards for a while, and then Grandma would say we had to have popcorn. She apologized for not having any oil, but could use some bacon grease. I said that would be just fine, remembering the times during the war when we loved her bacon-flavored popcorn.

The Haack-Earhart family has been blessed with longevity, both in lifespan and in marriages. Grandma and Grandpa Haack celebrated their fiftieth wedding anniversary. My parents, Kenneth and Mary Earhart, passed away just before their seventy-eighth wedding anniversary. At the time of this writing, my wife and I are well past the sixtieth year of our union.

The summer of 1962, after graduate school and just before my wife and I left for three years in Japan, both Grandma and Grandpa died.

Grandma and Grandpa Haack with many of their extended family at the time of their fiftieth wedding anniversary celebration. *From left to right*: Dora Mae (Eaton) Thornton, Clarence Eaton, Junior Brooks, Ruth (Haack) Eaton, Norma (Eaton) Brooks, Grandma (Ruth Haack), James Eaton, Grandpa (Charles Haack), Sylvia (Earhart) Heye, Mary Earhart, Rosemary (Earhart) Eilks, Kenneth Earhart, George Eilks, Virginia (Donaho) Earhart, Byron Earhart; in front are two children, Annette Eilks, and Kevin Eilks. FAMILY PHOTO.

A photo taken at the celebration party for our parents' 70th wedding anniversary. *From left to right*: Rosemary (Earhart) Watson, Mary Earhart, Kenneth Earhart, Sylvia (Earhart) Heye, Byron Earhart. FAMILY PHOTO.

The gravestone for Charles and Ruth Haack in Laurel Hill Cemetery, Havana, Illinois. AUTHOR'S PHOTO.

The gravestone for Kenneth and Mary Earhart, next to the stone for Charles and Ruth Haack. My wife and I will be laid to rest next to my parents. Joined in life, we will be rejoined in death. AUTHOR'S PHOTO.

Being separated from family for an extended period makes you all the more appreciative of what you don't have. Once when I was traveling around Japan, visiting Buddhist temples, and the Japanese visitors to this temple were buying incense to light for their ancestors, I bought and lit some for Grandma and Grandpa. Grandpa might snort at this religious practice. Grandma wouldn't mind mixing a little Buddhist ritual with her Baptist religion and Order of the Eastern Star pageantry.

Before going to Japan I asked mom and dad to save Grandma's old rocking chair for me. Now it's in our house, the only thing I have of hers, but every time I look at that empty rocking chair, it reminds me of the times she sat in it, when we lived at Grandma's house.

CHAPTER 34

Prewar, Wartime, Postwar . . . and More War

Those who lived through World War II clearly marked off time into three periods: prewar, wartime, and postwar. Before the war, America was recovering from the Depression, a difficult era economically, when people struggled to find work and raise families.

Wartime set apart the extraordinary situation that called most young men (and some young women) into military service. The entire population united in supporting the war effort and the military.

The first few years after 1945 marked the postwar period, when the nation shifted from producing tanks and planes to once more building cars and other domestic products. It was a time of healing for those who had lost loved ones, an occasion for rejoicing and reunion for those lucky enough to come home and for families to welcome these survivors.

I was too young to have vivid memories of the late Depression years and prewar times. My personal periodization of American history does not follow the familiar triad of prewar, wartime, and postwar divisions. My recollections begin with wartime experiences. Looking back on growing up in Havana while the war was raging overseas, I come up with two general observations. On one hand, it was a terrible few years of gut-wrenching uncertainty and anxiety. On the other hand, in spite of the terror of war, people were able to enjoy life. It was the worst of times, it was the best of times.

If the first period of my personal history is wartime, the second chronological unit is the giddy and carefree years of postwar America. Dad had returned home, and we left Grandma's house to live once more at our own home. Life passed through "the duration," and returned to normal. The country was victorious, new cars filled the streets, and confidence was in the air.

The Earhart Food Locker was doing well, because during the war people became accustomed to the new technology of frozen foods.

Dad and Mom still worked together, as they had before the war. The government implemented a program to help ex-servicemen make the transition from military to civilian life, paying for some of their occupational training. Under this program, Mom and Dad hired two former army men to help cut and wrap meat, and run the locker plant. In 1946 my folks purchased a three-quarter ton Chevrolet truck to bring slaughtered pigs and beef to the plant. By 1948 our family was doing well enough to buy a two-tone green Buick. It was the first car I had ever seen with flashing turn signals. For me, this beautiful eight-cylinder car with the fancy paint job, fender skirts over the rear wheels, and the new gimmick of electronic turn signals meant that we had arrived in the modern world. America won the war, Daddy came home, the locker plant was thriving, and we were comfortable in our South Orange house, which we began remodeling. All was well with the world.

I have read about the optimistic aftermath of the Great War, World War I, when people swore that "never again" would countries be so foolish as to squander the blood of their youth and the wealth of their nations for warfare. As a pre-teen and teenage boy, I shared that kind of exuberance following World War II. It was obvious that *this time* the world had learned its lesson. Even President Roosevelt said at the beginning of the conflict that we would win the war and we would win the peace.

My optimism seems to have been shared by many who survived the war. The first postwar issue of the *Democrat* is full of messages of peace. A chaplain on the USS Missouri at the time of surrender expressed his hope for lasting peace at the time of the Japanese surrender on the deck of the ship.

Much information and an oversupply of images from the war taught those of us on the homefront that countries—common people and government officials, as well as the military—had learned their lesson of the horrors of war, and would not repeat this terrible error. What we heard about the brutal treatment of American prisoners of war, what we saw in the newsreels of the unbelievable genocide of the Nazi concentration camps, and what we viewed in the pictures of the incredible devastation of atomic bombs dropped on Japan—all this convinced me that war was definitely not an option for humanity. I looked forward to an infinite span of peace and prosperity.

What terrified me about war was not just the distanced perception through newsreels of Dachau and Buchenwald, newspaper accounts

PRAYER AT THE SURRENDER OF JAPAN ABOARD USS MISSOURI

2 September 1945

by

ROLAND W. FAULK
Chaplain, U. S. Navy

Eternal God, Father of all living, we offer our sincere prayer of Thanksgiving to Thee on this day which we now dedicate to peace among the nations, remembering another Sabbath Day that was desecrated by the beginning of this brutal war. We are thankful that those who have loved peace have been rewarded with victory over those who have loved war. May it ever be so!

On this day of deliverance we pray for those who through long years have been imprisoned, destitute, sick and forsaken. Heal their bodies and their spirits, O God, for their wounds are grievous and deep. May the scars which they bear remind us that victory is not without cost and peace is not without price. May we never forget those who have paid the cost of our victory and peace.

On this day of surrender we turn hopefully from war to peace, from destroying to building, from killing to saving. But peace without justice we know is hopeless and justice without mercy Thou wilt surely despise. Help us therefore, O, God, to do justice and to love mercy and to walk humbly before Thee.

We pray for Thy servant, the President of the United States, and for the leaders of all lands that they may be endowed with wisdom sufficient for their great tasks. Grant unto all the peoples of the earth knowledge of Thee, with courage and faith to abide within the shelter of Thy sovereign law.   Amen.

This prayer offered by a U S Chaplain on the Missouri at the surrender of Japan echoes themes found in postwar American media, balancing a righteous victory with a just peace. My father and all sailors stationed on the USS Missouri received a copy. FAMILY COLLECTION.

of Hiroshima and Nagasaki, *Reader's Digest* accounts of the Bataan death march. In the late 1940s, from time to time, a veteran who was my mother's second cousin came into the locker plant to talk to her. He had difficulty speaking, and I could only follow a few words of his conversation. He had served in the army in Europe, and had been shot in the side of his head. Although not fatally injured, he spent many months in a hospital, as surgeons tried to repair the damage of a bullet. He had a glass left eye that did not track with his remaining good eye. The outline of his cheek was misshapen due to reconstruction of his jaw, which also made his speech difficult to understand.

Every time he came to the locker, he had visited a tavern first. His embarrassed wife cowered behind him, ashamed of his drunken condition. My mother always was nice to him, as they reminisced about old times before the war.

I could not bring myself to say anything. It upset me to look at this disfigured man, yet I could not help but glance at his grotesque appearance. In the immediate postwar period, this was the ugly face of war that I will never forget.

For me the "postwar" period ended abruptly on June 25, 1950. Although I was too young to remember clearly the attack on Pearl Harbor, I recall distinctly one day and one street corner in Peoria. Walking with my father while on a business trip to Peoria, passing a news stand, we saw an Extra edition of the *Peoria Journal Star* announcing hostilities in Korea. The sounds of warfare didn't need to reach my ears. Those headlines shattered my youthful innocence and naivete. The unimaginable, the inconceivable, had happened. Only a few years after the end of World War II, again we got caught up in military conflict.

The Korean "police action" was not called a war, but for me this marked the transition from postwar to a new wartime. In the next

ILLUSTRATION BY JOHN MICHAEL DOWNS.

few years some of my high school acquaintances enlisted for military service. One student left high school to join the army, was wounded, and came back to high school on the GI bill, graduating in my class. Like my mother's relative, this high school friend came home from war with a glass eye as a souvenir of warfare.

My brother-in-law was drafted, and I registered for the draft. In college, at my father's insistence, I participated in two years of ROTC (Reserve Officer Training Corps). In my junior year, because I wanted to go on for graduate work, I declined the opportunity to continue in ROTC and become an officer. Classmates who accepted this offer received a stipend during their junior and senior years, which obligated them to serve in the army for several years. My draft board annually renewed my deferment, enabling me to take up graduate work. Before the end of my graduate work, the truce between North Korea and South Korea had been reached.

The Korean War or police action made me dubious of the future and the prospects for a lasting peace. As the Cold War continued, we worried that either the Soviet Union or the United States would attack, possibly with nuclear bombs. Some homeowners built bomb shelters in their basements, while school children practiced air raid drills and huddled under desks. The Cuban missile crisis was another catastrophe that was narrowly avoided. Then came the Vietnam War, that divided rather than united the country. Amid minor skirmishes, such as Granada, there was the Gulf War, then the war with Iraq and Afghanistan. In recent years, the Middle East seems to be a scene of perpetual conflict, and North Korea has joined the nuclear bomb club that includes India and Pakistan.

In short, my personal history has the threefold compartments of wartime, postwar, and more war. The two earlier periods have ended, while the third seems to be an unending succession of military engagements. My optimism of "never again" has turned into the pessimism of "ever again."

Students who get lost in the chronology of American history or world history, instead of asking "what year is it?" might just as well ask, "what war is it?"

Some have called World War II the "good war," when the country was unified with very little opposition. Since that time, attitudes have become more fragmented, frequently polarized into staunch pro-war advocates and fervent anti-war proponents. I have quoted General

Sherman's famous statement that "War is Hell." A memory in Bordner's book by Lee Ann Ziener VanHooser rephrases this claim in twentieth century language: "War is outrageous behavior by humankind. Hopefully, all nations and all people will not continue to find themselves in devastating conflicts which maim us all. We totter on the edge constantly."

People wiser than the author will debate whether—if and when—war is inevitable, necessary, and beneficial; or avoidable, unnecessary, and harmful. As a senior citizen looking back on his youth, I can only comment that war is a terrible experience to live through, much more so for those who wage its battles, but also terrifying for those who remain on the homefront.

I consider myself fortunate to have spent the years of World War II at Grandma's house.

Ideas for Exploring the Homefront in Talks and Papers

Readers who want to know more about the homefront during World War II can scan the Suggestions for Further Reading for material on various topics.

Those who would like to give a talk or write a paper on the homefront may find helpful the following suggestions. These ideas fall into three possible approaches: personal interviews, internet searches, and library resources.

PERSONAL INTERVIEWS

1. *The veteran in your family during World War II (and other wars)*
   (Useful information can be found by googling "World War 2 veterans," and sites such as "Dad's War: Finding and Telling Your Father's WWII Story." Most veterans are men; the same questions can be used for women.)

Ask your family about someone in your family who is or was a veteran.
Did he enlist or was he drafted?
Where did he take basic training?
What war was he in? (World War I, World War II, Korean War, Vietnam War, or?)
What branch of service was he in?
What was his position and rank? (Infantry, pilot, mechanic, artillery; private, sergeant, lieutenant.)
Did he have any medals or service ribbons?
Does the family have discharge papers or other documents?
Look for pictures of this veteran in uniform.
Did this veteran bring home souvenirs from his place of service?
Did he see combat?

What stories does your family tell about this veteran?
What would you like to pass on to future generations of your family
   about this veteran?
Your talk (on video), or paper would make a nice family memento.

2. Women in Wartime

(Most World War II and earlier war veterans were men. For
the role of women in wartime and on the homefront, see Doris
Weatherford, *America's Women and World War II,* and Emily
Yellin, *Our Mothers' War: American Women at Home and at the
Front During World War II,* in Suggestions for Further Reading.
Another helpful book for considering stories of wartime women
is Pauline E. Parker, *Women of the Homefront: World War II
Recollections of 55 Americans.* Useful information can be found by
googling "American Women and World War II" and "History at a
Glance: Women in World War II.")

Ask your family about memories of women during the war.
Did this woman work during the war?
What did she do?
Did this woman relocate to be with her husband?
Did she bring back souvenirs of where she traveled?
Did she save letters she exchanged with her boyfriend or husband in
   the military?
What stories does your family tell about this woman?
How would you like to have future generations remember her?
Your talk (on video), or paper would make a nice family memento.

3. The military man or woman in your family today

(Reading about veterans may remind you of a family member or
friend now in the military.)

When did he or she enter the service?
What branch of service?
Where did basic training take place?
Position and rank?
What is the day to day activity the person does in the military?
Has this person served overseas?
Any medals or service ribbons?
Get a picture of this person in uniform.

Does this person have souvenirs from other regions or countries?
What is this person's most memorable experience in basic training?
What is this person's most memorable experience of military service?
Did he/she see combat?
Your talk (on video), or paper would make a nice family memento.

INTERNET SEARCHES

4. Veterans organizations

(The bonds that military personnel forged during war continued
in peacetime through the development of veterans organizations.
For the American Legion, look up www.legion.org; for Veterans of
Foreign Wars, look up www.vfw.org. These websites give information
on the founding, history, and activities of veterans groups.)

When were these organizations founded?
What is the stated rationale of these organizations?
What political policies do they support?
What charitable and humanitarian activities do they support?
You may want to contact a local unit of a veterans group and inter-
    view leaders or members about their activities.
Look up www.goldstarmoms.com for information on their founding,
    history, and activities. This site has slides and a video that can be
    used for public presentations.
When was Gold Star Mothers, Inc. founded?
What is their stated rationale?
What political policies do they support?
What charitable and humanitarian activities do they support?
You may want to contact a local unit and interview leaders or mem-
    bers about their activities.
Look up Daughters of the American Revolution at www.dar.org for
    information on their founding, history, and activities. The same
    questions can be pursued for DAR as for Gold Star Mothers.

5. Movies in the War

Find a movie made during World War II, such as "Destination
    Tokyo," or "Thirty Seconds Over Tokyo" on Youtube and watch
    it. (One internet source on Google for other movies is "world war
    2 movies.")
Sum up the story of the movie.

What does the movie say about America's purpose in the war?

What does the movie say about the purpose of enemies in the war?

How do you think the movie encouraged people at home to support the war?

What did you learn from the movie about the war that you didn't know before?

How can movies and actors/actresses help unify people on the homefront?

6. Songs during the war

Listen to some wartime songs, such as "Six Jerks in a Jeep," or "You're In the Army Now," or other songs mentioned in *At Grandma's House*. (One internet source on Google for other songs is "world war 2 songs.")

What is the message these songs express?

List some famous singers, such as the Andrews Sisters, Bing Crosby, Nat King Cole, or Frank Sinatra, and the songs about the war they recorded in the early 1940s.

Listen to some of these artists, and read the lyrics of their wartime songs.

How do you think these singers and their melodies influenced people on the homefront (and people in the military)?

How can the tunes and lyrics of singers help unify people on the homefront (and on the warfront)?

LIBRARY RESOURCES

7. Cartoons during the war

(Read the wartime cartoons of Little Orphan Annie, and follow the 1942–1945 adventures of Annie in Harold Gray, *ARF! The Life and Hard Times of Little Orphan Annie 1935*–1945. Two books about cartoons during World War II are Tony Husband, *Cartoons of World War II,* and Richard H. Minear, *Dr. Seuss Goes to War.*)

How did Annie recruit Junior Commandos to help her in collecting scrap metal and paper for the war effort?

How did Annie help locate and destroy enemy spies?

How can children be an important part of the war effort?

How can cartoons and humor help unify people on the homefront?

(The books by Tony Husband and Richard H. Minear offer other possibilities for exploring the relationship between humor and war.)

8. Rosie the Riveter

(Rosie the Riveter is considered one of the most important images of the homefront in World War II. A good resource for Rosie's image is Sherma Burger Gluck's *Rosie the Riveter Revisited: Women, The War, and Social Change*. Interesting facts can be found by googling "Rosie the Riveter.")

Give a brief description of the image of Rosie the Riveter, and explain why it became so important for women on the homefront during World War II.

Why is Rosie the Riveter still considered to be important today?

How did this image help change the view of women?

How do women today view Rosie?

What do you think Rosie meant when she said, "We can do it"?

9. Victory gardens

What is a Victory garden?

How did civilians in their Victory gardens help support the war effort? (A helpful book is M. G. Kains, *The Original Victory Garden Book*. Much information on Victory gardens can be obtained by googling "Victory Gardens During World War II," and variations of "Victory gardens.")

Re-read the chapter on Victory Gardens in *At Grandma's House*. How would you explain to someone today what a Victory garden was?

What can Americans today learn from Victory gardens about growing and preserving their own food?

Have you ever eaten fried green tomatoes? Googling "fried green tomatoes" or "fried green tomatoes recipe" will help you try this southern delicacy.

Have you eaten or fixed fried eggplant slices? The recipe is similar to the one for fried green tomatoes. Googling "fried eggplant" will give you several recipes.

How do World War II Victory gardens provide a lesson for us today?

10. The Ball of String

Read again the chapter, "The Ball of String." Why did Grandma save every piece of string wrapped around a store purchase? (For tips on saving and reusing, google "Use it Up, Wear it Out, Make Do or Do Without.")

How did Grandma use habits she learned during the Depression to help her save materials during the war?

How many materials did Grandma save, and how did she reuse them?

Explain the connection between Depression time frugality, wartime patriotism, and current day recycling.

What can Grandma's lessons about saving (instead of throwing away) teach us today about how to manage our homes better for recycling and conservation?

11. USO

Reread the chapter on the USO in *At Grandma's House*. What kind of help, food, entertainment, and friendship did the USO provide during World War II?

Today USO offices are found in major transportation centers such as airports. Googling "USO" will help you find a USO center in a major city.

Internet information lists the services provided by USO today. How does this compare with the services mentioned in *At Grandma's House*?

If you live in a major city, you may want to talk to a representative at a USO office and ask them about their experiences helping military personnel.

The USO also helps the families of military personnel who were wounded or killed. You may wish to volunteer providing these services or make a donation.

12. Hometown Homefront

Many towns, and especially county seats and larger cities, have war memorials, statues, and war material such as cannons and artillery pieces.

Choose a site such as your own hometown or a nearby city, and make a list of all the memorials to war.

Note the dates on these memorials.

Usually these sites are the location for Memorial Day events; attend an event, or look in a newspaper archive (often found online) for the last Memorial Day.

How did editors and reporters describe Memorial Day and the speeches?

How do these markers of war help define the city as a homefront support of distant wars (and some American wars such as the Revolutionary War and the Civil War)?

13. Race Relations

In *At Grandma's House*, race relations are touched on indirectly, in Chapter 16 and Chapter 31. For a fuller treatment of race relations during World War II, both on the warfront and the homefront, google "Race in World War II," "The Effects of Racism During World War II," "Race and World War II," and "Race relations on the home front."

What was the status of racism, especially segregation, at the beginning of World War II?

How did segregation affect the armed services, and how did segregation begin to change?

Who were the Tuskegee airmen and what role did they play in the war effort and in postwar America?

How did race affect the internment of Japanese Americans?

(The above internet sources provide information and suggestions for other topics on race and racism during World War II.)

Suggestions for Further Reading

For those who want to learn more about any aspect of World War II, the resources are endless. This war has been researched and described in detail by many people, both in personal accounts by the servicemen and civilians who lived through it, and by historians who have spent decades chronicling it. A public library will hold many popular or general accounts; a university library will house large sections on the war. Government records are extensive. For example, at the time of this writing, the British government just announced a project to digitize a collection of more than a million pages of World War I diaries. In the United States, the National Archives are a repository of many oral histories, documents, and images of World War II.

Out of this mountain of material, if one volume is singled out for how people experienced World War II, it is Studs Terkel's "*The Good War*": *An Oral History of World War II* (New York: The New Press, 1984). This collection of interviews with those who lived through World War II, has been praised as "The richest and most powerful single document of the American experience in World War II" (*Boston Globe*). Terkel's book covers the activities and attitudes of an amazing range of people, from the soldier in the foxhole to the airmen dropping the atomic bomb, from a conscientious objector to Washington administrators. Civilians in all walks of life, both from America and abroad, lend their voices. Great acts of valor and shameful moments of cowardice, selflessness and selfishness, are recorded as told by the people who lived through and observed these moments. Although almost 600 pages, the individual recollections of 3–5 pages each can be read as separate episodes.

A wealth of visual coverage of the war is available, some of it shown from time to time on various television channels. Ken Burns produced a seven-part, fifteen-hour documentary of the war and how it affected four American towns in his *The War*. Shown originally on PBS, it is available in many public libraries. Burns utilized extensive film footage and still photos of the warfront to provide a comprehensive visual presentation of Allied and Axis military and battle campaigns: it includes many combat scenes, images of the wounded and dead, the dropping of the A-bomb, and holocaust scenes. This description of the warfront is balanced with coverage of four American towns, their citizens who joined the military, and their interaction with family. Lengthy interviews with veterans of World War II provide a personal insight into the attitudes and actions of U.S. military during the conflict. See Ken Burns, *The War.* Available as "PBS Home Video," six DVD discs, 2007.

A comprehensive account of homefront conditions during the war is presented by Richard K. Lingeman in his *Don't You Know There's a War On? The American Homefront, 1941–1945* (New York: G. P. Putnam's Sons, 1970). Lingeman includes a wealth of information about government policies and statistics of people and production. He also covers the mood of the time with details of the movies and melodies that charmed the armed forces and civilians, as well as the failed artistic creations. Casting a critical eye on both governmental bureaucracy and civilian activities, he notes the cumbersome regulations of various departments and the extent of civilian conformity and participation in the black market. He adds perceptive analysis and comments on minorities and women during the war, and includes a useful bibliography.

Readers may wish to explore particular aspects of the wartime era. The publications listed below are offered as stepping stones to some of the topics mentioned in this book, starting with local, state, and regional information, and then moving to topics such as Victory gardens, rationing, and the role of women.

On the local level, a number of books have described Havana.

A rich account of Havana, the Illinois River, and stern wheelers by a man who came from a family of rivermen and once skippered the stern wheeler Gravel Gertie, is R. B. Hillyer's *Wooden Boats and Iron Men: A Saga of Havana, Illinois and the Rivers of Illinois, Missouri, Mississippi, Ohio & Kanawha.* Privately published. Pp. 204–209 give a sketch of gambling in Havana. I thank my late brother-in-law, Kermit Donaho, for giving me an inscribed copy of this book.

A rather romantic view of early twentieth-century Havana and the Illinois River by longtime Havana resident is Walter [P.] Hatton, *Back in Those Days 1902–1935.* (Edited and compiled by Susan H. McCoy,

Published by A. D. McCoy, 1988). Thanks to my classmate Helen Hatton Cross for providing a copy of this book.

A recent photographic narrative of this waterway is the coffee table volume by Daniel Overturf and Gary Marx, *A River Through Illinois* (Carbondale: Southern Illinois University Press, 2007).

An older work providing an overview of the early history of Havana, its people, culture, and activities (on pages 80–86) is Joseph Cochrane, *Centennial History of Mason County, including a Sketch of the Early History of Illinois, Its Physical Peculiarities, Soils, Climate, Productions, Etc.* (Springfield, Ill: Rokker's Steam Printing House, 1876).

A thorough chronicling of Mason County's early history is to be found in *The History of Menard and Mason Counties, Illinois* (Chicago: O. L. Baskin & Co., Historical Publishers, 1879); reprinted by Nabu Public Domain Reprints, no date. Author listed as "Anonymous." The early settlement and development of Havana is found on pages 501–536.

A more recent work is Ruth Wallace Lynn, *Prelude to Progress: The History of Mason County, Illinois, 1818–1968* (Havana: Mason County Board of Supervisors, 1968). This work is a comprehensive history of a century and a half of this county, its townships and cities, and its cultural, political, and economic development.

The development and activities of Camp Ellis are the subject of Marjorie Rich Bordner, *From Cornfields to Marching Feet: Camp Ellis, Illinois* (Dallas, Texas: Curtis Media Corp., 1993). This publication, once an expensive rare book, has been reprinted. Bordner includes the official *The Story of Camp Ellis* written by camp staff, then records 173 "memories" of the camp she collected from those who trained, lived, worked at, or came in contact with, Camp Ellis. *The Story of Camp Ellis* has been made available in a reprint, author listed as Robert O. Burton (London: Forgotten Books, 2018); the images are not clear. Mary C. Kerr in her *Washington's Homefront and the POWs* chronicled the presence of several hundred POWs from Camp Ellis in the city of Washington, Illinois, especially their work in canning factories. This book, privately published at GT Business Service in Tremont, Illinois in 2016, was not available to me.

Ron Stephenson's self-published *Camp Ellis* (2012) is a fictionalized account of his own and his brother's teenage years in postwar Camp Ellis as his father was in charge of dismantling the closed camp.

Roger D. Launius has provided a succinct overview of "Illinois in World War II," published in the April 1995 issue of *Illinois History*, and available online through Illinois Periodicals Online, Northern Illinois University Libraries. The address is http://www.lib.edu/1995/ihy950449.html. Launius writes that "the history of a locality cannot be treated as a separate entity because regional, national, and world events were of constant influence."

Mary Watters's two-volume work *Illinois in The Second World War* is "the state's official history of its participation" (quoting Launius). Volume One is Operation Homefront (Springfield: Illinois State Historical Library, 1951); Volume Two is The Production Front (Springfield: Illinois State Historical Library, 1952). The thousand pages of these two volumes chronicle the personnel, policies, conditions, and events of wartime Illinois in comprehensive detail.

The Illinois State Archives has prepared "Illinois at War, 1941–1945, A Selection of Documents from the Illinois State Archives," a teaching package of fifty documents made available to Illinois educational institutions. These teaching materials provide selective documents and teaching/learning tips for understanding the wartime experience in Illinois. This document was available at http://www.cyberdriveillinois.com/departments/archives/teaching_packages/illinois_at_war/home.html, when accessed March 14, 2015.

The University of Illinois, following up on Ken Burns' *The War*, recorded oral histories of Illinois veterans and civilians in *Central Illinois World War II Stories*, available at http://will.illinois.edu/wwii (accessed March 15, 2015). Included in these oral histories are the accounts of an African-American who was a steward on the USS Missouri, other African-Americans who encountered "institutional racism," and the wartime experiences of civilians.

Neighboring Indiana, especially the city of New Castle, is the setting for a detailed account of the war as seen through the oral history of several families; this book describes how these residents, their families, and neighbors coped with rationing, scarcities of products, and anxieties about loved ones. This is a detailed case study of a Midwestern community during wartime, which parallels much of the conditions and experiences in my stay at Grandma's house. See Bruce C. Smith, *The War Comes to Plum Street* (Bloomington: Indiana University Press, 2005).

Another regional work is R. Douglas Hurt, *The Great Plains during World War II* (Lincoln: University of Nebraska Press, 2008). This book does not touch directly on Illinois, but gives detailed information on

"Women at Work," "The Homefront," and "Rationing" that is comparable to the situation in wartime Illinois.

Louis Fairchild has compiled *They Called It the War Effort: Oral Histories from WWII Orange, Texas* (2nd ed., Denton: Texas State Historical Association, 2012). This extensive set of personal accounts of wartime experiences in a Texas community—transformed by the boom of wartime production—provides a portrait of wartime Texas comparable to what Bruce C. Smith has offered for Indiana. Chapter 3, pp. 71–116, "Children in a Unique Time," is the closest parallel to the account of my own childhood experiences at Grandma's house.

Lorraine B. Diehl, *Over Here! New York City During World War II* (New York: Smithsonian Books; HarperCollins, 2010). This book documents wartime New York City with many photographs; it includes sections on rationing and "New York's Riveting Rosies."

An example of a local collection of oral histories is Clinton C. Gardner, Managing Editor, *World War II Remembered* (by residents of Kendal at Hanover) (Hanover, NH: Kendal at Hanover Residents Association, 2012). This book is organized by accounts of war theaters and "Homefront." Those concerned with oral histories and local history may find collections such as this in city and regional libraries.

Harold Gray, *ARF! The Life and Hard Times of Little Orphan Annie 1935–1945* (New Rochelle, NY: Arlington House, 1970). With an introduction by Al Capp. A reprint of the daily newspaper comic strips of Annie; her role as "Colonel Annie organizing and leading the Junior Commandos" begins Monday, June 22, 1942. (This book is not paginated, but is organized by consecutive dates.)

Bruce Smith, *The History of Little Orphan Annie* (New York: Ballantine Books, 1982). This book covers "America's best-loved moppet from comic strip to Broadway to Hollywood"; see Chapter 5, "'We're Doin' War Work'" (pp. 46–63) for an account of Gray and Annie in creating the Junior Commandos.

James J. Kimble, *Mobilizing the Homefront: War Bonds and Domestic Propaganda* (College Station: Texas A & M University Press, 2006). A book critical of oversimplified and glamorized views of World War II as "the good war," Kimble discusses war bond drives in the context of propaganda: "the war bond campaign mobilized the public by attempting to convince homefront Americans that they were fighting the war, too." (P. X)

Guide for Planning the Local Victory Garden Program (Washington, D.C.: The United States Office of Civilian Defense in Cooperation with the United States Dept. Of Agriculture [1942]). This 13-page pamphlet is an example of government publications aimed at helping civilians cope with their lives while supporting the war effort; this guide advises states and communities how to organize local support groups and encourage and advise families to raise large gardens.

M. G. Kains. *The Original Victory Garden Book* (New York: Stein and Day, 1978). This book was originally published in 1942 under the title *Food Gardens for Defense.* Kains, author of the standard work *Modern Guide to Successful Gardening,* urges Americans to grow as much as they can to save valuable resources such as fuel for transportation and to conserve food for the troops. In this way, "we, as gardeners, should do our part." (P. vii).

Amy Bentley, *Eating for Victory: Food Rationing and the Politics of Domesticity* (Urbana and Chicago: University of Illinois Press, 1998). A critical examination of the "cultural and symbolic dimensions of food in wartime America," analyzing the propaganda and politics of rationing (and specific activities such as Victory gardens and images such as Rosie the Riveter), but also commenting on gender and race issues both during wartime and more recently.

Stephanie A. Carpenter's *On the Farm Front: The Women's Land Army in World War II* (DeKalb, IL: Northern Illinois University, 2003) discusses the debate over how the war changed the role of women in America: "The WLA effectively recruited, trained, and placed millions of women as labor on national farms" during the war. The book discusses the mobilization of women in the East, West, Midwest, and South.

Rudy Shappee, *Beef Stew for 2500: Feeding Our Navy from the Revolutionary War to the Present* (San Diego: South Jetty Publishing, 2007). A history of Navy cooking, with photos of modern ships and their galleys; my father was in charge of a galley on the USS Missouri. Many recipes are included, most of which are for whole crews.

Harvey C. Mansfield, *A Short History of OPA* ([Washington]: Office of Temporary Controls, Office of Price Administration, [1948]). The OPA, Office of Price Administration, was the government agency that controlled prices and rationing of goods; this is a detailed, 331-page official publication in the series "United States Government historical reports on war administration." The OPA is characterized as "the largest and best known of the civilian war agencies," (p. 7), and "very little was ever done by the office without controversy" (p. 7). This is one of a long series of official government publications of "Historical Reports on War Administration: Office of Price Administration."

John Bush Jones, *All-out for Victory! Magazine Advertising and the World War II Homefront* (Waltham, MA: Brandeis University; Hanover, [NH]: University Press of New England, 2009). Jones surveyed the ads in ten high circulation magazines from wartime to show how advertising helped mobilize people to support the military and aid the war effort. The many illustrations, some in color, help us see what Americans saw in their popular magazines during World War II.

For the homefront in general, with numerous personal recollections, see *The Homefront: America During World War II* (New York: G. P. Putnam's Sons, 1984). Edited by Mark Jonathan Harris, Franklin D. Mitchell, and Steven J. Schechter, it features an introduction by Studs Terkel that calls the war "a time indelibly remembered," one that brought about many changes in American life.

A fictional account of a boy growing up in California during World War II while his father is in the military, written for young adults, is Brian Kardashian's *A Flag in the Window*, available as an ebook. Although the boy is a character in a novel, the historical background has been carefully researched, especially through the use of the local newspaper. This work recommends itself to younger readers interested in war.

A googling or library search of World War II oral histories (or similar topics, such as "WWII children") will yield quite a few items; a number of people who lived their childhood through the horrors of war in other countries have penned their recollections. Although interesting in their own right, I make no attempt to include all of them in this brief list.

The role of women during World War II is not well known by many people, but historians have provided detailed descriptions and careful analyses of the subject.

The iconic figure of women workers is the topic of Sherma Burger Gluck's *Rosie the Riveter Revisited: Women, The War, and Social Change* (Boston: Twayne Publishers, 1987). Gluck offers an overview of the United States on the eve of the war, then utilizes lengthy oral histories of ten "Negroes, women, and aliens" to portray the actual workers who stood behind the image of Rosie.

A book dedicated "To the women who made history during World War II" is Maureen Honey's *Creating Rosie the Riveter: Class, Gender, and Propaganda during World War II* (The University of Massachusetts Press, 1984). Honey examines the creation of this wartime figure, then asks "How did the strong figure of Rosie the Riveter become transformed into the naive, dependent, childlike, self-abnegating model of femininity in the late forties and 1950s?"

Another book that approaches the war through oral history is Pauline E. Parker's *Women of the Homefront: World War II Recollections of 55 Americans* (Jefferson, North Carolina: McFarland & Company, 2002).

Denise Kiernan's *The Girls of Atomic City: The Untold Story of the Women Who Helped Win World War II* (New York: Touchstone, 2013) describes the development of the atomic bomb at Oak Ridge, Tennessee, highlighting the work of women in this process.

A book whose theme is "the liberating effect on women" is Doris Weatherford's *American Women and World War II* (New York: Facts on File, 1990). This book focuses on nurses, "The Military Woman," "The New Industrial Woman," and "The Homefront."

Emily Yellin, inspired by the diary and letters of her late mother, who was a Red Cross worker during World War II, thoroughly researched and interpreted the experiences of women like her mother. Her book is *Our Mothers' War: American Women at Home and at the Front During World War II* (New York: Free Press, 2004).

A book dealing with Alabama women during wartime, especially their employment and social conditions, is Mary Martha Thomas, *Riveting and Rationing in Dixie: Alabama Women and the Second World War* (Tuscaloosa: University of Alabama Press, 1987). Filled with illustrations of defense workers and government posters recruiting women, this book offers a balanced view of the continuity and change in women's role in postwar times.

Doris Weatherford is editor of *American Women During World War II: An Encyclopedia* (Hoboken: Taylor & Francis, 2009). This 552 page work documents the lives of women in military organizations, defense industries, and in "more traditional homefront roles."

Acknowledgments

While researching, writing, and publishing this book, I accumulated debts to many people for various reasons. Some thanks date back more than a half century, others are more recent. Some assistance with this project was unintentional and indirect, other help has been intentional and very direct.

The first acknowledgment should go to Grandma Haack (Ruth Haack), for she is one of the main inspirations for this project. In her shadow, but not forgotten, is Grandpa Haack (Charles F. Haack), who, with her, provided the home that is the major setting of these memories. Neither grandparent had any inkling that their household and their individual and collective experiences and activities would ever wind up in a book. Nevertheless, without them, this account would be an empty record.

The next recognition goes to my parents, Kenneth and Mary Earhart, who set a remarkable and courageous example of living through World War II with dignity and pride. My father served his country while in the Navy. My mother served the people of Havana and several counties by managing the Earhart Food Locker. Together, amidst severe hardships, without complaining, they worked hard in their military and civilian duties, while raising three children. In many ways, this book is their story. My parents were savers, seldom parting with any family picture or memento. They are the ones who saved items such as my ration book and savings stamp book. They would be glad to know that their lifelong saving has served a useful purpose.

On a more recent note, my wife Virginia (Donaho) Earhart has been a constant helper and supporter. She collected and organized both photographs and recipes for her 500 page *Donaho-Earhart Family Favorites Cookbook and Album*. This work, privately published, is now out of print, but a copy has been deposited with the Havana Public Library. Many of the photos in this book were first printed in her cookbook; other family photos that she assembled, but did not include in her book, were available for me to use. She has been of particular assistance in locating images and loading them on the computer.

Our son David C. Earhart read early versions of this story. He also provided a number of images. He has been a sounding board for this project, helping me formulate and improve the manuscript. He and Susumu Kamimura provided invaluable help in organizing and preparing the images for publication. David spent many hours helping me coordinate images with the text, and provided the idea for the cover.

Our son Kenneth C. Earhart provided key photos of his grandfather Kenneth H. Earhart and his Navy record. He followed his grandfather in a long Navy career. He also read a draft of the manuscript and made helpful suggestions.

Our son Paul W. Earhart helped resolve some computer problems in the process of transforming electronic files to a published book.

Nancy Glick, former Director of the Havana Public District Library, generously offered the resources of her library and personal collection to aid in the completion of this project. She helped locate photographs of wartime Havana, and provided important background information on the times. This library's microfilm copy of *The Mason County Democrat* was a valuable resource. Vanessa Hall-Bennett, current Director of the Havana Public District Library, secured permission to use materials from the library. It was a pleasure to return to this library, one of my favorite childhood places.

Bob Martin, Publisher of *The Mason County Democrat*, graciously granted permission to reprint materials from this newspaper, the major source of several chapters and the background for much of the book.

Marion Cornelius kindly guided me through the Easley Pioneer Museum in Ipava, with its collection of Camp Ellis materials. He allowed me to read through a scrapbook containing the 1944 *Camp Ellis News*. Thanks go to Glen and Becky Vanderveen for donating this scrapbook to the Easley Pioneer Museum. Cornelius also read the manuscript to check the account of Camp Ellis, and provided an endorsement.

Caroline McCullagh, a fellow writer from San Diego, graciously agreed to read and critique the manuscript. Her comments and suggestions have helped improve the language, organization, and clarity of the work.

Len Kube, who has written an account of growing up in Wisconsin during the 1940s, read the manuscript, and offered a number of helpful corrections and suggestions. He introduced me to John Michael Downs.

John Michael Downs provided illustrations that help make the text come alive.

David Dickason, a professor of geography, and colleague at Western Michigan University, read the manuscript and made many helpful suggestions.

Charles (Chuck) Schunk, a veteran of the Pacific Campaign and Iwo Jima, read the manuscript and wrote an endorsement.

Thanks to William Blessman for reading and commenting on the manuscript, and providing an endorsement.

Thanks to Chris Troxel for granting permission for the map of Havana.

Thanks to Richard H. Lederer for reading and commenting on the manuscript, and writing an endorsement.

Special thanks go to the Penny Dreadfuls Read/Critique group for providing helpful comments and suggestions: Randal Doering, Kevin Girard, Steve Rodgers, J'nae Spano, Doug Welch, and Kitty Welch.

Conversations with other family members, and Havana residents, have contributed to the completion of this project. Credits for particular images and documents are given in the text.

Acquisitions editor Kristine Priddy, chief clerk Judy Verdich, design and production manager Linda Jorgensen Buhman, project editor Wayne Larsen, coordinator of marketing Amy Etcheson, marketing specialist Chelsey Harris, graphic designer Tracy Gholson, administrative aide Angela Moore-Swafford, IT tech associate Jerry Richardson, and executive editor Sylvia Frank Rodrigue, all at Saluki Publishing, helped bring this book to publication.

Special thanks to my granddaughters: Michelle Bearheart for creating the website byronearhartauthor.com, and to Adrienne Earhart for setting up https://www.facebook.com/ByronEarhartAuthor/ as a Facebook account.

To all of the above, named and unnamed, my thanks to you for making this work possible.

Memories, both individual and collective, are selective and fallible. My hope is that any mistakes and oversights in this book will trigger the recollections of others.

THE END

About the Author

Born and raised in Illinois, H. Byron Earhart lived through the war
years in the small town of Havana
during World War II. In 1942 when
his father enlisted in the Navy,
he and his family went to live at
his maternal grandparents' home
(Grandma's house). After twelve
years of public school in Havana
he attended Knox College, before
receiving a Ph.D. from the University of Chicago in history of
religions. He taught courses on
Asian religions and world religions
at Western Michigan University,
which named him a Distinguished
Faculty Scholar for his many publications on Japanese religions. His
first book, *Japanese Religion*, in continuous print since 1969, is now in
its fifth edition. His most recent
monograph is *Mount Fuji: Icon of
Japan*. After retiring he returned
to his roots in Illinois and his early

interest in creative writing. He completed five novels with an Illinois setting;
No Pizza in Heaven is the first book of his Twin Destiny Series.

Other Publications by H. Byron Earhart

Academic Books

Religion in Japan: Unity and Diversity. First published 1969; fifth edition, 2014. (Cengage)

> Published review: "It is no surprise that H. Byron Earhart's classic textbook, *Japanese Religion,* has remained one of the only treatments of Japanese religious history truly suitable for use in undergraduate classrooms."

A Religious Study of the Mount Haguro Sect of Shugendo. 1970. (Sophia University) (also published in Japanese translation)

Gedatsu-kai and Religion in Contemporary Japan: Returning to the Center. 1989. (Indiana University)

Religious Traditions of the World: A Journey Through Africa, Mesoamerica, North America, Judaism, Christianity, Islam, Hinduism, Buddhism, China, and Japan (editor), 1992. (Harper)

Mount Fuji: Icon of Japan. 2011. (University of South Carolina) (also published in Japanese translation)

Novels

Twin Destiny Series, iCrew Digital Publishing

Book One, *No Pizza in Heaven.* (2016)

> Amazon review: "Earhart's *No Pizza in Heaven* is a fun, emotional look at growing up in religious middle-America, a look into religious exploration, and a feel-good suspense novel all in one."

Book Two, *Faith Finds Forgiveness.* (2017)

> Amazon review: In *Faith Finds Forgiveness,* H. Byron Earhart's follow-up to *No Pizza in Heaven,* Faith Armstrong attempts to reconcile her life by seeking out the man who fathered her twin sons so long ago. Readers of the Twin Destiny series will not be disappointed.

Book Three, *Meeting the Devil.* (2017)

> Amazon review: "My wife and I have enjoyed the three books of this series, and hope to continue to read more about Faith, her two diverse twin sons, and their amazing families."

Book Four, *The Devil Déjà vu.* (2019)

> Endorsement: "After devouring the first three books of the Twin Destiny series, I couldn't wait for a fourth book to appear on the scene. I wasn't disappointed!"

Book Five, *Canterbury Canticle.* 2020.

NOVELS BY H. BYRON EARHART

Earhart has penned a number of novels that have their setting in Illinois, including the five books of his Twin Destiny series, which follows the careers of twin sons and their mother for more than three decades of unity, separation, and reunion.

The Twin Destiny Series

In Book One, *No Pizza in Heaven,* when unmarried teenager Faith Armstrong has identical twin sons, her parents force her to give them up for adoption and insist on separating the babies. For thirty years this woman and her sons have no contact with one another, until an investigative reporter discovers the twins' identity and helps them locate their birth mother. This leads to the reunion of an unusual trio: an agnostic mother, a hot salvation preacher, and a cool New Age follower.

In Book Two, *Faith Finds Forgiveness,* Faith is happily reunited with her twins and their families, yet remains troubled by lingering doubts about the thirty years when she lived an unhappy workaholic life alienated from her parents and her religious upbringing. Book One traces an outer journey, Faith moving from downstate Illinois to Chicago and finding her twins. Book Two takes Faith on an inner journey, finding out who she has been, who she now is, and who she wants to be. The investigative reporter who discovered the twins' identity and located her, and also a priest, help her in this personal quest.

In Book Three, *Meeting the Devil,* Faith and her sons pursue complex medical and legal negotiations. Now Faith is happily married to Scott, and together they enjoy family events with the twins and their children. This idyllic scene is upset when Jeremy develops serious kidney problems, which might indicate his identical twin has similar hereditary tendencies. This forces Faith to locate Doug, the father of the twins, with whom she has not had contact in three decades; she never told him about the twins.

Book Four, *The Devil Déjà Vu,* finds Faith and her extended family quite happy. Doug, an aging Casanova who is estranged from his several families and live-ins, tries to weasel his way into this pleasant scene. Having found out that he is the father of twins, he tries to force Faith to divulge the names and addresses of his offspring so that he can at least enjoy some family togetherness in his old age. Faith and Doug engage in intense legal negotiations.

Book Five, *Canterbury Canticles,* revolves mainly around the Moms and Kids Foundation that Faith set up, and the Canterbury Academy that houses this project. Faith created a fund enabling single mothers to keep their children—a pleasure denied to Faith and her twins. When a dishonest financial officer threatens the future of the academy, Faith becomes involved in catching this crook.

Hiram Upright and the Good Time Feelin'.
　A Spiritual Journey from Hot Salvation to Cool Enlightenment . . .
　And Beyond

This completed novel awaiting publication follows Hiram Upright, a country bumpkin from small-town Illinois in his journey from middle America piety to California enlightenment, travelling across legendary Route 66 in the 1950s to find himself and spiritual fulfillment. He explores Christian piety, meditation, yoga, and Zen in his spiritual odyssey, hoping to avoid the coward's escape to self-destruction and to find a path to self-fulfillment.

For more information on the author and his publications, visit byron earhartauthor.com and byronearhart.com.